T

JAMES ROWLEY

OUT OF IVY

How a Liberal Ivy Created a Committed Conservative

2006

ISBN: 1-4196-3261-2

To order additional copies, please contact us.
BookSurge, LLC
www.booksurge.com
1-866-308-6235
orders@booksurge.com

To Mom and Dad, who taught me that there is a difference between right and wrong.
And to Kyle, Tyler, and Brendan—who taught me how to fight.

TABLE OF CONTENTS

FOREWORD

To say that our elite colleges and universities are mired in a toxic stew of left-leaning intolerance, indoctrination, and identity politics is to indulge in a cliché. Indeed, the decline and fall of higher education has been a recurring theme of conservative criticism, from William F. Buckley's God and Man at Yale to The Closing of the American Mind by Allan Bloom.

But it is not until the publication of this book that we have our first insider account of what it is like to actually live at one of these universities. In what follows, Travis Rowley will tell the wild tale of another world—a campus that blends the moral sensibilities of Sodom and Gomorrah with the political preferences of the Kremlin.

Readers will meet students who are as comfortable protesting the War on Terror as they are the heterosexism of Valentine's Day. They will become well acquainted with feminists who produce plays glorifying abortion, hold instructional workshops on sex toys, and graduate to become she-pimps. And they will encounter the Queer Alliance, a student group that sponsors on-campus sex binges that would make Woodstock blush.

One might wonder what happened to the adults in all of this. As Travis shows, they are right there in the middle of it all as eager participants, cheering spectators, or indifferent bureaucrats. They are the professors who dismiss their classes for anti-war protests. They are the disciplinary deans who excuse the mass theft of the student newspaper, but ruthlessly enforce campus speech codes. And they are the administrators who sometimes seem as concerned about crime as they are about the reaction of minority students to the arming of the Brown police.

The resulting account will be as humorous for readers as it is devastating for Brown. While previous works have focused on the flawed political and social attitudes of schools like Brown, Out of Ivy is sure to stimulate a debate on the deepening moral failure of the university. In so doing, it is destined to take its place among classics like God and Man at Yale.

Stephen Beale, Brown '04
Foundation for Intellectual Diversity, President

AUTHOR'S NOTE

I'm supposed to repeat the cliché. *I love Brown University, my dear alma mater.* People are going to ask what could have possibly compelled me to write such a destructive piece on an institution that has been so good to me. And I'm supposed to robotically respond, "I'm doing this *for* Brown—out of deep love and admiration for my dear alma mater—so that the University might correct itself."

But I don't *love* Brown University. And I don't say that to be intentionally inflammatory. I believe it is crucial to the purposes of this book that I continuously reveal how I feel, and how I felt at certain times. I do not *love* my alma mater. And I don't say that recklessly. I have thought long and hard about whether I can truly say that I love Brown. But I don't. I love my family. I love my friends. And I love my country. But even if I did hold a special place in my heart for Brown, I am beholden to the truth before I am loyal to any academic institution—especially one that swims against principles of discovery, and principles of liberty.

Besides, despite how it may appear, I am not picking a fight with Brown. I resent that portrayal of this book's release. *Brown* picked a fight with *me* a long time ago. But I'm supposed to show up to the annual reunions, and share the nostalgia of college memories. I'm supposed to hug my classmates and professors, and forget all about my objections for the sake of preserving everyone's ability to blind themselves to what Brown University has become, so that we can continue to celebrate ourselves and our Ivy League fraternity. Obviously, I have decided that there is something more important at stake.

With that said, and in all fairness, *Out of Ivy*'s first edition coincides with interesting and hopeful times at Brown University. Due to certain alumni, students, administrators, and professors, a number of healthy developments have taken place over the past several years that give hope to those who understand just how crucial a place Brown is to the nation. So I do *cheer* for my alma mater. However, Brown is governed by the political left, and there is always reason to be suspicious and doubtful when leaving important matters in the hands of liberals.

Go Bears!
Travis Rowley '02

The essence of the American dream is the understanding that we are here on this earth and in this land for a higher purpose: to discover—and develop to the fullest—our God-given potential. Anything that stands in the way of the dream, we must fight. Anything that enhances the dream, we must support.

Steve Forbes

The leverage of ideas is so immense that a slight change in the intellectual climate can and will—perhaps slowly but nevertheless inexorably—twist a familiar institution into an unrecognizable shape.

Irving Kristol, "On Capitalism and Democracy"

PROLOGUE

All of us were sent to a private, Catholic, all-boys high school. My brothers and I were forced to wear a shirt, tie, and sport jacket every day. Shaven, and hair kept above the collar. Our mother was a housewife. Our father, an Irish-Catholic, 6'4" 260 lb., Rhode Island State Trooper. I wouldn't know how to begin to describe what it was like growing up in our home. There is no single word that can accurately describe the constant episodes of childhood activity, and our resilience to cause unforeseen dilemmas for my parents. Drives to Little League practice. Pop Warner Football. A packed refrigerator immediately emptied. Fights. All-out brawls, in fact. Scabs and scars. Then, spankings. Unwilling babysitters. New bikes. Hugs. Baseball cards. Holiday meals. Grandma. Grandpa. Cookouts. Christmas gifts. Chicken wings. Nintendo and Wiffleball. Detention. Drivers' licenses. Car accidents. Proms. Girls.

A nice family, I guess. Four sons, the best of friends, excessively competitive amongst ourselves. Morning races to the bus stop. Afternoon races home. We were extremely hard on one another, competing in every facet of daily life. There were brotherly battles for victory and dominance of whatever the topic was at the time. Not just physical battles, but the more annoying and energy-draining intellectual exercises of argument. Of course, many of these did result in teeth being knocked out. Facial scars. We were a pack of youngsters with a seemingly endless supply of energy to eradicate any chance for a dull moment, and all under the supervision of the woman who would yell, "Just wait 'til your father gets home!"

Just like thousands of 18 year-olds every year, I graduated high school and left the comfort of home and family to attend college, arriving in 1998 at the doorstep of the Ivy League. I hadn't a shred of political knowledge, experience, or interest. I considered myself a pretty normal kid. I liked sports and girls. Any other passions or hobbies of mine were mild.

Ignoring politics in college, however, is virtually impossible. *Especially* at Brown University. Those who made up the framework of my alma mater were highly political, and they thrust their ideas and personal philosophies into the faces of as many as possible. So, without much say in the matter, I was forced to enter the political realm. Ironically, that is where I made my greatest contribution to Brown University, and for many at Brown, it is within that domain that they will remember me.

When I arrived on Brown's campus I believed I was an extremely good athlete. I was an all-state football and baseball player from Rhode Island, and thought I would find my time on Brown's football team an easy one, branded with many touchdowns and victories to speak of after graduation. That wasn't the case. It turned out that I was the slowest and weakest athlete among the group of thirty-five freshman that had shown up for pre-season football camp, and mere playing-time, rather than 20-touchdown seasons, turned into my primary goal.

I was also under the impression that I was a bright student. I had always received straight-As, and had graduated near the top of my high-school class. However, I would find out exactly how much intellect I lacked after encountering some of my Ivy League classmates. Right off the bat, Brown instilled in me a measure of humility, and it immediately became clear that in order to receive the most out of my experience, both athletically and educationally, it would take my best effort; something extra that I wasn't even sure I possessed. I guess you could say I was intimidated, but I was also a very confident kid willing to at least attempt to meet Brown's challenges.

I could never have predicted the culmination or conclusion of my college career. I ended up as the captain of the Brown football team, a controversial opinion-columnist for the school newspaper, a spokesman for Brown's silenced campus right, and a wildly unpopular campus celebrity. It took a lot of personal reflection to realize how I arrived at that point, and I found my story to be a telling one; the tale of a politically naïve adolescent thrown into one of the most activist communities in the world; the story of an all-American-type kid, raised with conservative values, and his clashes with an army of liberals with no patience for foreign opinion.

My alma mater was like a broken seesaw—permanently fixed in a position of political imbalance. Brown University couldn't escape academia's common criticism. Its schooling was better described as liberal indoctrination, rather than a true education. Brown's academic model was one that fostered educational sin, as it promoted collective thought, and restricted individualism. Intellectual limitations were placed on the students by denying us various perspectives, creating a culture that kept us out of touch with reality. The University's daily message was this: *Yes, there are other opinions out there, but the holders of those thoughts are either bigots, stupid, or not as enlightened as their progressive-minded counterparts.* "I really had no idea that entire states were against gay marriage. I thought it was just small, radical groups," a Brown student mused after the 2004 election revealed the overwhelming amount of support for a Constitutional Amendment to ban homosexual unions.(1)

The political oblivion of Brown's pupils wasn't their fault. It was the tragic end to a soft and deliberate scheme composed by today's modern left. For decades, students have been denied intellectual diversity to ensure the survival of a left-wing ideology in the outside world, and Brown University has been protecting that educational dishonesty. Currently Brown doesn't allow the ROTC (Reserve Officers Training Corps) onto its campus. This is due primarily to the military's "don't ask, don't tell" policy concerning homosexuality. Taking an unusual stance for a Brown student, one pupil argued that Brown *should* make room for this military presence in order to cause change "from the inside, giving future generals four years of liberal learning."(2) Even campus leftists recognized Brown's political imbalance, and the ability of such a place to help radically transform a nation.

While *Out of Ivy* seeks to reintroduce the sad state of academia, and to lucidly demonstrate the enduring tyranny of campus left-wingers, it also reveals a captivating conflict of two particular persuasions—a private struggle that not only validates previous warnings of higher education, but also offers a glimpse at one student's political development. At 18 years-old I didn't have the words to express my hesitancy to concur with modern-day liberalism. I just felt an uncertain negativity toward principles of the left, and also the people who were driving them forward. The values and virtues I was taught while growing up were not in sentence-form within my head, but rather in a collection of tiny life-lessons that formed my gut instincts—my own personal sense of right and wrong. Thrown into an activist whirlwind at Brown University, I was way out of my league—a political rookie amongst a rabble of seemingly intelligent and experienced liberals. I appeared just ripe enough for Brown's campus left to begin their brainwashing. But I detected something erroneous, dishonest, and absurd about the actions and beliefs of many of my classmates and professors. I just couldn't put my finger on exactly what it was that bothered me (and I wasn't allowed to either). With much trepidation and uncertainty, I set out to discover political truth, and the origin of Brown's political barbarism. That is the story that I will tell. A straight, white, male. An athlete. An outmatched, right-minded campus underdog doing everything in his power to resist the pressure that was forcing him to abandon all he was brought up to believe in, and follow the path of the liberal Ivy mainstream.

While *Out of Ivy* is peppered with the stories I wish to share, much of it is editorial. My opinions and my evaluations. My own gut feelings and political instincts. *Out of Ivy* is as much about me and where I'm coming from, as it is about Brown and the direction it steers tomorrow's leaders. This may seem to be the writer's obsession with himself, but it's really an attempt to allow the reader to evaluate not just certain events, but also the conflicting mentalities that were there.

Of course, one of those present mentalities was liberalism. Reflecting back on my college years caused me to see the recklessness of this ideology. It's a political philosophy that contradicts true Americanism, the nation that was intended. It alters the character of our country, not in any positive dimensions, but in ways that incrementally deteriorate our way of life, and diminish our national allegiance. Through resilient reflection and observation of campus occurrences that happened while I attended Brown—and then soon after I graduated—I became more cognizant of the battle I had engaged in when I decided to criticize the University's campus left by becoming an opinion columnist for the *Brown Daily Herald*, the university newspaper. During my final two years as a student I bickered with my classmates, finally defying their campus politics. Toward the end of my Ivy tenure I became aware of just how significant a step this was onto the battleground of America's ongoing culture war. Suddenly, liberal thought became one of the things I detested most. It was right up there with field hockey and the New York Yankees. I now saw Brown as a political weapon for radical progressives, a place intent on breeding the leftist mentality. I was suddenly fighting against the expansion of a mindset, one that I saw corroding a way of life that cherishes liberty. I was now confronting a mentality that was actually promoting hatred for America, and was turning the greatest nation in the world into a country of sniveling sissies.

Furthermore, upon graduating from Brown University I had learned to withhold credibility from anything spouted from the mouth of a liberal. Referring to the morality of Communist Russia, President Reagan informed the world that the communists would "lie, cheat, and commit any crime to further the goals of communism."(3) I wouldn't have to tone this line down too much to describe most components of Brown's campus left. How I came to hold this jaded perspective is the story I wish to share, and I invite anyone willing to listen to read the following pages.

Despite the fact that I graduated from Brown in May of 2002, I spent the next several years hovering around campus while I put my story down on paper. In a certain way I continued to attend Brown—not as a student, but as an observer of the campus structure. Therefore, some events I speak of within *Out of Ivy* occurred soon after my official departure. I have done my best to put together an honest and comprehensive book—one that is unique, informative, and entertaining. Within these pages you will read of certain accounts that were visible to the public, events that unveiled the state of Brown's academic atmosphere. These events often placed Brown in the public eye, as they sparked debate over free speech, political correctness, and the role of the academy in American society. However, much of my alma mater's intellectual prejudice flew below national surveillance. These are the episodes that I believe need to be revealed in order to chronicle the development of a political mind, and why I came to believe that the criticisms that have already fallen on our universities are not false admonitions, that the death of America begins on our liberal breeding grounds, our native institutions of the highest learning.

To Brown's current students: I want you to compare my description and dissection of the University with your own experiences. Indeed, I look forward to dissenting feedback. However, if my story begins to look unfamiliar to you, before assuming that I have intentionally exaggerated Brown's campus conditions in order to create a livelier book, consider the fact that many of my stories were born before you arrived on campus.

Within the past few years there have been slight changes brought about on College Hill, modifications that were prompted by events that happened while I was still a student. Brown's president, Ruth Simmons, was arriving just as I was leaving. If you have paid close attention, then you have noticed her immediate focus on issues of intellectual tolerance on campus. This may be one of President Simmons' favorite topics, but that's not why she has given it so much attention. It has all been due to several revealing episodes that you may not be aware of. Don't worry, *Out of Ivy* will divulge them. Trust me. You should also note recent University additions such as the Kaleidoscope Fund, a newly revived College Republicans, Students for Liberty, the Political Theory Project, and *The Brown Spectator*. Keep in mind that none of these existed when I was a Brown student. These additions, plus a sudden, lingering awareness of the importance of intellectual diversity have made strong improvements to the University's political climate in only several years. Soon, however, you will discover why I am not so confident in Brown's future. I only proceed with—to steal a phrase from a recent College Republican president—cautious optimism.

CHAPTER 1
America

When I was growing up I was fortunate enough to have three brothers, and a swimming pool. One thing all four of us knew was that my mother didn't like, what she called, the *In-and-Out*. *In-and-Out* was when my brothers and I would decide to go outside for a while, and then come back in to play Nintendo, wrestle, or watch television. Eventually we would get bored, so we would go back outside to play with our toy guns, play hide-and-go-seek, and roll around in the mud. Then, we would go back inside to hear my mother yell, "Knock off the *In-and-Out*!" We didn't know exactly why, but we knew we had to decide on a daily basis whether we'd be playing *In* the house, or *Out*.

Because of our mother's *In-and-Out* rule, my brothers and I were forced to become very creative with our time. We knew once we left the house we would not be allowed back in, so we came up with unique ways to entertain ourselves. My brothers and I found a game that we enjoyed very much, and precisely suited the character of the group. One of us would be tied up by the others using a rope that we had found in the woods behind our house. The detainee would be moved to the edge of the nine-foot deep-end of the family pool, and then thrown in to see if he would be capable of escaping death-by-drowning. The rest of us would watch and laugh as our brother squirmed for freedom, and life itself.

When we first originated this game, the youngster who was tied up would struggle out of the rope while pushing up from the bottom of the pool with his feet so that he could capture some air, and buy some time for his escape. This was unacceptable. It was too easy for the captive to evade death with an unlimited air supply. So we started to tie legs up to heads, and arms to feet, so that when our bounded bodies landed on the pool floor there would be no simple approach to gain more breath. I remember the rope being tied so tightly by my brothers that it would be difficult to breathe even before I had been thrown in, but for some reason (maybe a miracle) we always came out of the pool alive, only a tad out of breath. My mother never knew we played this game while we were outside, but I bet if she did know, then she would have tolerated a little more of that *In-and-Out* that she had such a problem with. At least if we were coming back *In* she would know that she still had four sons, and not three.

I often tell this story to remind myself of the irrepressible human spirit, a dignity in constant search for the pinnacle of one's potential. I tell this story to remind myself of that brave ingredient within all of us that understands what happens to the human heart if it's abandoned, and forced to settle for mediocrity. And I tell this story now to remind my readers of the nation that welcomed a constant condition of discord that unleashed this will to not only survive, but to become great, and to discover absolute truth. Demonstrating a powerful yearning for liberty, and an equal disdain for tyranny, an unprecedented faith was placed in the nobility of *The People.*

It was the rivalries of brotherhood, along with athletics, that taught me individualism and the American Way. And while my "pool story" certainly exhibits our misunderstanding of the physical world, it also demonstrates our *full* understanding of that portion of the human spirit that becomes inspired, that part of humanity that compels us to go beyond what others tell us is impossible. Believe it or not, our game actually evolved to the point where we would be tying each other up to plastic pool chairs before we were sent to the bottom of the pool.

I contrast this story with the one I will tell about Brown University. I had come from a place where if I wasn't being challenged, then I was taught to challenge myself. This new prism I was now to view the world through did not demand discourse, or even suggest it. At Brown University, as free-thinking, progressive-minded, and authority-defiant as my classmates were, their rebellion seemed to stall when it came time to question their politics. Frankly, I couldn't find a real fight, and for some reason I found that tranquility troubling. Some part of me wished to defy the silence, because somehow I knew that when discourse is denied, mediocrity and falsity are always the result.

Besides my inclination that political truth could never be discovered within a lopsided arena of debate, the unchecked mindset of the campus mainstream repulsed me in ways that I was not prepared for. They were calling it "liberalism"—a term originally intended to infer the enlightenment and open-minded spirit of those who exercised it. Today it has come to define a particular side of America's culture war because leftists hijacked the once-positive label of "liberal." Today, some *classical liberals* resent being confused with leftists. But hey, that's the evolution of words. And as a political newcomer, I learned to use "liberal" and "leftist" interchangeably simply because people at Brown referred to themselves as "liberals"—when they were really leftists.

Liberal or leftist, I would eventually realize that Brown's reigning ideology was enslaving the minds of the students, was empowered by fogging the history of our nation, and was turning the greatest country in the world into a bunch of whining weaklings. On liberalism's best days it was only un-American. Every other day, it was embarrassingly *anti*-American.

How could I sit by, and say nothing?

Yeh huh. Even Thomas Jefferson Said So.

The political imbalance at my alma mater was mind-blowing. Conservative opinion was not just held by a minority, but before time could be spent pronouncing it, you had to first remind everyone of the right you had to speak it. If somebody forgot to offer this reminder he would be doomed for what Brown members saw as the appropriate social consequences.

Even those who dared to stray from the Ivy groupthink did it apologetically. Someone who was willing to offer an alternative opinion would usually do so in the following fashion: *Don't get me wrong, I am a fierce proponent of gay marriage, but*...Or, *I also think that President Bush is as dumb as rocks, and should be impeached, but*...During these rare occasions of alternate expression, the slightest hint of conservatism was prefaced with a plea for tolerance. In November of 1999 a student wishing to express a libertarian perspective on discrimination laws began his column like so: "Before I begin, a quick request:...I...ask readers to read carefully and seriously. Without reading this column from start to finish, you will undoubtedly misconstrue my thoughts."(1) In 2001, the author of a conservative piece on homosexuality felt he needed to also say, "At the very least, I ask that [students] respect the views of those who, for either religious or moral reasons, believe that homosexual acts are sinful.

The social fabric of a university cannot otherwise survive without such tolerance."(2)

At Brown, engaging liberalism was like trying to feed a mean dog. *Is he going to take this food, or bite my freakin' hand off?!* This reality eventually forced me to investigate the meaning and purpose of our freedoms, the First Amendment, and the history of our nation.

Through my research, I found that since its inception our nation has understood the connection between free speech and American liberty, and the responsibility of its citizens to uphold the standard that was set when many sacrificed all they had, so that the America they envisioned might survive. After one of the more bitter Presidential elections in our country's history, one that rattled the unity of the new nation, Thomas Jefferson offered these words in his Inaugural Address:

> "All will bear in mind this sacred principle, that though the will of the majority is in all cases to prevail, that will to be rightful must be reasonable; that the minority possess their equal rights, which equal law must protect, and to violate would be oppression...And let us reflect that, having banished from our land that religious intolerance under which mankind so long bled and suffered, we have yet gained little if we countenance a political intolerance as despotic, as wicked, and capable of as bitter and bloody persecutions...If there be any among us who would wish to dissolve this Union or to change its republican form, let them stand undisturbed as monuments of the safety with which error of opinion may be tolerated where reason is left free to combat it."(3)

At a time when the notion of a free republic was the ideal that many had recently died for in order to create a way of life opposite a dictatorship, Jefferson realized that in order for true freedom to exist, and to be enjoyed by succeeding generations, that never should this cherished principle of liberty be compromised—even if this principle allowed room for lies and cruelty. When finding these words I perceived them as the true character of courage—to allow for the words of your most despised ideology, and to risk the loss of something proudly achieved, while having monumental faith that America's new standards of justice, peace, and freedom would prevail. Jefferson had an understanding that in order to reveal falsehood, bigotry, and evil, then the aforementioned ungodliness must be allowed to present itself. Only then can it be removed from our society.

Patrick Henry, one year before the start of the Revolutionary War, and within the same speech that he voiced his immortal words, "Give me liberty, or give me death," expressed a similar outlook to those who wished to appease the British, rather than take up arms:

> "No man thinks more highly than I do of the patriotism, as well as abilities, of the very worthy gentlemen who have just addressed the House. But different men often see the same subject in different lights; and, therefore, I hope it will not be thought disrespectful to those gentlemen if, entertaining as I do opinions of a character very opposite to theirs, I shall speak forth my sentiments freely and without reserve. This is no time for ceremony. The questing before the House is one of awful moment to this country. For my own part, I consider it as nothing less than a question of freedom or slavery; and in proportion to the magnitude of the subject ought to be the freedom of the debate. It is only in this way that we can hope to arrive at truth, and fulfill the great responsibility which we hold to God and our country. Should I keep back my opinions at such a time, through fear of giving offense, I should consider myself as guilty of treason towards my country, and of an act of disloyalty toward the Majesty of Heaven, which I revere above all earthly kings."(4)

During my senior year and beyond, I came to discover that our nation's greatest heroes are not so revered merely for existing in a time of historical achievement and prominence. They became our heroes because they demonstrated the bravery, and spoke the gospel of the dream for a new hope, and set a standard of courage and principle for all Americans to strive for long after they were gone.

Brown liberals had a difficult time upholding the courageous ideal of open political dialogue. I would eventually view their demeanor as behavior that our Founding Fathers would have firmly disagreed with due to their understanding of not only the preciousness of freedom, but also its fragility. For reasons I will speak of later on, the campus left was entirely disinterested in the valor of debate and dissension. For certain, this caused me to take a step back, and I imagined a time when Americans stood firmer on the grounds of freedom, and bravely accepted a state where error and insult would always be endured and confronted by an American spirit that would refuse to compromise this principle of liberty for the sake of compassion, or even survival.

The blackout of campus dissent is no small issue. Until I arrived on Brown's campus I had never before met a body of people as Machiavellian, as dishonest, as immoral, and as willing to behave with such vile contempt as were Ivy League liberals; all of this intended to solidify liberal supremacy, but disguised as healthy political activity. Unfortunately, the avoidance of campus discourse became habit. In the future we can look forward to leaders who are compelled to avoid democratic means whenever possible, those who will see nothing un-American with their despotic methods of political influence. This was the weakening of the American spirit, and the birth of a new order.

CHAPTER 2
Brown University: A Tradition Of Radical Liberalism

I suppose it is helpful to readers to have some historical background pertaining to the place they will be reading about.

Brown is one of the most elite academic institutions in the entire country, and numbers amongst the prestigious Ivy League. Somebody once told me that the origin of the term "Ivy" came from the first four schools in the illustrious collegiate conference; Columbia, Harvard, Princeton, and Yale. The Roman Numeral "IV" (four) when pronounced simply comes out of the mouth as "i-vee." When I investigated the truth to this trivia, it turned out to be highly disputed gossip, but I often spread the rumor anyway. It makes you seem a little smarter if you can throw tidbits of information like that out once in a while, as if you read a lot or something.

Brown sits atop College Hill in the historical city of Providence, Rhode Island. Many are drawn to the quaint city for its expression of art, culture, and diversity. Providence is frequently called the "Renaissance City," and has recently elected an openly-gay mayor (and as Jerry Seinfeld would say, "not that there's anything wrong with that").

Providence also boasts a great colonial history. It was founded by Roger Williams in 1636 when he fled Massachusetts Bay to escape the religious oppression of the Puritans. Freedom of religion became the hallmark of Providence as it was the founding principle of the new settlement. Almost four centuries later Brown, with its vastly diverse student body, has attempted to sustain Roger Williams' vision of a place where people are free to live without fear of persecution for their beliefs.

A Long History of Activism

I discovered early-on that Brown was no ordinary place for campus activism. In many ways Brown set the standard by which other colleges measured their activist role. The University resides in the esteemed Ivy League (a place wholly known for liberalism's cry), and Brown would host and sponsor regional discussions that invited renowned professors, government officials, authors, and other intellectual professionals to their campus. The national media coverage Brown received, and the political celebrities that visited the campus, inspired other schools to participate in the same type of activism in which the Ivy Leaguers were partaking.

In the 1960s Brown became well-known for its campus shenanigans, and the autonomy the University afforded its students. In support of demilitarization during the Vietnam era, students phased out Brown's ROTC program, and blocked CIA recruiters from visiting the campus. Black students ordered Brown to increase the number of minorities that would enter the student body each year, and the University quickly yielded to their demands.

Then, with the waning of the civil rights movement, the feminist movement, and the Vietnam era, college activism also subsided. Not as much at Brown, however. My alma mater achieved its activist reputation in the 1960s, but unlike other colleges and universities, Brunonians continued their activism in the years that followed. In the 1980s and 1990s they were organizing against things like sweatshops and the Gulf War. Long before I arrived there, political rallying had simply become a way of life for Brown students and faculty. On its website Brown University speaks of the overwhelming vitality of student activity:

> **"It is a testament to the special ethos of the College that, once at Brown, students quickly engage not only in the intellectual rigors of the classroom, but also in activities that complement and enhance their academic pursuits."** (1)

In the wake of September 11th this political agitation escalated, and was now at levels that matched notable times in the history of student activism. Professor Paul Buhle, who was a former student activist in the 1960s, and who now specializes in the history of the U.S. left, and who teaches a course titled *The Sixties Without Apology,* and who in 2003 said, "...we didn't go nearly far enough...we weren't able to do enough to democratize American society or even reduce the power of the military-industrial complex," said about Brown's current campus atmosphere, "I see an outpouring of activity and intellectual interest in ways that

I haven't seen on a campus since the 1970s."(2) I'm not sure whether to consider myself fortunate or unfortunate, but it was in this time period that I had the opportunity to witness the campus life Brown offers its students.

The Campus Left

The Brown faculty is marked by a 30:1 Democrat/Republican ratio, an informative statistic of the University's political imbalance.(3) Steeped in a tradition of radical liberalism, Brown has bred the likes of Amy Carter, Ted Turner, and John F. Kennedy Jr. The most recent Brown graduate to achieve his fifteen minutes of fame is Michael Newdow '74, the physician/law school graduate atheist who is now challenging the constitutionality of the Pledge of Allegiance because of its usage of the phrase *one nation, under God*, and he has already argued his case successfully in San Francisco's Ninth Circuit Court of Appeals. Mr. Newdow is also in the midst of a battle to rid our currency of the words, *In God We Trust.*

Even before they graduate, Brown students put on displays of liberal extremism that never fail to generate national media attention. Brown's radical feminism was nationally recognized when high-paying court settlements typified controversial sexual harassment and rape cases that sprouted up on Brown's campus in the 1990s. The origin of a national uprising over women's athletics also stems from Brown. One of Brown's own female volleyball players brought a class action Title IX lawsuit against the University when Brown attempted to cut women's gymnastics and volleyball from its budget. Even though men's golf and wrestling were to be cut as well, the U.S. Supreme Court ruled that Brown had discriminated against its female athletes. The debatable decision prompted the dismantling of men's programs throughout the country to make room for less lucrative and less popular women's teams.

David Horowitz, the former Black Panther turned famed conservative critic, also shook the halls of Brown in 2001 when his infamous and highly disputed ad, *"Ten Reasons Why Reparations For Slavery Is a Bad Idea—And Racist Too,"* was published by the *Brown Daily Herald.* The ensuing racial war gained national attention as the University was torn between those who believed that the ad was hate speech, and those who defended the right to print it. The nation watched as Brown's underground racial tension was exposed on a battlefield of justice and ideology.

After September 11th, and in the midst of the Iraq War, Brown seized the opportunity for national leadership of the opposition to the Bush Administration's efforts. *The American Council of Trustees and Alumni* put out a report entitled *"How Our Universities Are Failing America and What Can Be Done About It."* The report was a commentary on the anti-Americanism that emulated from the nation's campuses during this time of possible war, and much-needed patriotism. It reported a collection of over 115 anti-American quotations that stemmed from the country's college campuses. Among the 115 quotations, 14 were plucked from Brown's own private collection of unpatriotic statements, outnumbering all other schools, and demonstrating my alma mater's leadership role in campus activism across the country.(4)

Events such as these have allowed Brown University to require no introduction to high school students searching for a liberal activist community to be a part of during their college years.

The New Curriculum

Brown left the activist decade of the 1960s with a new mission, what came to be known as the *New Curriculum.* The notion of "relevance" had become a popular educational ideal, the idea that education should include less the study of traditional texts and subjects, and allow the students to choose their own course-load depending on their own values and interests. With a new University president, and a student body that had been dragged through the radical '60s demanding more "say" at their home campus, Brown discontinued its "outdated" educational procedure. The University implemented the *New Curriculum*, one that offered its students unparalleled educational freedom. In fact, it was two undergraduates who were responsible for the creation of the *New Curriculum*; Elliot Maxwell '68 and Ira Magaziner '69, who later became an advisor to President Clinton. Brown had begun its reformation, and was on its way to becoming one of the most liberal educational institutions the nation has ever known. I will say this right now, but *Out of Ivy* will explain later: The *New Curriculum* is a *bad* thing.

I discovered that the leftist mentality is thicker in the institutions of the *highest* learning, and we can see this by looking at the curriculum that these schools offer. Similar to the action taken by Brown in the 1960s, other schools began to liberalize their curriculum as well. *The American Council of Trustees and Alumni* found that among the top 55 universities in the country, students can graduate without taking a single course in U.S. History. Only three out of those 55 required one course on Western Civilization, and 78 percent of those 55 "top" universities allowed students to graduate without taking any history courses at all.(5) Within the short period that I attended Brown University, I would realize several times the drastic effects of deciding to radicalize a campus and its curriculum with liberalism, and only liberalism.

The freedom that Brown offered its students in the 1960s has expanded over the years, and in my opinion, has come back to bite the University. Brown began to allow its students to take partial control over the campus, a notion that initially sounded fine-and-dandy to me. I mean, it was our education, right? Why shouldn't we have had a say in what went on? What I witnessed at Brown, however, was a bunch of radical students who had learned to take advantage of the control they had over the administration, and abused that power so much that they often placed Brown in an embarrassing public spotlight. I would never blame anyone for stereotyping Brown students as a bunch of spoiled brats, even though I would be included in that characterization. Honestly, I would have to sympathize with those who get that impression. Time after time, I witnessed my classmates force the hand of reform with their protests, denouncing their school as one that fostered bigotry and prejudice in order to receive what they demanded. Of course, there was a history of this behavior. There have been six individuals who have served as the president of Brown University since the 1960s, and at least two of them have admitted that their resignations were—at least partially—due to the stress brought on by Brown's culture of constant campus upheaval from the students and faculty. In 1969 Brown president Ray Heffner said, "I have simply reached the conclusion that I don't enjoy being a university president."(6) In 1975, while facing the dilemma of a tight financial budget, Brown president Donald Hornig was also forced to deal with minority protests over admission policies, and a class-action lawsuit filed by a female professor who had not been assigned tenure. She made the claim that "the University discriminated against women faculty in its hiring and promoting decisions."(7) Hornig resigned saying that the "retrenchment 'has taken a toll on me and my family, as well as producing great stains on the fabric of the University.'"(8) A decade and a half later Brown had quintupled the number of its female faculty members. Oh woopee.

By the time I had arrived on campus the *Brown Daily Herald* was the recipient of ongoing remarks that outlandishly accused the paper of neglecting "to represent, in its staffing, in publishing interests and practices and in its values the diversity of the Brown community."(9) And despite the control student extremists had over the campus, despite their ability to convert College Hill into a leftist echo-chamber, and despite their tendency to drive university presidents to the edge of the cliff, they still reserved for themselves the right to chuck preposterous firebombs such as this: "Issues of race and class (and sexuality, sexual identity and gender) are not looked at deeply, critically and courageously enough on this campus. Brown is not immune: We too are racist...sexist...homophobic," said one of my classmates in a *Herald* letter entitled, "*Racism Exists in Many Subtle Forms*."(10) Continuing to malign the University, Jason Lambrese, a member of the Lesbian Gay Bisexual Transsexual Alliance (LGBTA), once said, "The University has proven itself unwilling to confront the impact of hate crimes on students of color, lgbtq students, and other targeted communities..."(11) Administration officials, whether because they were cowering from my classmates' zealotry, or were too concerned with possibly offending some of them, seemed to lack the courage to stand up to those pupils who persistently smeared them. Shaun Joseph '02, a member of Brown's thunderous *International Socialist Organization* once said, "My method of dealing with [Brown] administrators is that when they do something good, I'm behind them, and if they do something bad, I'm behind them to kick them in the ass."(12) That's nice, Shaun.

As I came to discover, student dominion was one of Brown's tactics of indoctrination. A majority of the administration and faculty actually agreed with my classmates' politics and protests. And fanatical pupils were crucial to the scheme of silence.

Censored Conservatives

Brown University was supposed to be my "marketplace of ideas," and was to provide room for the broadening of my intellectual horizon by collecting various perspectives. However, a political ideology called "liberalism" was corrupting the university-medium to advance its own agenda. The education promised to students, and their intellectual potential was what needed to be sacrificed.

Somewhere along the way Brown adopted the leftist tactic of political correctness as well. However, once Brown had custody of this tool of conservative tranquility, they heightened its ability to succeed in political debate by mastering the practice that ensures one-sided politics. Brown's campus became not only a shrine for student activism, but was now marked by the totalitarianism of the political left.

I watched as prominent liberal lecturers were trucked in by the dozen each year to speak to the Brown community while conservatives were invited on the rarest of occasions. Just within recent years, Brown has hosted the lectures of Howard Dean, John Kerry, Bill Clinton, Spike Lee, Woody Harrelson, Mikhael Gorbachev, Chris Matthews, Howard Zinn, Noam Chomsky, Cornel West, Carol Moseley Braun, Ted Turner, Dan Rather, Jesse Jackson, Charlie Rangel, Ralph Nader, etc. Despite Brown's intellectual inequality, that a list of speakers helps to reveal, the few orators of traditional thought that made it past the Van Wickle Gates (Brown's symbolic entry to the community) while I was there were almost assured of boisterous protest, and were forced to spend their lecture-time defending their right to speak, rather than declare their beliefs (figures such as Ralph Reed and Richard Perle can attest to this). Many of us just learned to accept the intolerance of the campus left. Too many examples had been made of those who dared to challenge their authority. As you will soon discover, many Brown students simply passed through their college years viewing a political puppet show, having contributed little, and gained even less.

Like many other university handbooks, the language in my alma mater's "Principles of the Brown University Community" and "Student Rights and Responsibilities" contained language that established an acceptable code of speech for my classmates and I to abide by. One possible offense that a student wishing to offer his/her opinion might have had to answer to involved:

> **"...subjecting another person or group to abusive, threatening, intimidating, or harassing actions, including, but not limited to, those based on race, religion, gender, disability, age, economic status, ethnicity, national origin, sexual orientation, gender identity, or gender expression."** (13)

The groundwork for fierce debate over the definition of *free speech* or "abusive" or "threatening" or "intimidating" or "harassing" was always set when my alma mater would draw these lines of decent and respectful speech. During my time upon College Hill, Brown would often run the risk of appearing as a hypocritical institution for their constant claim to fostering an open-minded education. From the same source comes this quotation:

> **"Brown strives to sustain a learning environment that supports individual exploration, creativity, and accomplishment and that promotes and protects the free exchange of ideas."** (14)

I found out just how dishonest these declarations of uninhibited thought and campus individualism were as I encountered example-after-example of protected liberal bombardment that was always surrounded by an administration claiming to safeguard the speech of a minority.

Brown doesn't sit alone in this pool of criticism, but it surely resides in the deep end. Many universities have been found guilty of sheltering campuses that are philosophically sealed, but throughout the years Brown has taken a leadership role in the indoctrination of America's youth. There might not be a university with a comparable reputation of liberal antic. Even the high-profile, lesbian, feminist professor, Camille Paglia, had to admit about my alma mater, "Brown is the most viciously intolerant campus that I ever visited as a lecturer." (15) It was at this place that I was meant to discover political truth.

CHAPTER 3
So, You're a Pimp.

One of my early encounters with liberalism at Brown University wasn't even on campus. I met a girl while I was at a bar called the Yellow Kitten on Block Island, a small, old-style, colonial island off the coast of Narragansett, Rhode Island, my hometown. The area is a popular tourist spot in the summer, and thousands of people show up from all over the country to enjoy the beaches, fresh seafood, and tourist activities. It was the Fourth of July, and as you can imagine, a setting such as Block Island makes for a great celebration spot for that specific holiday. Thousands of people flocked to the island.

I was 19, and in the bar. (Give me a break, I'm Irish.)

Across the bar I saw an attractive female, and anyone who knows me would also know that I would waste no time in making a move. You learn pretty quickly in your pubescent years that the pretty ones don't stay lonely too long. This girl looked slightly older than me, and the only thing I found bizarre about her looks was that she was wearing some sort of alternative-style skirt that seemed to be made out of paper. I remember thinking that it looked as if she had made it herself in home-economics class in the third grade or something. Still, like The Flash, I was right next to her introducing myself. She appeared slightly miserable.

The typical starter questions were asked. What's your name? Where ya from? Where do you go to school? What do you study? Is your boyfriend within a 100-foot radius? Her name was Katie. Katie or Katy or Kadi or Kaity or K.D. I don't know how she spelled her name because I never got the chance to send her a love-letter.

Things went great at first, though. I remember making her laugh, but I don't remember exactly what I said. I think I might have told her that I liked her paper skirt. That would have been funny.

She said she had graduated from Brown University. Great! Any competent womanizer knows that it always helps to have one common piece of ground for both of you to stand on, and I was going into my sophomore year at Brown in the fall. We were getting along great before I asked, "So what do you do now that you've graduated?"

"I moved back to San Francisco and I run my own business." At 19 years old I didn't know any better. I couldn't see the warning signs back then. Brown University. San Francisco. The paper skirt. I wasn't going to get along with this chick. Oh, and I better not call her "chick" either.

"Oh yeah!? What's your business?" I asked, pretending to care.

"I provide troubled women with sexual pleasure."

"What!?"

"Forget it. I don't want to get into it," she said.

"No, no. I want you to tell me about it." This 19 year-old was suddenly very interested.

"I provide men for women who have trouble with their sex lives. Sex toys just don't cut it. People need another person there to really be fulfilled. Ya know?"

No. I didn't know. Proudly. A million thoughts ran through my head at once, and I began to stutter because all of them were trying to come out at the same time, and I also wasn't sure if I should say some of them.

She could tell I was having a problem with what she had just told me, so she cut my stuttering off and said with conviction, "Do you realize that there are thousands of women out there who have never had an orgasm?!"

"Um, no," I said. Actually, I don't even think I knew women could have orgasms.

"Well, I help women who have those types of problems."

"By providing men for them?"

"Yeah...well...sometimes other women too." She said it so matter-of-factly.

I had gathered all of this information and thought I had it all figured out when I said, "Sooooooo....... you're a pimp."

"No. I'm not a pimp. I help women who are very frustrated and unhappy people." She was becoming agitated and slightly insulted by my confusion about her "business."

I had to get away from the controversial side of the topic. So, I asked her, "Oh, I see. Well...ummm...Do you make good money?"

"I do okay."

"And do you pay the guys you set these women up with?" I asked.

"Yeah, of course."

"Sooooo...you're a pimp." I couldn't help but press the issue.

She looked at me with a decided face and said, "Ya know what, forget it! I believe in what I do!" She walked away. That's okay. I could handle the rejection, and I never dreamed I'd marry a she-pimp anyway. She'd probably wear a white paper dress to our wedding. Not my type.

At 19 years old, I didn't fully appreciate what had just happened to me. Back then it was just another girl walking away from one of my valiant efforts to approach. At that point in my life, I was not interested in politics. As I spent more time at Brown, however, campus events would convert me into a committed conservative. Only then was I able to realize who my Pimp Girlfriend really was. She was a liberal.

It's a Mindset

After meeting the she-pimp I came across an article in the *Brown Daily Herald* that would jumpstart my reflection on the differences in human thought. A columnist for *The Herald* submitted an article on the USA Olympic Basketball Team that declared just how awful it was that the United States was allowed to send its BEST players (those in the NBA) to COMPETE in the Olympics. The article was entitled, *Dream Team a Real Sleeper,* and it has hung on my bedroom wall ever since it was printed.

I cut the article out and taped it to the wall of my dorm-room. Each year as I moved into a different dormitory, the article came with me, and onto a new wall in my new room. When I first read the article I hadn't a full understanding as to why I despised it so much. For my remaining years at Brown I would read it over and over, pondering its message, and wondering about the character of the writer.

The writer felt that it wasn't "fair." She *really* said that. It was not "fair" that the United States was allowed to send its BEST players to COMPETE for the Gold Medal. These were the types of notions that went virtually uncontested at Brown. They were continuous and unopposed. My classmates were ferociously defiant to so many opinions, yet when this thought was placed in front of them they saw no need for an uproar. Why? Part of the reason probably lied with the fact that, in her *sports* column, the writer just couldn't help but bring her argument into the political spectrum (an area I was unfamiliar with at the time I had first read this). She stated:

> "There are those who would disagree with me, those who would call me a whining liberal who wants to support the undeserving at the expense of the strong. These are the people who are truly sold on the capitalistic, Darwinistic notion that the fittest should and will outlive (or outplay) the weaker of the species."
>
> "I root for America. I want America to win, but only by playing fair. I don't want to be the bully who beats up the scrawny kid down the street for his lunch money just because he can. It's just not fun that way."(1)

She was right. There were those who would call her a "whining liberal." Now I'm one of them. More important than how I feel about her opinions, however, were the undertones of anti-capitalism, anti-Americanism, and the liberal monopoly over high intellect that permeated from almost all of Brown's popular campus sentiments. If you were an open-market conservative, you were "truly sold." Stupid, if you will.

Leftist indoctrination was just that subtle. It was everywhere. It was within what people wrote. It was within how people spoke. It was within the classroom. But it also boomed from student activities. It saturated student discussion. It was solidified by invited guest speakers. It was on flyers, pamphlets, posters, and bumper stickers. It was presented as smart, progressive, moral, and harmless. And it was almost never challenged—not *just* because campus liberals practiced the art of intentional political silencing, but also because every vocal component of the campus was like-minded, and Brown simply didn't offer anything but left-leaning activities. In fact, the College Republicans were just being revived as I was about to graduate.

Much of Brown's chatter and commotion confused me—and certainly, some of it bothered me. At first, it was this writer's hostility toward true competition that I found unsettling. She wrote, "Olympic basketball no longer promotes competition." I thought to myself, *Why? Because there is a dominant team? Does she think that other teams are going to stop trying to win? Did the NBA no longer promote competition when Kobe Bryant, Shaquille O'neal, and the LA Lakers were running the table several years in a row? Or, would somebody eventually figure out how to defeat them? Don't "the best" always fall at the hands of an over-achiever, someone striving to surpass the boundaries of high achievement that their predecessors previously established?* Those were *my* thoughts. But this Ivy League student didn't want to be the "bully." It wouldn't be "fun."

I actually felt a little bit of anger when I read her column. And I felt more anger the more I thought about her opinion, and how many people she may have influenced. However, I also felt that all it would take was one person with a shred of understanding of competition and the American Way, someone who still believed in the concept of the American Dream, to publicly refute her. That's all it would have taken to overcome this weak, discouraging, and un-American opinion. But nobody, for some reason, felt compelled to do so.

On a sidenote, most people must have noticed the struggle the rest of the world forced on our 2004 Men's Olympic basketball team. In the 2004 Summer Games, the entire world seemed to have caught up to the USA as we were forced to scuffle with every team we played, and actually lost to teams such as Argentina, Lithuania, and Puerto Rico. PUERTO RICO! A once dominant team was forced to settle for only the Bronze.

Now, I often wonder if the writer of *Dream Team A Real Sleeper* would have looked a foreign Olympian in the eye before the game, and told him that she was opposed to sending our best players overseas to compete against him and his countrymen because it would be impossible for them to beat us. She would probably expect a big hug and a warm thank-you for being so understanding and sensitive to his lack of skills, height, and strength. Instead, she would have received a big glob of foreign spit in her eye for her insult, and she wouldn't understand why. After all, she was just trying to help.

Back then I could sense it, but couldn't explain it. This girl was discouraging any hope, faith, or optimism that may have been swelling in the hearts of others. And essentially what she was telling the entire student body on this average day upon Providence's College Hill was that she supported the worldwide regression of the game of basketball. She was supporting the lowering of standards within the level of play on a global basis due to her compassion for those who were finding it difficult to win the Gold. It irked me so.

Looking back, it doesn't surprise me that it was an opinion generated within the athletic spectrum that was able to get under my skin. Athletics had played such a large part in my upbringing, and the things I had a comprehension of were the lessons and values that resonated from the playing fields. Yes, I thought, by sending only amateur basketball players to the Olympics it would allow other countries to win once in a while. We would most likely see some more exciting buzzer-beating games too. What we would miss out on is the knowledge of just how good we can become. We would never reach our full capabilities. Others across the world would be trained to believe that a very possible goal was actually unattainable. As for Americans, even we would be held back. Because our best players would no longer be chased by others, there would be no reason to further develop their skills. As a result, the entire world would settle for mediocre play, and this girl would feel good about herself for accomplishing true *fairness.* Was I the only one experiencing this agitation from her column? It seemed so.

This was the aspect of leftist thought that troubled me the most—it never demanded a fight. It never asked people to do better, or be better. But it offered an infinite amount of excuses, only causing the perpetual lowering of standards: athletic standards, military standards, educational standards—and perhaps worst of all—our moral standards.

After a while it became crystal clear to me exactly how campus liberals pushed their philosophy onto others. All of their ideas were driven by the same insanity—the shortsightedness of sensitivity, and an incessant pandering concern for people's feelings. This was a difficult outlook to accept for a football player who had spent the past ten years of his life being taught that his personal feelings were of little importance—especially when up against a backdrop of something larger than himself.

Nevertheless, coming from the same mindset as the student who wrote *Dream Team a Real Sleeper*, my Pimp Girlfriend, in the name of compassion for women who couldn't achieve orgasms, thought it was appropriate and righteous to sell sexual favors, including homosexual sex, to other women. She had graduated from Brown University one year earlier, and her mind had been programmed to see her "business" as something other than promoting prostitution, something other than the perversion of intercourse, and something other than the corruption of society itself. As a young Ivy League student, I had to wonder: Are pimps the graduates that Brown is most proud of?

Individually, liberal propositions seemed so harmless. So, some women get to have some orgasms. Big Deal. So, some other countries get to win the Gold once in a while. Who cares? Well, for some reason I cared immensely. I won't go overboard and say that, somehow, I just knew that what always dictates the survival of a nation is the mentality and culture of its people. But certainly, it was something like that. The "Olympic Basketball" instance was not an opinion generated within a social or political realm, but rather a notion derived within the *Brown Daily Herald*. However, I saw this train of thought being echoed into all walks of life, those parts of life that set the standards of justice, morality, and the American Way; areas that were deciding life or death, vice or virtue, freedom or bondage. This opinion on the U.S.A. Dream Team was only a microcosm of the leftist thought that loomed inside Brown halls, and I think the she-pimp confirmed that Brown students graduate, and take their liberalism with them.

CHAPTER 4
Don't Worry, They Will Save Us All From Our Own Inferior Intellect

While I have come to realize that universities and their students do achieve remarkable things (for the most part within the halls of scientific research), I can't help but still feel that the typical student body of elite institutions often receives far too much recognition for their intellectualism than they deserve. Nevertheless, the students accept that notoriety, and as I began to pay closer attention to my classmates, I began to see a common conviction jutting from most of their opinions—that all others were relying on them for their intellectual guidance, and remarkable ability to empathize.

My classmates seemed to think of themselves as more intellectually elevated than everyone else, and that they were the heroes of, whom they saw as, the needy and stupid. They were in the forefront of so many movements that claimed to be in response to grave injustices inflicted upon the poor, or minority groups, or anyone with a claim to victimhood. They protested in the name of sweatshop workers, all types of discrimination, and they even rallied for Brown University workers such as those involved with the food services, library functions, and janitorial duties. While sticking up for the "little guy" is a noble endeavor, I found that my classmates were using this nobility to authorize their elitism.

My assessment of my classmates' elitist attitude did not just come from their constant will to lead who they viewed as less-fortunate and less-intelligent, but it also came from their views of the political opposition. Anyone who wasn't along side them they considered one of the Big Three: Racist, Sexist, or Homophobic. But you see, it was okay. It was understandable for conservatives to be those things because they just didn't get it. They weren't as enlightened as my progressive classmates. Not as understanding. I was told all of the time, *You think that way only because you're white. You've never been poor. And you have never had to experience real hardship due to your "white privilege."* My classmates (???many who were also white and more privileged than I???) were smarter than me I guess. They could see beyond their fortunate upbringing, while I could not. But there was no need to be upset with people like me. Rather, they pitied conservatives for their ignorance. We were the understandable, and forgiven bigots. They were the compassionate, heroic apologists. Pure elitism.

I began to find this elitist attitude emulate from other campuses as well. Responding to the observation of Democrat-heavy faculties within our top universities, Lawrence Evans, Duke emeritus professor of physics, informed the intellectually-deprived as to why leftists dominate these institutions. "True, and rightly so" he rationalized. "Universities want people of some depth, subtlety and intelligence. People like that usually vote for the Democrats. So what?"(1)

Professor Evans was not alone in his thinking. Within the same debate, Robert Brandon, chair of Duke's *philosophy* department, told *The* [Duke University] *Chronicle*, "We try to hire the best, smartest people available. If, as John Stuart Mill said, stupid people are generally conservative, then there are lots of conservatives we will never hire."(2) I don't know this "Stuart Mill" guy, but somebody should tell him that there's a job waiting for him at Duke.

George Lakoff, a linguistics professor at Berkeley, may have exposed leftist elitism best when he declared that liberals, "unlike conservatives... believe in working for the public good and social justice."(3) Yes, it's true. We conservatives only care about ourselves.

Here is where I saw a gleaming contradiction within leftist philosophy. All leftist ideas were being advanced simply by appealing to the sensitivity of the masses. In fact, liberalism was spreading more easily on college campuses because of the idealistic political impulse of the compassionate youth. But despite liberalism's immense influence over millions, leftist ideology was still streamlined with negativity, insinuating that mankind lacks compassion, and is inherently cruel. Racism! Sexism! Homophobia! These were the reasons why the nation required leftist policies. But how could an ideology that required the compassion of the majority be advancing such a philosophy if the majority actually *was* characterized by cruelty and selfishness? This political paradox caused liberals to exude a distasteful arrogance, an attitude that assumed the bigotry of everyone but themselves.

Custodians of Compassion

I know *Out of Ivy* is supposed to be the story of *my* experiences at Brown University, but what happened to my little brother (also a student at Brown) during his freshman year is much too relevant to this chapter to leave out. I tried to warn my brother, Tyler, what he was in for at Brown, but I don't think anything could really have prepared him for what awaited him.

Tyler was a freshman, living in a freshman dorm with a roommate. At one point during his first semester the hallway community bathroom had been disgustingly dirty, and hadn't been cleaned for at least a couple of weeks. Now, Tyler is no neat-freak. Trust me. But even *he* told me that the bathroom, and the community kitchen were getting pretty disgusting. The dorm janitor seemed to be nonexistent all of a sudden. Once Tyler found the situation unbearable he decided to leave a note for the janitor on the bathroom door. It read:

Dear Custodian, I was just wondering if you could spend a little more time in this bathroom. Particularly the bottom of the showers, and the sink area. Also, the kitchen has gone without a cleaning for a couple of weeks. Thanks a lot.

Tyler, Room 309

Tyler left his dorm to go to class, and when he returned he noticed that his note had been taken off of the bathroom door, and put back in his room. His roommate and neighbors had disapproved of the note, and made sure that the janitor would never see it. When Tyler asked one of his neighbors why they had removed his note, he replied, "Do you know what it's like to clean bathrooms for a living?! Have you ever been a janitor before?!" There it was! It was Tyler's first encounter with Brown's shame-filled class warfare, and the truth-obstructing sensitivity that he would be forced to offer those who his classmates saw as petty, incompetent, and pathetic. It was the elitist Ivy attitude that I had just escaped from, only to have it take more hacks at the mind of one of my family members.

Ironically, Tyler had spent that summer cleaning nasty beach bathrooms to earn some spending money for that semester. Something told me that it was actually his neighbors who had never held such an occupation. Plus, our mother was a housewife, so we had learned to equally respect those who cleaned up after others for a living. We had seen the yellow gloves.

When Tyler told me about this incident, he expressed his utter confusion. The situation would have confused me as a Brown freshman as well. My brother wasn't being insensitive. He just wasn't looking *down* upon the dorm janitor. He saw him as an equal. An equal with a job to do. If a police officer was sleeping on the job, wouldn't everyone be willing to say to that officer:

Excuse me, sir, could you please stay awake to make sure nobody steals from me, or murders me? Thanks.

Tyler, Room 309

But because it was a *janitor* who was being asked to do his job, suddenly someone had to come to his rescue. Why? While many liberals are the result of bleeding hearts, I found that those bleeding hearts were the offshoots of feelings of shame, a desire to appear intellectually sophisticated, and strong feelings of superiority.

Because the janitor was one of his elders, Tyler tried to treat him with as much respect as possible within his note. Tyler's classmates, shocked at his audacity, were only shocked for one reason—Tyler was not *appearing* sensitive enough to this man's lowly occupation. A custodial job could never be a profession of choice, right? And the low-paying occupation could never be a result of the man's own shortcomings, right? He must have been *forced* to take such a job. And how dare Tyler *remind* him that he's a janitor! He was likely ashamed of his own profession, and was probably an unhappy person tinkering on the brink of suicide. There's no way a man of custodial duties could possibly be at peace with himself!

If there was anyone disrespecting the dorm janitor, it was my brother's neighboring students. Tyler saw the janitor as an equal, but they viewed the janitor as someone who needed someone else to stick up for him, and all janitors throughout the world. While they were acting delicately toward the janitor's feelings, their sympathy stemmed from their own outlook of superiority. So, they pitied the janitor, just as they pitied my brother for his inability to understand the feelings and hardships of others.

Tyler's neighbors were so appalled that they removed the note even though Tyler had signed *his own* name to it! Tyler felt no shame. He didn't care if the janitor knew he had written it. He didn't spinelessly write an anonymous note because he felt uncomfortable asking a man to do his job. Still, his classmates would have been embarrassed if anyone knew they even shared a hallway with such a person as my brother. Perhaps others would think they too shared the same unenlightened outlook. *Quick, get rid of that note before someone thinks we don't care about poor people!*

This occasion seemed so familiar to me. My own classmates also felt that others were of a lower caliber, not as capable of success or happiness. Many of their thoughts suggested that they were needed to guide the rest of the populace to joy and prosperity, and to even save them from truth that could insult them. This was the most intellectually arrogant mindset I had ever come across, and it was keeping all Brown members grossly disconnected from true Americanism. An individual right to the "pursuit of happiness" made no sense to them. "Happiness" was not something that actually needed to be "pursued." It was an entitlement. So, Brown liberals spent most of their time teaching others to rely on them for peace, comfort, and success. That was their calling.

What always annoyed me the most about liberals' sentiment of superiority was that it was hidden behind the mask of sensitivity. Compassion—an emotion exempt from criticism. It was always their tenderness that veiled their elitism, and Brown's political correctness protected them from anyone who dared to dissect their mentality. At Brown I was meant to perceive political correctness—obedience to sensitive speech codes, and the political alignment with self-declared victims—as proof of the left's monopoly over empathy and moral uprightness. Unfortunately for the campus left, I discovered that, in fact, PC was merely a dishonest political strategy, not their very own cartel of compassion.

This is how the liberals walked around campus:

Ooh, there's a black guy. Act normal. Ooh, there's a gay couple. Pretend as if you have plenty of homosexual friends. Ooh, there's a janitor. Act as if you don't think he's a lower species than you. Don't insult anybody. I have to watch what I say. Be careful now. Be very careful. Say something nice. Act smart. Act enlightened.

How none of my classmates ever dropped dead from their paranoia, I will never know. They seemed to be so wary of their words. I found that conservatives, on the other hand, were not ashamed of their beliefs or who they were. At Brown they would remain silent in fear of the campus reaction, but they wouldn't alter their opinions (or pretend as if it was not a janitor's duty to clean the toilets and empty the trash). Liberals, on the other hand, seemed uncomfortable with who they were. Wealthy. Privileged. Perhaps a straight, white, male. The truth about them could never be told. They would rather run from that truth than ever be seen for what they were. Arrogant elitists. Meanwhile, all the toilets were clogging up.

"The best men have their blind spots, and sometimes they feel almost crushed at how little respect logic can show them."
Victor Hugo, *Les Misérables* (1862)

Yeah, as if I have ever seen Les Miz! Really though, I just love that quote because it reminds me of my classmates and professors. I truly was sharing a campus with people who considered themselves superior scholars, and they all craved an admiring audience. Notice all the protests.

Without a doubt my classmates' intelligence went unmatched, but liberalism did not discriminate between the minds it infected. In fact, where I began to see the great danger of the left's dominance within universities was when I realized it was tainting the minds of the over-achieving intellectuals with the quickest avenue to societal influence, those students of the prestigious Ivy League. For four years I witnessed a bunch of like-minded students whose only talent seemed to be that they were able to reiterate—with great accuracy—notions that they had heard from others. Better than anyone, they had the ability to regurgitate liberal clichés such as, *It's a Woman's Choice*, *We Must Separate Church and State*, *The Rich Get Richer and the Poor Get Poorer*, *We Have to Level the Playing Field*, *Iraq for Oil*, and *Save the Whales*! It became evident to me that most of them hadn't known the logic (or lack of it) that was behind these notions, and rarely did I meet or witness an intellect deserving of great respect. This is because Brown students only learned to protest, and to silence their political opponents. Because the University never forced them to confront a challenging opinion, they never felt compelled to think a little deeper, to actually have to consider an alternate philosophy before subscribing to a serious political agenda. I never witnessed any of them live up to the standards that I thought an Ivy League institution should expect of them. They congratulated each other on their campus activism, but all I ever saw was a riffraff of highly intelligent students settling for mediocrity.

Not only were my classmates poor thinkers, but they were also a group of people lacking humility (the same can be said for Brown professors). A bunch of know-it-alls. They were the smartest. They were the free-thinking, open-minded heroes of the world. Anything they believed must have been on the side of the righteous simply because... well, it was them! This was my overall impression, and I'm not sorry for it. I would see flyers and posters all over campus calling on everyone to come see one of my classmates, or one of Brown's student-activist groups, give a lecture. They would speak (or have a renowned guest speak) on abortion rights, on discrimination, on proper methods of anal sex, on pornography, on diversity, on trans-gender bathroom use (not kidding), on masturbation and female ejaculation, on the evil Bush Administration, etc. You probably think that I was so turned off by some of these topics that I never attended any of them. But I did. More than I'd like to remember. And without any opposition to their lectures, they congratulated themselves on a job well done. So proud they always were to have enlightened their interested classmates, to have graced them with their staggering amount of knowledge. Sickening.

Brown professors, of course, offered unfailing support for anything sermonized by the left. No doubt did students see this as powerful credibility for liberal ideology. In 2001, students who wished to deny the opportunity for David Horowitz, a conservative author, to come speak at Brown posted flyers all over campus that read, *"Even Brown professors agree: Silence David Horowitz in order to save democracy..."*(4)

Oh, well, if the professors say so...

Faculty support for student activism helped ensure that liberal supremacy remained uninterrupted. Upon leaving Brown I had learned the reasons why liberalism propagated there. Not only were popular campus notions backed by the vast majority of campus adults, but all liberal ideals were painted as progressive and compassionate, and were advanced with bigheaded authority. Therefore, they always took advantage of the politically anxious, the politically inexperienced, and youthful idealism. This made certain that liberalism had a monopoly over spontaneous and hasty opinion. Its landscape was inarguably unflawed, and the University provided a perfect opportunity for self-serving professors to retain a consistent, and always changing, wide-eyed audience; a bunch of students eager to listen, learn, and act on what they were told.

At Brown, progressive ideals were more attractive to students than hallucinogenic drugs. When my classmates and I had finally reached our prestigious university, and were now in a phase of life that revealed pressure to achieve some relevance to important matters, and earn some intellectual weight amongst our peers, liberal causes were meant to serve as our means to accomplishing that. As soon as we stepped onto campus we were met with a swarm of activist groups offering us dozens of seemingly worthwhile causes that were all based on the same righteous mentality, and always seemed in response to some injustice. We could join the International Socialist Organization, or the Brown Feminists, or the Brown Democrats, or the Lesbian Gay Bisexual Transsexual Alliance, or the Young Communist League, or any special-interest group that appealed to us. It was likely that at least one would. I could not help but notice that Brown was assembled much like the Democratic Party, a society made up of a bunch of tinier communities. Just as the Democratic Party is known for its representation of a large amount of special-interest groups, Brown is made up of a collection of campus activist crowds dedicated to the advancement of their own agendas. Yes, we were being programmed to be Democrats.

Unfortunately for me, I understood that anyone who decided to stand by the morals and values of their conservative upbringing would be seen as ignorant, insensitive, or just plain dumb. But unfortunately for the campus left, I started to find conservative thought to, in fact, be the ideology that required more brain-power to understand. It seemed to command a historical understanding of the question "why." My classmates' spontaneous boarding of the liberal bandwagon did not require the prerequisite of deep thought—or any thought for that matter. But to have to consider *why* society had naturally been structured a certain way, *why* the nuclear family is seen as an important component of our culture, *why* so many cringe at the thought of abortion, *why* people for so long have deemed homosexuality as immoral, *why* people resist reform that comes disguised as "equal rights," and *why* so many of us remain traditional were questions that entailed contemplation, research, reflection, and debate to answer. Brown's populace lazily and effortlessly explained these questions with the same charge every time. Bigotry. Oh yes, it seemed that up until the exact moment my classmates were born, the Earth had been overrun with the morals of cruel, sexist, racist, and homophobic Christians. And now, Brown's liberals were going to show everyone where we had all gone wrong.

The intellectual arrogance of Brown's liberals was something they would try to conceal, and was usually something that could only be detected through keen observation. Well, either keen observation, or being forced to share the same campus with them for four years. Despite their attempts to mask their Ivy egotism, you could always rely on a few to unwisely spew a few of their honest thoughts: "The people who want to go to war are these white trash who will follow whatever the government says," a member of the Brown Communist Party informed the campus about those Americans who supported retaliatory attacks after 9/11.(5) Also speaking of mainstream America, another student echoed a similar comment during the aftermath of 9/11: "They just stand behind the flag no matter what, and it seems they will blindly follow the government."(6) In a *Brown Daily Herald* opinion column, the day after President Bush's victory in 2004, one Brown student called all those who voted for Bush "ignorant fools."(7) Speaking of the overwhelming support for a ban on gay marriage one student reasoned, "It seems like people do not understand the issue and are not ready for it."(8) And one of my classmates said about my objection to campus posters portraying graphic sexual imagery, "I hope he never goes to Europe, where depictions of sex and sexuality are far more common—he'd discover that his repulsion about 'pornography' is not much more than parochial American narrow-mindedness."(9) You see, campus liberals considered those who disagreed with them on any issue bigoted, unprepared, overly patriotic, blind, or were people who had simply never been to Europe.

CHAPTER 5
Diversity University

As I walked through Brown's campus there were often times when I couldn't help but be reminded of Disney World's amusement park ride, *It's a Small World After All.* Brown is exactly as advertised, populated by students from various ethnicities, cultural backgrounds, religious sects, and even sexual orientations. The Brown student body contains students from all 50 states, and just as many foreign countries. Ten percent of undergraduates are international students, and over 25 percent are students of color.(1) Brown didn't just *talk the talk* when it came to the University's firm conviction that an education could only be enhanced when students are immersed into a community of ethnic variance.

Multiculturalism was much more than a nicety that Brown tried to offer its students. It was the University's Golden Calf. I have never witnessed anything so constant in my life—the repetitive assertion by Brown members that diversity was an invaluable virtue. It was often bragged about, and used as a selling point in order to lure students to Brown. Then, once students passed through the Van Wickle Gates, for the next four years they would be unable to escape the steady commentary and symbolism of diversity's importance. On its website, the Office of Student Life says that Brown fosters "effective life skills for living and working in a diverse community."(2) Sheila Blumstein, the University president, told the campus in 2001 that Brown cherishes "community values that honor diversity and respect."(3) "A commitment to pluralism and fair play lies at the very heart of the Brown ethos," a student echoed.(4) An administrative declaration in 2004 stated, "As we reflect on what we have observed...we are struck by the many wonderful characteristics of our community, not the least being our richly diverse campus."(5)

This endless accentuation, I must admit, annoyed me. You would think that just by walking around Brown's campus an Ivy League student would be able to recognize the fact that he is in a diverse place, but for some reason there were frequent reminders of diversity's existence and importance. The University seemed not to trust me to casually appreciate campus diversity. Certain campus sects sought to control how often I would observe cross-cultural issues, how often I would discuss them, and also how I would view them. So as time passed my annoyance developed into a quiet skepticism about the proclaimed intentions of Brown's multicultural community.

My suspicion would be confirmed. Brown's obsession with multiculturalism had severe consequences. My classmates became engrossed with the concept of pluralism, seized control of it, and used it as a political weapon. It was their intellectual premise from which they launched almost all of their activist efforts. I have no problem with diversity, but I also have no problem explaining how my alma mater took a largely positive ideal, and smudged it with over-emphasis, and political interruption.

Victims of the Ivy League

Why did diversity get accepted as the 11th Commandment at Brown? We can be certain that part of the reason rested with the attempt by certain liberal sects to corrupt the educational ideal by using it to their political advantage, to highlight their victim-hood in order to gain political leniency.

I began to notice after some time at Brown that almost every time one of my alma mater's student-groups claimed to be offended by an opinion, that opinion was not necessarily racist, homophobic, sexist, or even unkind. It just had the ability to suggest that certain special-interest groups might not be as victimized as they claimed to be, a notion that apparently wasn't open for debate. Special-interest student-groups *needed* their victim-hood, and they *needed* to persistently remind others of it. It was unaffordable to have it stolen, or even downsized—due to the fact that it forced the silence of their political opposition.

Multiculturalism became leftist indoctrination's most powerful gadget because liberals simply retained a monopoly over the topic. Established intellectual boundaries forbid anyone to stray from the way in which they demanded everyone to view a world of pluralism. This included the forbiddance of criticism toward certain people who fell into certain categories. I'm talking primarily about minorities.

And homosexuals. And sometimes women. But only if they were black feminists. Who were pregnant. Or poor.

Another tenet of the diversity platform was the suffering that "whiteness" had caused. One popular sentiment was that white individuals should feel sorry (and even apologize!) for the sins of their ancestors who took part in an expansionist movement across North America, killing Native Americans and enslaving Africans. I would hear it often with no rebuttal, the sole opinion that America was born of grave injustices. This was something that had not been previously exposed to me on such a regular basis.

It was powerful indoctrination—a historic perspective of self-loathing that accomplished the guilt that was needed to achieve all liberal reform that contradicted true Americanism. "This country was founded on racism, genocide, and theft," one of my classmates informed me.(6) Another Brown student: "The red states used it [starvation] against the Indians when they wiped out the buffalo and the antelope."(7) "Slavery went on for longer and killed more people than the Holocaust…and its victims are just as deserving of compensation," a visiting lecturer told the campus.(8) There is no doubt that this relentless rhetoric effectively influenced the student-body, teaching us that minorities were victims, and all whites were wealthy and privileged. We certainly weren't a group worthy of laying claim to victim-hood (unless you were a janitor).

Unlike many of my classmates, I wasn't ready to apologize for being white, or feel sorry for the ways of my great-great-great grandfathers. To feel ashamed for sharing the blood and skin tone of men who acted according to the methods and morals they were born into didn't feel right to me. It was insisted, however, that I conform. The victimization of others was an outlook that could not go unaccepted at Brown. It was persistently emphasized either by forthright opinion, or by soft campus imagery. The MPC. The MPC. The MPC. The MPC. The MPC. One more time, the MPC. The Minority Peer Counseling program. Everywhere I looked, the MPC. The MPC. The MPC. If it wasn't the MPC, it was a similar program advertised or promoted around every corner. The WPC, for instance. The *Women's* Peer Counseling program. After a while I had to wonder why there wasn't just a generic "Brown Counseling Program" for any student with a problem. Why was I being informed as to which particular students were in need of their own therapy sessions—so much so that Brown actually required separate programs aimed at assisting that specific group? Well, it turned out that counseling programs were just another piece of the campus puzzle, serving to segregate the student body into visibly discernible groups, reinforcing Brown's message that only particular groups of people had a claim to victim-hood.

At Brown, everyone was a victim—except straight, white, males. We had no counseling group to turn to. Apparently, we required no such program. Oppression. Isolation. Depression. To have to endure, persevere, or struggle. To be discriminated against. To feel trapped. These were only the problems of minorities, gays, and women. We had "white privilege," and they were "underrepresented." Brown liberals wouldn't always openly declare that whites were to blame for others' misfortunes, but their actions, opinions, demands, and ethnic-based counseling programs always suggested that if minorities were victims, then there must have been a perpetrator to inflict such harm. If minorities were the victims, who was left to be the perpetrator?

This campus climate caused me to start thinking a lot about—what liberals were calling—"social justice." How was I to decipher who should be considered a casualty of American society, and who wasn't so deserving of that title? I reasoned that there were *many* factors that could cause someone adversity, but Brown was teaching me to assume the victimization of only select groups of people.

I may have been influenced early-on, but I ultimately found this collective racial premise difficult to accept because there was no shedding of personal responsibility where I came from. That is, a life of athletics, demanding parents, and a strict schooling. Individual effort. Individual success. All of a sudden, however, I had suddenly stepped into a world of group-identity and hyper-sensitivity. I had overcome so much to earn my passage into the Ivy League, only to have my achievement diminished the moment I arrived on College Hill. Because I was white, acceptance to Brown was an easy handout to me. I simply faced less obstacles than others to arrive there. Even if that was true, my values of work ethic, responsibility, and individuality taught me to reject all forms of entitlement or pity whenever possible. They also taught me to refrain from offering it to others. To do so preys on weakness, causes dependency, is outright insulting, and is not the key to true success. Somehow I knew that. Thank God.

Brown's "policy of pity" just didn't resonate with me. Initially, I saw it as an insulting lesson to white students. And eventually, I saw it as a crippling lesson to minorities. It was the dogma of groupthink and group rights, and it was painfully diminishing the importance of individuality. But you didn't dare speak so plainly on campus. Certain opinions might have resulted in truth, and the undermining of the victimization of all Brown's special-interest groups.

The Sham of Multiculturalism: White Liberals, Black Liberals, Asian Liberals, Gay Liberals, Straight Liberals, Male Liberals, Female Liberals, Young Liberals, Old Liberals, Skinny Liberals, Fat Liberals, Paraplegic Liberals

Lee Bollinger, Columbia University's president once declared:

> **"Diversity is not merely a desirable addition to a well-run education. It is as essential as the study of the Middle Ages, of international politics and of Shakespeare. For our students to better understand the diverse country and world they inhabit, they must be immersed in a campus culture that allows them to study with, argue with and become friends with students who may be different from them. It broadens the mind and the intellect—essential goals of education."**(9)

You can be assured that Brown University would concur wholeheartedly with president Bollinger's sentiments. And while I agree with the second portion of Bollinger's statement, that attending a school comprised of varying viewpoints can challenge students and help them better understand the world they live in, this idealism was certainly not the result of Brown's diversity. In fact, at Brown, diversity was one big lie. Perspectives never wavered, only the skin tone of various students.

No doubt was there a deliberate effort at Brown to organize people into groups, and then stress vehemently that some groups were unduly injured by America's past and present. Certainly, every one of these factions *looked* different, but they were all subscribers to the leftist doctrine of victim-hood. Still, ethnic variance among the student body gave liberals an orgasmic reaction. Their delight was so strong that they had come to view something as insignificant as a color just as important as History and Shakespeare. *Son, put down that book and come meet this nice Asian fellow.* What a crock.

The University encourages students to enroll in a number of its *Diversity Perspectives Courses*. Keeping up with the harmless and unindictable rhetoric of multiculturalism, Brown describes these classes—numbering well over 150—as courses that "represent the dedication of the Brown faculty to examine knowledge from perspectives of groups often not represented in traditional disciplines." They are "courses that treat...the knowledge and experience of previously underrepresented groups...or courses that examine the ways in which disciplines, histories, and paradigms of knowledge are reconfigured by the study of diversity-related intellectual questions."(10)

Unsurprisingly, an overwhelming proportion of Brown's *Diversity Perspectives Courses* focus on race, class, and gender studies. For the full list readers can acquire the *Brown Course Announcement* to view my alma mater's love affair with cultural plurality, and its fixation with specific groups of people. Here is just a short list of some student course options:

Africana Studies
–(AF 9) Intro to Africana Studies
–(AF 17) Afro-American History and Society Before 1800
–(AF 19) Caribbean History and Society Before 1800
–(AF 21) Blacks in Latin American History
–(AF 76) Rastafarianism
–(AF 99) Black Lavender: A Study of Black Gay and Lesbian Plays
–(AF 102) Freedom in Africana Political Thought
–(AF 106) Africa Since 1950
–(AF 106) Black Leadership in Ethnic Communities
–(AF 111) Voices Beneath the Veil
–(AF 113) Black Feminist Thought and Womanist Theology
–(AF 114) Women, the State, and Violence
–(AF 115) Afro-Caribbean Philosophy
–(AF 121) Afro-Brazilians and the Brazilian Polity
–(AF 141) Africans and the West: Studies in the History of Ideas
–(AF 170) American Radicalism: The Black Panther Party
–(AF 175) Eastern African History

American Civilization
–(AC 75) Society and Culture in America
–(AC 161) Asian America Since 1945
–(AC 161) Women and Social Activism
–(AC 161) Making America: 20th Century Immigrant/Ethnic Literature
–(AC 161) The Civil Rights Movement: History and Legacy
–(AC 161) African American History, 1876 to the present

Anthropology
–(AN 105) Peoples and Cultures of Southeast Asia
–(AN 106) Race, Culture, and Ethnic Politics
–(AN 111) Africa in Anthropological Perspective
–(AN 112) Peoples and the Cultures of the Americas
–(AN 114) From Coyote to Casinos
–(AN 116) United States Culture
–(AN 118) Japanese Culture, Society and Performance
–(AN 120) Ethnonationalism, The Asian Arena
–(AN 122) Ethnic American Folklore: Continuity and the Creative Process
–(AN 134) Comparative Sex Roles

Education
–(ED 102) The History of American Education
–(ED 121) Public Education and People of Color in U.S. History
–(ED 143) The Psychology of Race, Class, and Gender
–(ED 158) Cross-Cultural Perspectives on Child Development

English
–(EL 65) From Pamela to Bridget Jones: Writing Women in Diaries and Letters
–(EL 71) Intro to African American Literature
–(EL 73) Intro to Asian American Literature
–(EL 171) Harlem Renaissance
–(EL 176) Race, Writing, and Manhood
–(EL 176) Literary Africa
–(EL 176) Chicana/o Cultural Studies
–(EL 176) Mediating Color in African American Literature
–(EL 151) American Women's Writing

Ethnic Studies
–(ET 50) Intro to Ethnic Studies
–(ET 102) Race and Language in the U.S
–(ET 187) Latino/a Communities Seminar

Gender Studies
–(GN 10) Intro to Feminist Studies
–(GN 12) Intro to Gender Studies and the Disciplines

History
–(HI 51) American History to 1877
–(HI 197) Red, White, and Black in the Americas
–(HI 197) Gender and Sexuality in European High Middle Ages
–(HI 197) Indian/Black Individuals and Communities in the Americas

Modern Culture and Media
–(MC 120) African Cinema
–(MC 150) Television, Gender, and Sexuality

Music
–(MU 129) Music in Ethnic America
–(MU 134) Jews, Blacks, and American Musical Theater

Political Science
–(PS 131) African American Politics
–(PS 182) Women and Politics

Portuguese and Brazilian Studies
–(PB 150) Esthers of the Diaspora: Female Jewish Voices from Latin America
–(PB 160) Africa and Anthropology from Colonialism to Postcolonialism

Religious Studies
–(RS 5) Introduction to Islam
–(RS 88) Muhammad and the andQur'an

Sociology
–(SO 13) American Heritage: Democracy, Inequality, and Public Policy
–(SO 164) Social Exclusion and Inequality
–(SO 187) Immigration and Ethnicity
–(SO 187) He, She, or It: Sociological Perspectives on Gender
–(SO 127) Race, Class, and Ethnicity in the Modern World

Theatre, Speech, and Dance
–(TA 128) Theatres of Feminism: Performing Sex, Race, and Gender

My classmates ensured the survival of this diversity-push by acting on

Brown's encouragement to take advantage of its welcoming campus. As a result, the students ended up adding to this doctrine by creating a non-stop mirage of various ethnic events, and sponsored discussions. Among the most notable periods of expressed multiculturalism were:
–African-American History Month
–Asian-American History Month
–Women's History Month
–Latino History Month
–Queer Pride Month

–National Coming Out Week (for homosexuals)
–Cape Verdean Heritage Week
–Puerto-Rican Heritage Week
–Multiracial Heritage Week
–South Asian Identity Week
–Caribbean Heritage Week
–South East Asian Week
–Semana Chicana.

This schedule didn't leave much time for History or Shakespeare.

After decades of multicultural education, Brown had mastered the art of harnessing student enthusiasm. My classmates were merely expressing themselves under the impression that their skin tone and sexuality were the most vital components of self-expression. They never realized that the University was channeling the majority of their energy into a world of false assumptions and political fallacy.

Only Whites Need Diversity

The mysterious absence of a month or week reserved for the sole purpose of recognizing *White History* could only infer one thing to Brown students: Brown's multiculturalism rode along a one-way street, with no intent to offer minorities a chance to better understand their Caucasian counterparts.

Proof of diversity's double standard was the undeniable reality that, while diversity was being presented as indispensable for everyone, I could have never declared to one of my minority classmates that he couldn't be properly educated without my presence. Political correctness ensured that an opinion running counter to liberal doctrine was never heard. *We best keep our opinions to ourselves*, was the protective thought of the straight, white student.

White students were always at the mercy of vocal campus groups, who demanded recognition of their people's plight. That commanding sense of victim-hood—craftily injected into the student body—is what suggested that diversity was more essential for whites than it was for minorities. White students needed to practice a little patience and tolerance, and assume the agony of our minority classmates. They had all had it so rough.

I actually started to find a contradiction in the assertion that diversity is as essential as my right arm when I started to reminisce about my old high school. Without a doubt my high school offered a wonderful learning opportunity to its students. Yet, it was extremely un-diverse. No female students attended. No one other than Catholics attended. Because of the high tuition, rarely did any poor students attend either. Yet, parents were knocking down the doors of the admissions office in order to get their sons accepted into the school. As a Brown student I had to wonder, *How could that be? Maybe ethnic variation isn't necessarily a key component to a great education after all. Brown University established itself as a great university long ago when it only accepted rich white boys, too. And all-black schools such as Morehouse College boast a long history of great learning without the presence of whites.* But revealing this sentiment to another Brown student would have earned me stares of puzzlement, shock, and anger. You just didn't say such a thing within an earshot of Brown's campus.

The University might as well have come right out and said it to my face. Because I attended a private, all-boys, Catholic school that was comprised of mostly middle-class white students, the University had to assume my bigotry. Racist, for sure, and likely sexist as well. *Not to worry, young man. Nothing a little diversity can't fix.*

Help me, Brown! Save me!

Most students didn't seem to be as insulted as I was. Not that I had decoded Brown's scheme of indoctrination right away, but after a while it became clear to me that white students were meant to graduate with diplomas in their hands, and guilt in their heads. It bothered me that other white students were quick to apologize, and I began to respect them less and less. It seemed to me that a lot of my classmates had come to Brown for just that reason, to take up arms against injustice. But that's not why I had come to Brown. I was recruited to play football. I didn't expect to be pressured toward particular intellectual avenues, especially ones that sought to make me feel ashamed of my heritage. So while others allowed liberals to give them their direction, I just kept my head down and my mouth shut—all the while developing a quiet scorn for multiculturalism as a result of Brown's suggestion that minorities need not diversity, but it is only whites who need a little more color in their lives.

White Guilt: A Catalyst for Socialism

The wirings of liberalism were often traced back to the same source. I can't pretend that I even knew what socialism was when I arrived on Brown's campus, but my investigations into certain campus happenings seemed to always bring me back to this one guy, Karl Marx.

While proofreading *Out of Ivy* I realized that, wow, a lot of my stories deal with race. There was a good reason for that. Almost everything portrayed as important on Brown's campus dealt with racism. Therefore, many of my own campus tales involve issues of ethnic prejudice. Not *my* obsession. Brown's.

The topic of race was Marxism's best mechanism. Its job was to tune the mind of the student body onto a socialist frequency. As my classmates set off to save the world, racial Marxism was the left's leadoff batter. Politically inexperienced college students were less likely to immediately tackle such issues as healthcare and tax-cuts just due to their prior lack of involvement in these matters. But anyone at any point could take a stand against meanness.

Late into my time at Brown, I would come to understand how important victimization is to the leftist uplifting of Marxist theory, that "capitalism produces poverty, racism, famine, environmental catastrophe and war," according to Brown's International Socialist Organization.(11) My classmates and I needed to be reminded that it was white people who were responsible for this oppressive capitalism, and that certain ethnic groups were unjustly grasping the butt-end of a white world.

If you don't believe that Brown's multiculturalism was a device for the left, then check this out.

Toward the end of my junior year, Brown's Young Communist League sponsored a panel discussion to address the current "dominance of conservative ideologies in modern political and racial discussions."

Brown professor of Africana Studies, Anthony Bogues, was a featured member of the panel. *The Herald* reported him as saying, "Even when leftist governments come to power...the conservatives 'run the terms of debate.' This new ideology...espouses small governments and the belief that 'social justice is an unrealizable goal in human society.'"(12)

What, then, was Professor Bogues' solution to this *problem*? Well, first he derided the policies of Margaret Thatcher, "who broke the power of British unions and halted British immigration, and former President Ronald Reagan, who promoted a free-market world economy to the detriment of third world states." Then, Professor Bogues criticized current studies "which suggest the troubles of undeveloped nations are due to problems of geography or culture." These were "ideas he compared to European justifications of slavery two centuries ago." These studies, according to Bogues, were saying, "These peoples who can't participate in the market are diseased individuals."

Conservatives still haven't learned the lessons of slavery, and think people of the Third World are diseased. *Primitive. Unenlightened. Bigoted.*

The article continued. "Bogues said in order for an effective socialist response to take place, progressives must recognize the racial underpinnings of today's political ideology." It was *all* about race for these "progressives." They needed to prove that *someone* was being treated unfairly. Professor Bogues went on to say, "The theory must also come from what are the everyday experiences of those that are engaged in struggle." Minorities, that is.

Another featured member of the panel was Anthony Monteiro, assistant professor of sociology at the University of the Arts in Philadelphia. Monteiro "related his philosophy to questions of class struggle by claiming that in America the race issue underlies most of the problems confronted by the Marxist tradition." He went on to incriminate the United States for producing a society that has "assassinated" five black men in Cincinnati, and that "jails over 1 million black youth—the same in terms of percentages as 11 million white youth behind bars." Monteiro believed that there were active "forces of state power against black liberation," that there was a "need to take back a black popular culture that has been dominated by white establishments," and told his audience, "My charge to the broader feminist and class forces is that they must unite with those...facing the most intense forms of repression."

Victims Unite!

It's no wonder my classmates were so obsessed with race. All of their energy and intellect was being channeled in that direction by campus commies. Going forward, all solutions to inequality would only be seen through the prism of socialism. The world was awaiting my classmates' creation, a utopia of peace, justice, and humanity accomplished through the redistribution of the riches bestowed upon the lucky and undeserving.

Sensitivity Training 101

My first taste of Brown's lesson on diversity was during *Freshmen Orientation*, the period of several days before classes begin. I always told people that they should call it *Freshmen Brainwashing*, but nobody would listen. First-years were required to show up a few days before everyone else to get familiar with the campus, and to also go through a series of required meetings with their unit, the group of students that closely surrounded them in their dormitories.

It was the second day of *Freshman Brainwashing.*

I had already been on Brown's empty campus for about a week for pre-season football camp. Camp was more overwhelming than I expected. It was intense as hell—fast-paced and intellectually rigorous. While being screamed at by overgrown monsters with whistles, battling injuries and the heat, we were required to be out of bed by 6am, watching practice film by 7am, on the field by 8am, watching practice film by 11am, back on the field by 2pm, watching practice film by 6pm, studying our plays by 8pm, and in bed by 10pm. And repeat.

Toward the end of football camp the campus began to fill up with about 1500 of the brightest 18 year-old from all over the world. I had just finished morning practice of double-sessions, and was required to attend another *Freshmen Brainwashing* meeting.

Each of these meetings was run by our Resident Counselor (RC). RCs were the upperclassmen living in the freshmen dorms pretending that their purpose for being an RC was to help some of the new students with some of their common, everyday problems. Their actual purpose for becoming RCs was to have first dibs on the new batch of young college chicks that just arrived on campus. Those guys never fooled me. I knew what they were up to.

I found most *Freshmen Brainwashing* meetings either annoying, or entirely arduous. One meeting was held just to make sure everyone was doing okay, and that our room keys were working. *Yea yea. Can I go now? 90210 is on.*

Another meeting's purpose was to tell us where the condoms could be found. They could be found in a pocket that hung on all of the RC's doors. The RCs only asked that we replace each condom taken with 15 cents to defray the cost of the community condoms (I know of some people who *never* put the 15 cents in). Not only were they so nice as to tell us where to pick up our condoms, but they also demonstrated how to use one using a banana for a prop. Everyone really appreciated the demonstration. It didn't make anyone uncomfortable or anything.

But it was the meeting after my morning football practice on the second day of *Freshmen Brainwashing* that actually angered me. Actually, I wasn't *angry*. It's important that I am accurate with my emotions. I was too ignorant to be *angry* over what was about to happen. *Embarrassed*, is more precise.

This meeting gave me my first taste of what I was truly going to experience for the next four years at Brown University. I showered, grabbed a sandwich, and went off to the 12:00 meeting. My unit (which was comprised of whites, blacks, girls, boys, Hispanics, Asians, Christians, Jews, Indians, etc.) was forced to watch a one-hour film about diversity. The video served as an eyewitness to a retreat taken by several older men in open discussion about equality and race. The film's liberal programming was disguised with the upfront message that it was acceptable and important to take part in racial discussions on Brown's campus. However, the film successfully framed what Brown considered to be acceptable speech by telling its viewers, *But if you are going to have a discussion, this is what it should look like.*

The film operated from the premise that bigotry was thriving and spreading. An important first step was to gather a representative from every ethnic background, and then have them share their personal pains with the rest of the group. The film featured several characters including a gay man, an Asian-American man, a black man, and a white man. Every character present (besides the white male) spoke of their fears, concerns, and troubles brought on by being a minority. I had just come from a place comparable to boot camp, where one-hundred enormous men were trying to maim one another, and coaches were calling us names that I'm not allowed to print in this book. So I'm not ashamed to say that the first thing I found unsettling about this film was the large amount of weight and relevance it afforded to people's feelings.

More disturbing, however, was the bias demonstrated against whites. The most notable conflict that arose in the film was between the white man and the black man. The black man became extremely angry during the discussion, and he yelled loudly at the white man whom he had just met, but had no trouble blaming him for his hardships. The white man defended himself as much as he could by explaining how he had never been a racist, and had never judged anybody by the color of his skin, and also couldn't understand why he was being targeted as the evil one of the group purely for being white. I agreed. In the end, though, the black man's angry demeanor was too much for him to handle. His fury ultimately forced the white man into tears as he apologized for his racism—that must have been brewing in his subconscious. He had no idea how much pain he had caused the black man.

Of course, the film ended with the entire group holding hands and singing. The black man *forgave* the white man. It was supposed to be a beautiful moment, but I felt *embarrassed.* Yes, *embarrassed.* What was all this expression of hurt? All this coddling of people's emotions? And what was a white kid to say? I'm sorry too?

I guess the film's message was that there is hope for diversity—that all races, genders, and people of various sexual orientations can get along and learn from one another. Blah, blah, blah. What was actually being taught was: yes, we can all get along, just as long as all whites acknowledge the racism that exists in their hearts, and the emotional pain they cause for minorities on a daily basis. If you don't acknowledge it, you will rightfully be subjected to the anger of others who disagree with you, and also be blamed for others' misfortunes. The lesson was clear; blacks are angry and whites should apologize. This was only the beginning of my liberal education.

Imagine the scene. There were a bunch of timid freshmen of all different backgrounds. Nobody knew anybody, and everyone wanted to kickoff their Ivy League experience by saying something intelligent. During the film, and at its conclusion, a feeling of mistrust swept across the room. I no longer wanted to express my *true* feelings about what I had just been forced to watch. I wasn't even sure what they were. Now I just wanted to say the *correct* thing, and get the hell out of there.

Surprisingly, when we were asked at the end of the film by the RC if anybody had any comments on what we had just seen, nobody had one. The act of asking the group if anyone had a comment was disingenuous, because no open discussion could be withdrawn from the group. At best, it was a symbolic gesture telling a group of freshmen that, at Brown, open discussion is encouraged. But the film had instantly outlined an acceptable code of speech for us to abide by. *Be careful what you say. This is how angry someone might become when you express your true feelings, and that just might be you weeping in front of your peers.* Under the guise of attempting to encourage open racial dialogue, Brown had accomplished the exact opposite during *Freshman Brainwashing* by attempting to control the level of sensitivity in which we approached matters of race. This was a difficult situation for a student who a) didn't care about race, and b) wasn't very sensitive.

Beyond my own personal reaction to being ordered how to think and how to feel, I eventually had to notice the severe institutional effects of such mind reform. In a room filled with wide-eyed eighteen year-olds, who were ready to make friends with anyone regardless of their race, suddenly there was a lingering distrust of everyone in my unit. At the meeting's dismissal all of us began to create our closest circle of friends with those we knew we could speak our honest minds to. While freshman dorms may have personified the diversity of the student body, the following three years were typified by our segregation. The creation of cultural student-groups, the drift of African-American students into all-black dorms, the isolated Hispanic Machado House, the fraternity scene being dominated by Brown's white athletes, and the cafeteria's dining tables being able to be described as white, black, or Asian couldn't have more perfectly demonstrated how phony and politically correct Brown's diversity-push actually was.

Racial conflict seemed everlasting during my time at Brown, and the biggest barrier to racial harmony that I saw was the liberal cure to ethnic mistrust, and the silencing that those who disagreed with it had to endure. This video only helped increase racial suspicion to remarkable levels, and I resented this thought-arrest, because it suggested that any obstacles toward healthy diversity were white people's fault. But for the next four years we had to suppress our resentment, obey our speech codes, and give way to the sensitivities of campus victims. That was the true end result of Brown's film on diversity, and several times during my time at Brown I saw exactly what the fallout is when years of honest racial dialogue are suppressed for the sake of not offending anyone (except whites).

Skin Deep

In the following years Brown attempted to build on *Freshman Brainwashing* as they changed the film that first-years watch. Now, they watch an hour-long film called *Skin Deep*, a popular film now shown by hundreds of universities during their respective freshman periods of mind reform. I had to research the video to see what my alma mater now forces upon its freshmen. I found out that *Skin Deep* even comes with a study guide that exposes the foundation from which the "honest" dialogue is set. The video operates from the assumption that there are "racial inequities that permeate our institutions and communities,"(13) and that there is a "growing wave of racial hatred and violence in this country." The study guide goes on to explain the need for affirmative action policies, and the "myths" of reverse discrimination and balkanization. However, it doesn't fail to emphasize the very real existence of "white privilege." To believe that the filmmakers did not have a political agenda is to be slightly naïve. Yet, they assert that their film was designed only to "stimulate... dialogue."

Skin Deep's characters videotaped on a retreat are students of our own age group, and a conversation of similar style occurs during the film. However, exhibiting their enlightenment, the white students immediately expose their family's prejudices. A white student remarks, "It's a tough choice, choosing what's right and choosing your family."(14) However, when the white students declare that they have never personally inflicted pain or prejudice upon minorities, a black student argued back, "One thing that you must definitely understand is that we're discussing how this country was founded, and because you are a white male, people are going to hate you." Justice served. Deal with it, Whitey.

Within *Skin Deep*, a film that's purpose seems to be to spread the concept of minority victim-hood and a disgusting sentiment of anti-Americanism, the minority students make broad and outrageous statements. I mean, at best their declarations are controversial. A Hispanic male remarks, "I want you to know that because of the system, my cousin was shot...and then another cousin was shot." One black student makes the claim that slavery still exists in America, and an Asian student remarks on how whites are taught in society to love themselves while minorities are taught to hate themselves. Concerning white people, that same Asian student also stated, "If you don't know that you have shit in your head, you'll never deal with racism." Wait, there's more. Another girl just goes off. "I will not stop being angry, and I will not be less angry or frustrated to accommodate anybody. You whites have to understand because we have been oppressed for 2000 years. And if you take offense, so?"(15)

After the film that reminds 18 year-old freshmen that our nation has been oppressing blacks since the birth of Christ, the RC will attempt to initiate some "honest" dialogue. Yeah, good luck.

———

Just to offer you a better idea of how vast multiculturalism exists at Brown, and how much campus activism is offered to its students, here's a short list of some of Brown's campus groups.(16)

African Students Association (ASA)
African Sun (African-American literary magazine)
American Civil Liberties Union (ACLU)
Amnesty International (dedicated to freeing political prisoners)
Animal Rights Coalition, Brown (BARC)
Anime Brunonia (Japanese animation club)
Anti-Racist Action
Arab-American Anti-Discrimination Committee (ADC)
Asian American Student Association (AASA)
Brotherhood, the (black student organization)
BUAD (Building Understanding Across Differences, for Brown first-years only)
Campus Alliance to End Gun Violence (CAEGV)
Cape Verdean Student Association
Catalyst, The
Catholic Pastoral Council at Brown
Catholic Community of Brown-RISD
Celtic Cultural Organization
Central American Solidarity Organization (CASO)
Chinese Students Association (CSA)

Chinese Students and Scholars Association, Brown University (BRUCSS)
Christian Fellowship, Brown (BCF)
Christian Science Organization
Coalition for Social Justice (CSJ)
College Hill for Christ/AIA (part of Campus Crusade for Christ)
College Democrats
College Republicans
Concilio Latino, El
Cuban American Student's Association
Cultural Activities Board (CAB)
East Asian House
East Timor Action Network (ETAN)
Environmental Action Network
Federacion de Estudiantes Puertorriquenos, La (FEP)
Feminist Majority Leadership Alliance (FMLA)
Filipino Alliance (FA)
Free Burma Coalition
Free The Children
Friends of Israel
Friends of Turkey
Fuerza Latina, La (La Fuerza Latina)
Green Party
Habitat for Humanity
Hawaii Club
Hellenic Students Association (HSA)
Hi-T (queer social group)
Hong Kong Students Association
International Socialist Organization
International Students Organization
Japanese Cultural Association (JCA)
Jewish Student Union (JSU)
Korean Adoptee Mentoring Program
Korean American Students Association
Korean Graduate Students Association (KGSA)
Latin American Students Organization
Lesbian, Gay, Bisexual, and Transgendered Alliance (LGBTA)

Mandarin Enrichment, Student Assoc.
MEChA (Movimiento Estudantil Chicano de Aztlan, El)
MEZCLA (Latino performing arts group)
Model United Nations Club
Muslim Students Association, Brown (BMSA)
National Pan-Hellenic Council
National Society of Black Engineers (NSBE)
Native Americans at Brown (NAB)
Next Thing, the (TNT) (for queer students of color)
Not Another Victim Anywhere (NAVA)
Nuestra Gente Mexicana
ONYX (support group for African-American seniors)
Organization of Multiracial and Biracial Students, Brown (BOMBS)
Organization of United African Peoples (OUAP)
Organization of Women Leaders (OWL)
Orthodox Christian Fellowship
Pakistani Society at Brown (PSAB)
Portuguese-American Cultural Association (PACA)
Shades of Brown (multicultural singing group that focuses on African music)
Sisters United, Brown (student group for black and Latina women)
Society of Women Engineers (SWE)
Somos (Latino Literary Magazine)
South Asian Students Association (SASA)
Student Homeless Action Campaign (SHAC)
Student Labor Alliance
Students for a Free Tibet
Students for Choice
Students for Liberty
Students for Life, Brown/RISD
Students of Caribbean Ancestry (SOCA)
Taiwan Society, Brown (BTS)
Thai Student Association (TSA)
third world ACTION
Third World Coalition (TWC)
Vietnamese Student's Association (VSA)
Women in Science & Engineering (WISE)

Women Students at Brown (WSaB)
Women's Empowerment Workshop Group
Yarmulkazi! (international music group)
Young Americans for Freedom
Young Communist League (YCL)
Young Minority Investors Club
Ze French Club
Zen Community at Brown

CHAPTER 6
Campus Adults

The Brown professorate was the body of people the students looked to for guidance. They were a renowned group of opinionated intellectuals, who had control over which texts would be read, which perspectives would prosper, and how much vigor the students would use to shape the face of Brown University. The faculty often seemed more politically active than Brown's students, and they served as powerful role models for the campus left.

Criticism of college professors' political bias is most often focused on what happens inside the classroom, where certain professors seem unable to restrain themselves from advancing their leftist ideals, teaching a one-sided view of history and politics. However, you won't meet a professor who believes his classroom is one where any student could possibly feel unwelcome to speak his mind. But I think it is reasonable to suspect that classroom bias is not only possible, but probable. One only has to look at the party affiliations of most professors, and the political passion of the college make-up. If this line of reasoning is not enough to convince someone of the likelihood of classroom indoctrination, then there is a collection of disclosed accounts where professors have not only expressed their political outlooks, but mocked others in the process. More than a few times I saw political cartoons taped to professors' private office doors that ridiculed right-wing policies. One public statement criticized political science professor, Terance Hopmann, for tearing "into the current Republican dominance of the political scene like a dog into a shoe."(1) Another student reported, "My history professor last semester: Continuous commentary on the war with Iraq and the stupidity of our president. Sadly, it was only met by the self-righteous giggles of the students."(2) This is how politically one-sided Brown's campus was. Right-minded thought, or Republican support, was so rarely given vocal expression that many professors assumed it just wasn't there, or cared little that anyone who thought differently would have to cower from the majority's intimidation.

Not that intimidation is a bad thing. *Out of Ivy* argues that Brown should be brought to a healthier level of debate, and the essence of debate *is* intimidation. It's just that Brown professors should *also* be intimidated. If Brown had a more balanced political atmosphere, where students had access to resources that could help them confront teacher opinion, there would be less of a problem because professors would not be able to recklessly shoot from the mouth. Currently, however, professors uncontrollably slip their slant into their lectures, and then their students scurry across campus to a Young Communist meeting. The faculty can sleep well at night knowing that their indoctrination is secure.

The morning after John Kerry's loss in the 2004 Presidential Election some professors felt the need to open classes with a somber expression of *assumed* collective depression, presuming the agony of *everyone* in the classroom. Other professors, even if they tried, were unable to refrain from expressing their misery the morning of November 3, 2004. One student reported that political science professor Jennifer Lawless, who is running for U.S. Congress in 2006, was "really depressed" and "in a funk" during her 8:30am political science class, "Campaigns and Elections."(4) And professor of History, Carolyn Dean, "definitely had problems giving her lecture…she was obviously very flustered," one of her students reported. The simple fact is this: Brown's professors are so politically passionate that they are incapable of avoiding the indoctrination of their pupils.

Professors don't appreciate being challenged, either. When certain right-wing organizations compiled evidence of anti-American thought emulating from college campuses after 9/11, professors complained that these reports were too similar to McCarthyism. Brown professor Kevin Lourie said, "These kinds of attacks will only discourage professors from speaking out and opening up dialogues about what's happening overseas, and why."(3) We should be so lucky. But there was one thing I learned at Brown: you *can't* stop the professors from speaking their mind. Engaging their rhetoric would only intimidate them, thereby forcing them to think a little deeper before espousing their left-wing ideals. God forbid.

Short of the University making a concentrated effort to balance the faculty with an equal amount of conservative professors, I think this problem's cure is difficult to prescribe. There are some who argue that it is justified to monitor exactly what certain professors say in their classrooms, and also to set specific guidelines that detail what is acceptable speech for a college teacher. While I initially cringe at the strategy of micromanaging professors' speech—because I feel like a free speech hypocrite (basically, a liberal)—I can't argue against an effort to remind professors that they are not there to make their students agree with them on the issues they find dire.

The grounds for speech-policing the faculty are actually compelling. A professor who continuously teaches his *opinions*—say, on current political issues—would be violating the University's promise of an open-minded education. He wouldn't be teaching his students how to confront issues, but rather teaching them exactly what to think about specific events. Conventional wisdom says that the best teachers are the ones who teach their students *how* to think, not *what* to think. Even the most arrogant liberals aren't willing to defy such a pretty cliché.

If one proceeds in this debate from the premise that professors are not supposed to be teaching their students *what* to think, then one is recognizing the possibility that some professors may be doing a poor job of teaching. If this is possible, why can't their work be policed?

Objectors will say that monitoring the professors will create a detached faculty, one that would hesitate to personally engage their students. And surely, one great thing about Brown was the enthusiasm of the faculty, and their accessibility. However, I wouldn't hit the panic button as readily as others because, again, you *can't* stop professors from becoming heavily involved with student learning. After all, they became professors to do just that. Chaos is an overblown prediction when talking about the effects of monitoring the faculty's teaching methods. I think it is more likely that a strict teaching policy will serve as an effective reminder and warning to professors. While a few disputes over whether or not charged professors have actually been corrupting the educational model may occur, it may be a worthwhile nuisance that prevents professors from promoting certain political philosophies within the classroom. After all, you can't fire your professor. But if your drycleaner derides capitalism every time you stop in, you can go somewhere else to starch your shirts.

I'm not exactly sure what the proper solution is to the concern over faculty bias, but one thing is for certain—it's time to intimidate the professors.

Okay, Take it Outside

The majority of Brown's professors—like the majority of the student body—were not leftist intimidators. However, also similar to the student body—and almost as indictable—professors allowed a radical handful to reign over College Hill.

There was much more to the faculty's campus influence besides just being able to put a liberal twist on any topic covered inside the classroom. As you will continue to see, most of my encounters with radical leftism and political intimidation pertained to my classmates. It was the student body that had the most vocal and intimidating voice on campus when it came to the viciousness of political name-calling and character assaults. There was a reason for this: Professors wishing to add their voices to campus disputes had to be much more tame, and therefore, they had an understated method of contributing to Brown's political indoctrination by continuously aligning themselves with rallying student leftists outside the parameters of the classroom.

It was outside of the classroom where I found undeniable proof of faculty bias. Professors primarily contributed to the University's political imbalance with their consistent support at student rallies, with their written contributions to the *Brown Daily Herald*, and any other way they could find to let it be publicly known how they felt about political matters. You will notice within my upcoming stories concerning campus quarrels that my professors never failed to share their sentiments of support for those on the left side of any of these issues. On the rarest of occasions was a professor willing to make a public conservative argument, or take a stand against the actions and thoughts of radical students.

The sight of professors assisting the causes of Brown's student groups, and the lack of any professors standing against them gave credibility to liberal opinion, and told nonconforming students that if they were to ever find themselves in conflict against a liberal sect of the Brown community, they would find no assistance from within the faculty. That was the careful manner of campus adults, and exactly how they added to the culture of fear and intolerance on campus. They tactfully made it known on whose side of the political aisle they stood, and used the vigor of the student body to ensure that they would never be bothered with dissenting conservative viewpoints. A conscious conspiracy? Perhaps not. But that's the way it was.

More proof of the campus' uniformed politics came when Brown's 30:1 Democrat-heavy faculty held a meeting in October of 2003 in the midst of the War in Iraq, and took their official University position at its conclusion. They declared publicly:

> **"The Faculty wishes to go on record as opposing the doctrine of preemptive war. Force should be employed only as a last resort and even then, only in accordance with international law. We believe strongly that the present invasion and occupation of Iraq do not fulfill these requirements."**(5)

You can see just how much Brown liberals thought of themselves. The faculty actually thought that President Bush got a devastating newsflash that day. *Um, sir. We've got trouble. I hate to break this to you, but the Brown University faculty is collectively opposing the War in Iraq.* My professors actually thought that their collective opinion would send a statement of such an overbearing reputation of intelligence, that the highest offices in our land would reconsider their national decisions. If this wasn't the case, then what was the point of collectively announcing their political views? Why not remain as individuals? It was because not one of them wanted to go on record as Mr. or Mrs. So-and-So, but rather as a member of the *Brown* faculty. In their eyes, that held much more intellectual weight, and could possibly influence national opinion on the war.

Forget for a second about faculty arrogance, and consider this: What happened to diversity? Why would an institution that takes great pride in its open-minded education take a public stance on an issue that had divided the nation? Why did Brown's administration allow its faculty to represent the school with a sweeping characterization of the University? What about the professor that believed in the cause for war? The student? The janitor? The coach? The dean? Did Brown not represent them? Did they not represent Brown?

The University also declares on its website:

> **"Brown University has been and will continue to be committed to a policy of equal employment opportunity**

> and to the principles of affirmative action. The University endorses the goals of equal employment opportunity and affirmative action as supportive of the University's values. This commitment extends beyond ensuring neutrality in employment opportunities with regard to race, color, sex, age, religion, national origin, veteran status, disability, sexual orientation, gender identity and gender expression."(6)

Asserting the values of affirmative action on Brown's website wasn't the only way administrators alienated certain students. In October of 2003 after right-wing pundit David Horowitz offered a controversial speech on race relations to the Brown community Brenda Allen, Associate Provost and Director of Institutional Diversity, said to a group of students, "If anyone left there feeling they learned something significant about anything, that's a shame. That man doesn't have a clue about race in America. He's a waste of time."(7)

If the point I'm trying to make just isn't resonating with you yet, then try this. Years ago most of our elite universities expelled the ROTC (Reserve Officers Training Corps) from their campuses. Brown students, like many others, ensured the removal of the ROTC from College Hill in the 1960s in support of Vietnam protests and demilitarization. Apparently, this distaste for the U.S. military still defines the overall campus sentiment. In fact, most of the Ivy League schools have still not invited the ROTC back onto their campuses. Harvard outright prohibits ROTC recruiters from school grounds, and students at Yale, Columbia, etc are forced to travel off-campus if they wish to participate in this program. But why hadn't the question of the ROTC's presence on Brown's campus been revisited since its expulsion years ago? And why did Brown's quest for diversity end at the footstep of a military lifestyle? As I would discover, it is primarily the gay and lesbian community that now serves as the primary obstacle to achieving the campus presence of the ROTC. The military's policy toward homosexuals is the reason for their objection. Yet another politically loaded issue not open for debate on the Ivy League campus.

The forced absence of the U.S. military from Brown's campus may be the most shameful example of intellectual prejudice within Providence's hotbed of liberalism. My classmates and I weren't given the opportunity to participate in the ROTC program, but Brown funded student-groups such as the Young Communist League, and the International Socialist Organization, who openly declared that they stood in the "revolutionary tradition of Karl Marx, Vladimir Lenin and Leon Trotsky," and "believe that capitalism produces poverty, racism, famine, environmental catastrophe and war."(8) Yet, symbols of the U.S. military on campus might have offended someone?

Few campus adults were ever present to help confront such intellectual discrepancies. There was very little concern over the fact that students who may have dissented from affirmative action policies, anti-war sentiments, or disgust for the U.S. military were being told that they were not welcome on Brown's campus. So, without any identified faculty friends, dissenting pupils would just have to abide being the intellectual underdog for their entire undergraduate life.

It was quite a sight. That is, for an Ivy League school to have become so blinded to its own blatant hypocrisy. The charming and hypnotizing rhetoric of diversity and individuality habitually rolled from everyone's lips, even as the University was clearly functioning as a one-dimensional political robot. And I began to believe that the poor state of Brown's academic atmosphere was not entirely spawned from administration/faculty blindness, but by an ethic that told them that it was moral to willfully keep their eyes shut.

The Professor

In April of 2003 Brown's campus hosted and sponsored a public affairs conference titled, *A Time of Great Consequence: America and the World.* A portion of the conference was a public forum that featured experts on international security issues. Paul Kennedy, director of International Security Studies at Yale, and Joseph Nye, dean of the Kennedy School of Government at Harvard were two participants. Also present was Richard Perle, chairman of the Defense Advisory Board leading up to the War in Iraq. In the months leading up to the war the University had already revealed its strong opposition to the Bush administration's efforts, so of course, Perle met Brown's natural resistance. While people entered Salomon Hall (the building on the Main Green where the discussion took place) they were met by students holding up signs that denounced the Iraq War, and the presence of Mr. Perle on campus.

Kennedy and Nye were both critics of the war. When they spoke the audience had the opportunity to listen, but when Perle began to speak campus protesters sitting in the balcony section of Salomon Hall dropped leaflets onto the crowd that condemned his visit to Providence. Perle tried to continue speaking, but the protesters then released a banner from the balcony for everyone to read. It said:

YOU'RE A WAR CRIMINAL, MR. PERLE.(9)

As if the student protesters hadn't already made their point from their outdoor rally, their leaflets, and their incredibly insulting banner, they also forced Mr. Perle to consistently hurdle their vocal obstructions for the rest of the event. Later on, Perle called the student protest a "significant departure from politeness."(10) How could anyone disagree?

Professor of English William Keach disagreed. When the protest came under scrutiny, he defended the protest with a letter-to-the-editor in *The Herald*. He wrote:

> "...Free speech is an important principle—one worth fighting for. But applying the principle in an abstract, absolute way to protest, which involves disrupting the speech of very powerful, very wealthy, very widely represented members of the establishment like Richard Perle simplifies and diminishes political reality. Was Perle prevented from speaking at Brown? Were members of the audience prevented from hearing what he had to say? Should those of us who believe that Perle is importantly responsible for the development and execution of a genocidal U.S. military policy in Iraq and elsewhere in the Middle East accord him our respect and civility?... Is there anyone whose speech you would be willing to disrupt for political, moral or practical reasons? Must this form of protest be absolutely condemned no matter who the speaker is, no matter what the speaker has done or plans to do?...Speaking for myself, I'm very sorry that a meeting in Boston prevented me from joining in the protests against Perle. I would have eagerly joined in the verbal attacks on him and felt that by doing so I was in no way violating his right to speak or to be heard."(11)

It was an intriguing defense of the protest. And I must admit, it seduced me. Keach simply believed that Richard Perle was a reprehensible character. The worst of the worst! Not only was he "very wealthy," but he was also a member of the Bush administration! Obviously I am mocking the professor's opinion, but he still had a solid argument. *Certain* people to *some* people are just intolerable, and therefore don't deserve "our usual customs of respectful debate"—as professor Keach said about David Horowitz, the conservative author who had caused a controversy on Brown's campus in 2001. The Professor had a real problem with him as well. After all, Horowitz was also "well-funded."(12) "The principle that such disruptive protest can be morally and politically justified in some situations needs to be recognized," The Professor stated in another letter to *The Herald.*(13)

As a free speech fanatic (and a civilized person) I instantly had a negative reaction to an uncivil protest during an organized debate. However, The Professor's letter was challenging me to consider whether there was "anyone" whose appearance on campus would force me to set aside values of decency and free speech for the sake of upholding my own personal "political, moral, or practical reasons." These subjective conditions were the basis of Keach's fierce objection to Perle, and I realized that I had not attempted to truly understand the feelings of the Perle protesters. They *strongly* objected to Perle. So did The Professor. He believed the current Iraq War (that Perle was largely responsible for developing) was a "form of terrorism."(14) And I reasoned that there was probably *someone* who I would feel the exact same way about. No doubt about it. *Some* people are just insufferable. I just couldn't think of who that person might have been. But there must have been *somebody.* For The Professor, it was Richard Perle and David Horowitz. I needed to understand that.

So I began a personal search for the individual whose ideas and values repulsed me so much that I would be in favor of obstructing not only his speech, but also his presence on my alma mater's campus. It wasn't an easy search. I'm a pretty lenient person. I mean, I never vocally objected to the pornographers, racists, anti-Americans, and the most left-leaning liberals whenever they visited Brown. But again, it seemed logical that I should be able to think of just *one person* who could boil my blood that much. I just needed time to think about it. The Perle protesters, according to The Professor, had strong convictions, and they were merely sticking up for them. And having strong convictions is admirable. The Professor had *very* strong convictions. At a student anti-war rally in 2001, several days past 9/11, Keach told the crowd, "What happened on September 11th was terrorism, but what happened during the Gulf War was also terrorism."(15) He extended this sentiment to the current war in Iraq: "If 'Shock and Awe' is not the name of a terrorist strategy, I don't know what is" and "U.S. military terrorism is not the same as al-Quaida terrorism. But they're both forms of terrorism."(13) The Professor had inspired me with his passion, and I yearned to discover that one individual whose speech I would be willing to interrupt with a protest—somebody whose opinions absolutely disgusted me! Hmmm.

Again, after reading the The Professor's letter I began to understand where the Perle protesters were coming from. When do principles of liberty fall behind one's personal taste? When you *really* disagree! When you just *know* you're right! Or when you believe someone is "importantly responsible for the development and execution of a genocidal U.S. military policy..." Following the Horowitz controversy Keach said he "stood against those who either actively or passively perpetuate oppression by claiming that all acts of speech are equally entitled to legal protection..."(16) Certainly, the noble cause of freeing oppressed people also warrants the restriction of certain words and thoughts. So is punishing mean people for using harsh language. During the Horowitz controversy Keach and other faculty members urged the administration to "take strong action" against particular individuals who posted "injurious racist insults" onto The Herald's on-line discussion forum.(17) Of course, The Professor was rightfully the arbiter of what was considered to be "racist" and "moral" and "oppressive" and "practical." And during these times of elevated moral confidence certain circumstances just didn't matter to The Professor—for instance, the opinions of his inferiors.

Another circumstance that didn't matter to The Professor was the fact that the Perle incident took place at a setting that was the least fitting for a protest—an academic institution, the supposed home of open-minded thinking. Not to mention that the event was designed as a debate, and the essence of debate is—pretty much—the absence of protest. The parties in opposition to one another have already agreed to a lack of disturbance for the sake of an academic occasion (granted, they hadn't checked to see if that was okay with The Professor). Perle was sharing the stage with two anti-war, Ivy League liberals, who were well-equipped to dispute Perle's ideas. The event had all the makings for a great scholarly occasion, but academic decorum correctly takes a backseat to the personal views of a righteous individual. The Professor, acting accordingly with his own "political, moral...practical" purposes, *really* objected to Perle. Remember, Perle was "very wealthy."

It also didn't matter to Keach that he was ignoring his employer's philosophy. Brown University's creed is one of intellectual tolerance. Just go right to the University handbook: *"Brown strives to sustain a learning environment that supports individual exploration, creativity, and accomplishment and that promotes and protects the free exchange of ideas."* (18) Surely, however, exceptions can be made when you *really* disapprove of particular outlooks. Keach understood this better than anyone else. That's why he ignored the fact that somebody else within the Brown community (obviously someone less important than The Professor) found Perle's presence worthwhile. We know this just by the fact that Perle was *invited* to attend. At Brown, it was always so important to make everyone feel safe and comfortable when expressing personal viewpoints. Suddenly, this wasn't such a vital principle to The Professor when an important member of the Bush-team was doing the talking on behalf of someone else within the University. Applying double standards to the Brown community was suddenly a necessary evil because...well...because The Professor said so.

Another stubborn fact is that a majority of the nation at this time agreed with the deployment of U.S. troops into Iraq. However, because certain students so vehemently objected to Richard Perle, the entire Brown community was forced to tolerate a disruptive rally. It didn't matter if the rest of the student body would be kept out of touch with this "political reality" because, again, these student protesters *really* hated Perle.

Keach constantly gave the necessary lip service to principles of free speech, but he was still "left wondering about how they applied to situations in which the institutionally protected attacks and insults of powerful people collide with the militant protests of students and ordinary people." (19) Yes, free speech, of course. Unless dissent comes in the form of "attacks" or "insults" toward "ordinary people." Despite the fact that The Professor was admitting that there is a trade-off between principles of free speech and principles of disruptive protest, he somehow found the logic to make the contradictory claim that Perle was still able to speak his mind. *No harm, no foul*, he was now suddenly saying. Now, I was meant to perceive the protest as a mere symbolic effort that was well worth it, and should have been tolerated simply because other activists around the world were likely "strengthened by this show of defiance," or maybe they "took heart from reports of these protests," said The Professor.(20) It didn't occur to The Professor that bigger issues might have been at stake—for instance, that the ethos of the University was being violated; that conservative students were being told that their values were not welcome; that perhaps The Professor's elitist, self-indulgent mindset was eroding a culture of civility, fairness, liberty, and democratic ideals.

Liberals—as well-intentioned as some of them may have been—refused to acknowledge any code of ethics that might have stood in their way as they attempted to advance leftist causes. Truth and morality were expendable. It was "everything goes" and "what can be done for me?" No doubt about it, the liberal mindset was a totalitarian one.

CHAPTER 7
A Normal Point Of View, Finally!
How I became a columnist for *The Herald*

I hadn't figured out what was truly going on around me when I finally decided to speak out against my classmates. I had something to say, but I just didn't know what it was. I just couldn't take...it...anymore. But I didn't have the knowledge, experience, or the words to criticize what I didn't like about Brown University.

Looking back at my Brown experience we can see that this is true. My very first column for *The Herald* was a vague criticism of my classmates, and their life of protest. However, it wasn't merely as in-depth as my current understanding of why they had subscribed to such a lifestyle.

At Brown I felt as if I was in driver's training school as a 16 year-old, and the teacher kept instructing the class to drive on the left side of the road, and that Green meant STOP, and Red meant GO. Now, even though I would not have had any driving experience, and much less knowledge than the teacher, I still could have sworn that those teachings should have been the other way around. Feeling slightly inferior and insecure, I would have decided to keep my mouth shut until I investigated the truth myself, and had taken a few spins around the block. At Brown I went for a political ride, observing the backwardness of liberalism the entire time.

As I was leaving the cafeteria one particular day I noticed a sign that read, *Brown Daily Herald Opinion Columnists Needed.* I immediately considered this opportunity to express my frustration only because I had just read an article in *The Herald* that got under my skin. The story served as a specific incident at which I could focus my criticism. We'll get to the story soon, but for now just know that I had decided to give this "writing thing" a shot.

I went back to my dorm room and got to work. About 30 students handed in columns, but only a few of us would be chosen as regularly appearing columnists in *The Herald*, a distinction I wasn't even sure I wanted. But I began to write. I wrote as best as I could. I had never before written anything quite similar to an op-ed before. I had no real writing experience, and it certainly wasn't as easy as I thought it would be. Fortunately, as it turned out, the most important weapons needed to fight the campus left I had in abundance. Decency and common sense.

When You Lose Elections, Just Give Bush the Finger

It was my junior year, and I had just returned from winter break when I finally decided that enough was enough. I had just returned from a nice, relaxing break from school. I went skiing for a week in Maine with a bunch of close friends, and had spent the rest of my vacation doing some odd jobs to earn a little bit of spending money for the Spring semester.

I guess it is surprising that my little temper tantrum over Brown's liberal assault came on my first day back from a vacation. Like a slap in the face, however, in the first edition of *The Herald* for that semester an article appeared on the front page entitled, *In Washington, Brown Students Join Protesters at Bush Inauguration.* Even during our winter break my classmates refused to stray from the picket line. That January, following the controversial 2000 presidential election, dozens of my classmates joined thousands of others at the largest inaugural protest since President Nixon's second Inauguration. (One thing my alma mater taught me was that Republican victories will always cause the largest protests).

The Herald's front-page article placed the students who went down to Washington in an admirable light for all of the school to admire. I didn't buy into the glory of their charge as everyone else did. I thought it was embarrassing that some of my fellow students attended the protest that included signs that read, "Bush=Racist" and "Hail to the Thief." The way they proudly handled themselves was especially embarrassing as the article included quotations from certain students who boasted about giving President Bush the middle finger as he walked by them.(1) But the article was written in such a way that I'm sure that the students who were highlighted cut it out and hung it on their tiny dorm refrigerators.

By the time I was a junior at Brown I had already begun to see my classmates as a bunch of spoiled brats whose purpose in life seemed to be to protest at all costs, and at all levels of indecency. I wasn't against political activism, but the peculiar absence of conflicting viewpoints on

Brown's campus had resulted in diehard narrow-mindedness. So rather than confront issues with a moral and mature sense of political debate, my classmates inherited a childish activist routine that was never subjected to criticism. I suspected most of them had overlooked why attending the rally was not a good idea. So, I told them why.

A Normal Point of View by Travis Rowley

Brown Protesters Embarrassment to Community

> I was upset to be informed by the Brown Daily Herald on my first day back from winter break that some of my fellow Brown students took a large part in a classless protest at the Inauguration of President Bush on January 20...Dozens of Brown students, including representatives from the College Democrats and the International Socialist Organization, joined the largest inaugural protest since the second swearing-in of President Nixon..."I went pretty much to say F-you Bush," one Brown student bragged. "When Bush passed the National Archives had he looked to his right, he would have seen a sea of middle fingers," he added proudly.
>
> Thoughtlessly, {the protesters} went down there with the same intent that most young, energetic people have always had when joining a cause, to express their views for the sake of saying they did no matter what the repercussions of their actions may be..."Oh yes son, I protested at George W.'s Inauguration. I even flipped him the bird." This is what these students hope to say some day...I am sure President Bush is a lot like everyone else, and he is more likely to listen to a group of mature protesters, rather than a 'sea of middle fingers."
>
> Your actions represent, and also help spread and solidify, a scornful disunity that this nation needs no more of... George W. is not your enemy anymore, but rather your tool

for political and social improvement because, as unfair as it may seem to you, Al Gore lost the presidential election of 2000. President Bush speaks a lot about uniting this country, but your ignorant actions may only lead him to believe that his efforts may be futile. If he has any of your qualities he may just give you the bird.

Tagline: Travis Rowley is a junior from Narragansett, Rhode Island.(2)

I received a phone call that night after the entire campus had a chance to read my column. On the other end of the phone was the president of the Brown College Democrats. Oooooh.

"You're going to write another f-ing column apologizing to the College Democrats! And you're going to recall what you wrote in your column today!" he demanded.

He claimed that his problem was that in my column I included the fact that representatives from the College Democrats attended the protest.

"Where did you get your information?" he asked me.

"I got all of my information out of the article in *The Herald* last week" I told him.

"That's impossible because the article didn't say anything about representatives from the College Democrats being there."

Now I was confused because I was pretty sure that I had read the article correctly. About a minute of awkward and confusing dialogue had gone by before he decided to come clean and clarify his point—one that even he knew was slightly dishonest.

He said to me, "The article stated that *members* of the College Democrats were there. We sent no *official representatives*." Even he had to put the word "official" in there to enlarge the difference between the two synonyms.

Do you see the type of people I had to go to school with for four years? I don't know about you, but I believe wherever I go in life I am *representing* every group that I am a part of. My behavior is a reflection of any organization that I am associated with. My family, my school, my teams, my company, etc. That was why I used the word "representative" in my column, not because I believed the College Democrats instructed their people to go down to Washington and raise hell. *Give Bush our worst, fellow Dems! Give him the middle finger for me!* That demand would have been unnecessary anyway because untamed, juvenile politics was their lifestyle. Those students in Washington *represented* the College Democrats, and they *represented* Brown University, and I was embarrassed by their behavior. I pictured them in my mind. They had traveled enthusiastically down to the Capital, their faces bright red from hollering chants that kindergarteners could have come up with, sporting their Brown outerwear, and waving their middle fingers toward the President of the United States. My classmates.

Of course, being the stubborn Irishman that I am, I refused to apologize or recall anything that I had written. The phone call ended with him yelling, "Listen, if you're going to be a f-ing hard-on about this, then I'm just gonna call the editors of *The Herald* and have them remove you from their staff!"

Hard-on?

The next day in *The Herald* appeared a letter-to-the-editor from a member/representative of the Brown Democrats, my victims of slander. This representative/member, in a letter titled, "College Dems Not Official Protesters," explained to the Brown community how upset he was with me, and that the College Democrats did not send "official representatives to the protest of President Bush's inauguration."(3) Again, they had to stretch the difference between "members" and "representatives" by using the word "official" to describe the type of representatives they were talking about. I could only see their argument as intellectually dishonest as they knew that I never claimed that "official representatives" were sent down there, only that students who *represent* the College Democrats were at the protest.

I never even accused any particular person from any organization of acting improperly. I only mentioned that College Democrat reps/members were there, just as the previous article had done. "Dozens of Brown students, including representatives from the College Democrats and the International Socialist Organization, joined the largest inaugural protest since the second swearing-in of President Nixon." That's the sentence that sent the Brown College Democrats into a fit of panic. I couldn't believe how willing they were to appear so lame and pathetic.

I wish they had just been honest. What the College Democrats were really upset about was that an article was written that didn't exalt their activism. They saw no need to get upset over the article that *complimented* childish opposition to the Republican President, and it wasn't because the article used the word "member" when describing the College Democrats that were there. They were upset because I criticized their trip to Washington, rather than glorified it.

Think about it. Had they reprimanded the members/reps that acted so inappropriately down there? No. In fact, the rest of this student's *Herald* letter went on to *defend* the protest! Not once did he denounce any of the protesters' behavior. He only refuted my belief that "public demonstrations are illegitimate and ineffective means of political participation." I thought I was just making a call for decency to those who were choosing to exercise their right to free assembly. Oh, but I offered no "consistent ethical argument," he claimed. Admittedly, at the time I was ignorant to one thing; the fact that liberals would actually argue that flicking the President off was "ethical."

My classmates often dispensed this type of deceitfulness. Their true intentions, thoughts, and agendas were often disguised by propaganda, political correctness, and diverting people's attention away from the meat of the issues—for instance, their whining over the usage of a word. That was my first personal encounter with their intellectual dishonesty. There would be plenty more.

I had to be understanding, though. At Brown University, the College Democrats just weren't used to disapproval. As long as the letter "D" was next to your name, then you were safe from scrutiny no matter what you did. I'm sure they also weren't happy to find out that the editors of the *The Herald* made me a regular columnist after this dispute. Nah nah-nah nah-nah naaaah!

I must say, the College Democrats' harassing phone call and *Herald* letter did not have the effect on me that they were hoping for. I only recognized their objections as devious and dishonest. From then on, my columns were even more abrasive and uncompromising, certainly never concerned with political correctness or the inevitable campus wrath. I was angering people even more than I thought I would, and I enjoyed stirring up political controversy at Brown, some sort of intellectual campus challenge that I felt was nonexistent. Not only that, but I felt that I was on the right side of the debate as I got under people's skin. President Democrat's phone call only motivated me to write more. And I did. The College Democrats were only the first among a long line of enemies I would make for my remaining years at Brown. For two more years I submitted columns to *The Herald.* I called my column *A Normal Point of View,* a title that many of Brown's liberals had a problem with. Who was I to say what was *normal* and what was not?

I'm Normal

Having strong opinions is one thing, but Brown's political one-sidedness was only creating a body of youngsters who were detached from anything even pertaining to truth as they graduated into reality. "I really had no idea that entire states were against gay marriage. I thought it was just small, radical groups," a Brown student said, expressing her shock caused by the 2004 election results.

My alma mater had an astonishing ability to make certain students feel intellectually isolated, but as a junior I began to realize that the mind of mainstream America shared the same fundamental principles of humanity, justice, fairness, and freedom as I did. Coming into my own politically, I could finally feel the warmth of the majority I was residing in. In that sense, yes, I had come to think of myself as part of the norm. Normal. Off of College Hill I was simply part of mainstream America, and in many ways the campus left had portrayed it as stylish and smart to hate the American mainstream, anything white or Christian.

One of my classmates, objecting to my arrogance, told the campus, "Only a white male could use the word normal in that context without using quotation marks."(4) In fact, only a politically correct liberal would actually think that quotation marks could solve all of our problems.

After another column of mine defended the Brown Police Department from allegations of practicing racial profiling, one of my classmates told the campus that "it was incredibly bold for a Caucasian male from Suburbia to tackle the issue of racial profiling...Rowley has no idea what being racially profiled (especially wrongfully so) feels like, due to the fact that he never has, and never will, experience this particular phenomenon."(5) This is like me getting perturbed when a black guy suggests that white people should use sun-block at the beach. How does *he* know what a sunburn feels like?! How incredibly bold! Oh, the nerve!

My classmates didn't realize it, but it was them who first labeled me as *normal.* If I had no "special interest," then the only thing left to be was *normal.* In no way did I consider it a complement to be *normal.* It's just who I was according to Brown's liberals. I was simply a member of the mainstream. Normal. I wasn't *special,* and therefore undeserving of any extra sensitivity for any problems I might ever have to endure. Just a normal guy. Well, for the most part, it was the normal guys who weren't allowed to voice their opinions on campus. It had been restricted from the ears of Ivy League students by the liberal guidebook of political correctness. So, I decided to show Brown what *A Normal Point of View* sounded like, and my classmates hated me for it.

"I never give them hell. I just tell the truth and they think it's hell."
Harry S. Truman

I can't imagine someone more insecure than myself when I began to confront the most thunderous components of the campus left. As you'll soon discover, my columns were written with over-confidence, and even had a mocking tone. The arrogance that radiated from my columns, however, was paper-thin. I was under the impression that my classmates were much more knowledgeable than myself when it came to political matters. So, as a defense mechanism, I attempted to express my opinions unapologetically, and with overbearing confidence. If they knew just how phony my certainty was, they may have been able to beat me back with argument. All I really knew for sure was that I was not a cruel individual, and that waving your middle finger toward the President was not the antic of a scholar. So when the campus left fired back at me with petty word games and character assaults, my political confidence began to embolden, as I began to realize just how intellectually vacuous their rhetoric and activism really was.

It's a strange phenomenon. That is, people's over-animated reaction to a previously quiet truth, and our intuition that tells us that when a seemingly casual comment triggers such a deafening uproar, we can assume that we're probably onto something. Even as an 18 year-old, I knew that whenever someone becomes defensive without a serious initial attack, it is always a signal of guilt or uncertainty. I learned that *before* I arrived at Brown. Believe me, never on campus was there a threat that conservatism might take over as the school's mainstream ideology.

Yet, whenever an individual showed the slightest hint of conservatism, campus activists would get so up-in-arms that I used to think hostile alien invaders must have landed on College Hill. That defensive behavior always suggested to me that there must be some legitimacy attached to right-minded thought, and I set out to see what it was that got liberals in such a tizzy. Do you know what I found out it was? It was the truth.

Just look at the College Democrats' reaction to my column that criticized the protest in Washington. Their president actually called me up screaming, cursing, and saying things such as, "members, not representatives!" Come on, give me a break. How childish did he want to look? How *defensive* did he want to look? Richard Perle, during Brown's public affairs conference in 2003, not only was forced to hurdle incessant heckling from the crowd, but had to ignore a student banner that read, "**You're A War Criminal, Mr. Perle**." Rumors of violence echoed through the Main Green when the College Republicans invited David Horowitz to campus. The list of examples goes on and on. Do you remember the she-pimp? We were only one minute into the conversation about her "business" before she yelled at me and ran off (out of my life forever...sniffle, sniffle). I simply stated that it appeared as if she was running an escort service and she walked away from the conversation. "I believe in what I do," she shouted at me. *I'm not so sure that you do, my love. Because if you did, you probably wouldn't have yelled at me and ran away.* She was really pretty, though.

Somewhere along my journey through Brown University I discovered why the leftist movement had resorted to the tactic of political correctness to attain campus authority. It was because the left could not deny the foundation of common sense that conservative thought lies upon. The only way to advance leftist ideas was to stigmatize certain viewpoints, effectively achieving liberal domination by silencing the opposition. My classmates' behavior, as it turned out, was entirely attributable to the quality of their ideas.

If my classmates and professors *really* had faith in their beliefs, if they *really* thought that conservatism was as absurd and offensive as they dressed it up to be, then they would have craved expression from the right. *Please, oh please, somebody challenge us!* A conservative argument would have gratifyingly revealed all of that bigotry that liberals insisted was boiling within traditional theory. But how could they convince anyone of this if they kept obstructing the voice of conservatism? They should have unzipped those conservative lips! Liberals could have finally relaxed! The protests, the rallies, the marches, and their thought-policing would no longer have been necessary. They could have spent more time worshipping themselves.

But let's face it—traditional thought was given no such entryway because liberals were lacking faith in their ability to influence others with conservatives always peering over their shoulders. It's no wonder I could only recognize political correctness as defensive paranoia, rather than confident activism. This only led me to one conclusion—there was more to the story that Brown University was not telling me.

CHAPTER 8
Only Allies Were Welcome

The campus left found it to be efficient activism—to teach others how to *speak* like a liberal, before teaching them how to *think* like one. For strategic reasons, the language came first.

In an opinion column printed in *The Herald* a white freshman student reported his personal experience after being forced to view *Skin Deep*, the sensitivity-training video shown to first-years during *Freshmen Brainwashing.* He described the film and the setting just as I have at the end of Chapter 5. After the film that was intended to set the guidelines for racial dialogue was over, and it had created an awkward atmosphere of racial mistrust, the students were expected to discuss their feelings about what they had just seen. The upperclassman Resident Counselor (RC) asked questions that were supposed to make sure that the appropriate dialogue continued. One question asked was, "How can you become an *ally* to minorities?" The student telling of this account asked the RC what exactly he meant by "ally?" He wrote, "I asked him to clarify it for me. Instead, he blew up at me and repeated the word back to me in an abrasive tone, as if I were hopelessly racist by asking for a clarification."(1)

I always had a huge problem with campus activists' usage of the word "ally" as well, and I came to realize that the campus left had adopted this word with arrogant political intentions.

The word "ally" was stamped on every corner of the campus—within the rhetoric, and within the literature. Posters that advertised upcoming events hosted by certain minority groups frequently employed the word. The message would always appear at the bottom of the advertisements: ALLIES WELCOME.

In a lecture called "Queers and the Greek System," *The Herald* reported that the invited speaker told his audience that "many fraternities have not addressed the issue of gay membership...but queer people can still rely on straight allies—'you just have to find them.'" Yeah, like an Easter-Egg hunt.(2)

Hi-T was a Brown student-group that utilized the word in its own self-description.

> "Hi-T is a study break and social for the queer communities at Brown and RISD. Straight *allies* are always welcome. The group meets for an unstructured period to eat, meet other LGBTQA students, and relax. Our primary goal is to provide a safe space for queer students to socialize. Meetings occur every other week on Wednesdays nights from 10 pm to midnight in the Faunce Memorial Room" (emphasis added).(3)

I can't choose a more perfect example of soft indoctrination, and intimidation. And by hearing just how often liberals felt compelled to evoke the word "ally" I learned just how important it was to them. ALLIES WELCOME was much more than an invitation to all who were interested in supporting liberal causes. In fact, the last thing that it served as was an invitation. It was more often used to suggest the presence of *enemies*—that the campus left was on the victimized side of an ongoing campus war. It was used to convince the Ivy League's most impressionable of severe injustice happening right under their noses, thus motivating the nation's brightest over-achievers to join the latest rebellion.

ALLIES WELCOME was also a revolting political statement that stared students in the eyes and said, *If you're not with us, then you're against us.* It forced me to make a decision. Was I going to be an ally, or an enemy? A righteous liberal, or a self-centered conservative? *Well, which one?!* For my first couple of years on campus, I followed the path of many Brown students. I didn't make a peep.

This understated intolerance actually helped create more resistance toward activist organizations. But don't go feeling sorry for Brown's activists. This was the result they desired. ALLIES WELCOME was a powerful political tactic, an actual attempt to agitate campus onlookers. Because liberal agendas required the *image* of conflict, my classmates actually craved episodes of hate that would justify their activism. To this end, the campus left didn't truly desire an abundance of "allies." Instead, they hoped for conflict because their agendas demanded the impressions of *white vs. black*, *queer vs. straight*, *men vs. women.* As long as the public perception was one of inequitable struggle, my classmates would have retained their appearance as political casualties, and therefore entitled to all the perks that come with the label "victim." Their most powerful weapon in their political arsenal—their victimization. In no way could they ever allow it to be diminished or downplayed. And by the time I had arrived on College Hill, the word "ally" had already been institutionalized into the rhetoric of radical student-groups for the purposes of maintaining their wounded status, to secure hostile relations between them and their political adversaries, and to hopefully ignite an incident that they could spin into an act of bigotry. This would give their yelps irrefutable integrity so their cause could live on, so they could continue to organize, rally, and protest. Remember, that's what many of them were at Brown to do.

Agendas

Here are some examples of public self-descriptions of some of Brown's student activist groups.(4)

The Brotherhood

The Brotherhood shall exist to provide a space for Black men to discuss and express the views, which we see as socially and politically significant. The Brotherhood seeks to support and strengthen the bond between its members by sharing our common and diverse experiences as Black men. We as Black men find that this communal space is severely inhibited within the walls of Brown University. Thus we will help to foster a sense of friendship and unity among the Black men to ensure that this space is a safe haven for its members to express their political, social, academic, spiritual views and experiences at Brown.

Arab-American Anti-Discrimination Committee (ADC)

AAADC is intended to promote the Arabic culture on campus and to present the Arabic heritage and traditions, forming a comfortable atmosphere for both Arab students and Arab-Americans.

Asian American Student Association (AASA)

To build a conscious, inclusive Asian American community through a commitment to reclaiming our identities as Asian Americans and people of color by critically examining our histories of colonialism and immigration and actively defining a space for Asian Americans in the struggle for Third World liberation. Furthermore, AASA is dedicated to challenging all forms of oppression, including racism, sexism, heterosexism, and classism, and recognizes their historical and current manifestations in systems of imperialism and the exploitation of people of color.

Lesbian, Gay, Bisexual, and Transgendered Alliance (LGBTA)
The LGBTA is an umbrella organization for queer groups at Brown. We are committed to creating a space that is comfortable and welcoming to people of all identities (sexual, gender, ethnic, racial, and otherwise), and to provide relevant social and educational resources and programming in a socially responsible manner. We publish a weekly anonymous email newsletter (subscribe at our website).

Feminist Majority Leadership Alliance (FMLA)
The Brown University Feminist Majority Leadership Alliance (FMLA) is a part of a nationwide network of pro-choice feminist student-run organizations. In coalition with the Feminist Majority Foundation, we strive to raise awareness about issues affecting all women, in this country and abroad, by educating ourselves and other students, raising money, and engaging in political activism. In the past, we have worked on issues such as reproductive freedom, women's health, and violence against women, both in the United States and in other countries. We invite all progressive activists committed to equality between women and men to get involved! If you are interested in joining us, please email us at fmla@brown.edu and visit our national website at www.feministcampus.org.

third world ACTION
third world ACTION is a coalition-building group formed in response to the absence of third world activism at Brown University. Through third world ACTION, students of color proactively strive to address issues at Brown, including racism and institutional injustice, in order to substantively effect change.

Why Protest? To Justify the Activist Existence

It was odd to me whenever a minority group at Brown declared that they did not feel comfortable expressing their views on campus. All I *ever* saw were minority groups expressing themselves. This contradiction forced me to conclude that they were simply being dishonest.

It became so obvious to me. My classmates were protesting *not* to object to injustice, but to validate their existence. There was no doubt—a perpetual state of grief was actually more important to the campus left than actually achieving their stated goals. Brown's culture of protest was simply a selfish and self-fulfilling lifestyle only practiced to make the protester feel substantive within his own world. Examples of bigotry were few and far between, so campus ringleaders were forced to make mountains out of molehills, always declaring how offended they were by unfamiliar opinion. The level of cruel consciousness that liberals wished to expose just didn't exist on Brown's campus, so they were forced to pretend it was there, or to provoke it themselves. And anyone who wished to avoid being tagged as an *enemy* was forced to adhere to their ludicrous indictments. If you wanted to be an *ally*, you would keep your mouth shut, and recognize that you were the offspring of "white privilege" (another slogan of leftist vocabulary). This was the complex political game I would be forced to play if I wished to criticize any portion of the University.

The entire basis for forming *The Brotherhood* was built upon the fundamental belief that Brown was not a safe place for African-Americans. That meant, that in order to warrant the existence of *The Brotherhood*, they had to prove that this was true. Quite frankly, it was not true, and they knew it. So they were forced to blow every occasion out of proportion, and modify their speech to include words such as "ally"—all to relentlessly exhibit their oppression.

The Brotherhood declared that Brown was not a "safe haven" for them to express their political and social concerns. Right off the bat in their own self-description they marked themselves as victims, telling me that their "communal space is severely inhibited" at Brown. Nevermind the fact that there was an entire Afro-American Studies Department at Brown dedicated solely to the study of black America's unique culture and history. Apparently that wasn't sufficient enough to be considered a "safe haven." For some reason a classroom setting, where white students were welcome as well, would not do. It probably would have been too difficult to determine which whites were *allies*, and which were *enemies*.

Sometimes you could catch certain students, who were unaware of the campus left's fundamental exaggeration of oppression, admitting how friendly and accommodating of a place Brown actually was. One of Brown's international students wrote, "I love being here, and I think that most, if not all, international students would agree with me that our campus is definitely not hostile to foreign students. If anything, I feel very welcome and at home here."(5) And a homosexual student told the community, "In four years on this campus, I have cross-dressed regularly and kissed both men and women publicly. I have found most of my nervousness about these actions came from my own fears, not from other Brown students treating me badly. In fact, Brown students have been overwhelmingly supportive."(6) During my time at Brown I came across countless straight, white students perplexed by those minorities who claimed they didn't feel "safe" at Brown. If minorities couldn't feel safe at Brown, then where could they feel safe?

The *Arab-American Anti-Discrimination Committee* would declare the same thing right there in their title. Discrimination? I just didn't see the discrimination, or the need for a group to be formed to create a "comfortable atmosphere" for Arab students. The *Asian American Student Association* also suggested that they suffered from campus prejudice with their description as a group that challenged "all forms of oppression, including racism, sexism, heterosexism, and classism." The *Brown Feminists* welcomed anyone to their meetings who was committed to "equality between women and men." The LGBTA claimed that their main purpose was to create "a space that is comfortable and welcoming to people of all identities?" All of this was intended to tell me that Brown was failing to offer a welcoming community to any student that happened to be female, gay, black, or Asian. And Brown's student-groups cleverly, deceitfully, and successfully convinced others that this was true. Simply amazing.

Undoubtedly, I'll be the one attacked for unfairly criticizing Brown University. *Out of Ivy* will be considered too harsh. An exaggeration. A book of lies. When in reality, it was members of the campus left who were constantly smearing the face of the University. By listening to Brown liberals, it was a wonder anyone would want to enroll at such an awful school. Their false campus agendas prompted them to shout with annoying resilience, "racism, sexism, homophobia!" According to liberals, bigotry was everywhere—so much so that they were forced to conduct an untiring search for "allies"—so much so that they were forced to organize themselves into small comfort groups where they could feel "safe," and where they could speak openly without having to worry about being lynched or gay-bashed. Disturbingly, the campus left's right to rule College Hill wasn't validated by truth, facts, or evidence—but by their incessant submission that Brown was the home of bigotry.

I was in Loonyville.

The Third World Center

While I have criticized the actions of my classmates, it is important to realize the role the University played in encouraging and influencing their campus lifestyles.

In 1976 an influx of under-qualified minority students admitted into the student body under affirmative action policies sparked the formation of the *Third World Center* (TWC). The purpose of the TWC was to "meet the needs of all students of color." Among an assortment of activities, the TWC's Minority Peer Counselors help promote "cross-cultural awareness" by organizing "racism, classism, sexism, heterosexism and homophobia workshops."(7) At least liberals were consistent.

The term "third world" is not meant to imply that the TWC is comprised of students from economically poor countries. According to the TWC's website, they use this term "in the sense of a cultural model of empowerment and liberation...to describe a consciousness which recognizes the commonalities and links shared by their diverse communities. Using the term 'Third World' reminds students of the power they have in coalescing, communicating, and uniting across marginalized communities to create a safer and more open place for all individuals. This consciousness at Brown also reflects a right, a willingness, and a necessity for people of color and others to define themselves instead of being defined by others." *Third World* was adopted in place of *minority* because of "the negative connotations of inferiority and powerlessness with which the word 'minority' is often associated."(8) Referring to themselves as "Third World" made my minority classmates feel better about themselves.

At Brown it was "ally." It was "class struggle." It was "marginalized." It was "underrepresented." It was "social justice." It was "marriage equality." It was "heterosexism." It was "white privilege." It was "safe and welcome." And it was "Third World"—certainly not "minority." You could have hurt somebody.

The pitiful level of political correctness that infected Brown's campus was all too real. You could only say certain things, at certain times, in certain ways. And the TWC was just another apparatus of the liberal language, and the leftist outlook. Each year the TWC ran a separate (but equal, for sure) *Freshmen Brainwashing* prior to the regular *Freshmen Brainwashing* that all first-years attended. It was called the Third World Transition Program (TWTP). Only incoming minority students were allowed to participate in this program designed to introduce them to "the issues they will encounter at Brown as minorities in a predominantly white institution"—according to TWTP's mission statement.(9) I remember finding it difficult to understand how anyone could have the audacity to imply that Brown, with all of its splendor that was racial diversity, was a "white institution" when it boasted the first black president of the Ivy League, and a significant percentage of the administrators, professors, and students were of minority status. Yes, a majority of the students were white, but to suggest that this majority was somehow "predominant" was absurd when talking about a university that worshipped its own ethnic diversity, and the fact that the most vocal and respected groups on campus were of minority status. Could that boldness to assert whites' dominion over Brown's campus have come from a deliberate effort to remind minority students that they were, in fact, minorities—and to suggest that because of that they would be routinely subject to discrimination and other forms of oppression at Brown?

Well, you decide. To the dismay of the Third World Center, one of my minority classmates told of her experience at TWTP.

> "I was told to give my experiences of 'oppression' by white people...I was told not to write for the college daily newspaper, having been told that they are 'biased' and 'against minorities'...In addition, we were given advice on how to 'deal' with a white roommate...My group in particular was told to come to the Third World Center if there were any problems with white roommates and was told specifically that there was a history of problems with white students not understanding concerns like student work, being on financial aid, or minority activities and groups...One participant in the program joked that the University would soon be 'whitewashed,' and some of the leaders laughed at that...Several leaders expressed liberal

> **views, and the idea that we should all support affirmative action programs was assumed...The underlying current of the program was to perpetuate a feeling of 'otherness.'"** (10)

So much for diversity and understanding.

Right away as Brown freshmen, my minority classmates were taught to remain exclusive, and the University prepared them for the discrimination that would surely be waiting for them. I can only assume that this fueled many minority students' drive to become active in the battle against campus bigotry as soon as they arrived. It certainly would have fueled *my* will to become active. However, when minority students didn't find the racism that they were told they would unquestionably encounter, they went searching for it, or any incident that could have appeared as bigoted. TWTP only spawned separatism at a university that claimed to be some sort of racial blender.

Of course, separatism was the hidden design of diversity drivel. As much as liberals praised multiculturalism, they wanted nothing of it. They wanted liberalism. No matter what shape, color, socio-economic status, nationality, or handicap that you were, the campus left wanted nothing to do with you unless you agreed to echo their politically correct poppycock for the next four years. Another TWTP graduate informed the campus that "after it ended there was no sense of trying to connect us with the rest of the Brown community."(11) And one non-participant said, "I have seen people I know who were in TWTP and who are in my unit, but I don't really hang out with them because they already have their own group of friends who they met at TWTP."(12)

The prejudice and deviousness of TWTP and other campus groups was exactly what some students suspected was going on behind the scenes, that campus anxiety over the topic of race wasn't really due to a legitimate fear of white racists hiding among us, but was actually the result of the campus left's willful attempt to keep certain people quiet, and to make *everyone* suspicious.

These days the TWC blatantly exposes itself as a promoter of radical ideologies. Beyond organizing a segregated orientation period, promoting feelings of racial mistrust, instilling sentiments of victim-hood, and coddling the emotions of budding adults—the TWC's website also declares allegiance to the writings of Frantz Fanon, a black intellectual of post-colonialism who advocated violence as a "cleansing force" that "frees the native from his inferiority complex and from his despair and inaction."(13) In the upcoming chapters the reader should always keep the TWC in mind, and attempt to determine for himself whether or not this administration-run program is a positive or negative campus entity. Personally, I believe the TWC has reached its final days.

Perhaps the best reason, however, to re-think the entire existence of the TWC is not its hidden political agenda, but the fact that it doesn't even accomplish any of its publicly stated goals. According to its website, in 1976 the TWC was "designed to serve the interests and meet the needs of all Third World students and to promote racial and ethnic pluralism in the Brown community."(14) Today the TWC serves "to provide an environment in which Arab, Asian, Black, Latino, Multiracial and Native American students can feel comfortable in celebrating their cultural heritages."(15) Thirty years later, and minorities still don't feel "comfortable." Maybe it's time to can this thing.

Reform

TWTP has recently been put under the microscope, and been highly criticized for their separatist solution to knocking down racial barriers. And after legal mandates in 2003 regarding the University of Michigan required that students be accepted or rejected on individual merit, rather than ethnicity, Brown and other schools were motivated to adhere to this legal demand. The "attempt" to reform TWTP may best reveal the duplicity of the program's aims.

In the Fall of 2003, with all eyes on the upcoming decisions concerning TWTP, its doors were officially opened to incoming white students as well, and the program's self-description was altered to state that the TWTP is "a forum *primarily* for students of color...designed to help entering students of color identify and increase their awareness of issues they will encounter at Brown as minorities in a predominantly white institution" (emphasis added).(16) David Greene, Interim Vice President for Campus Life and Student Services, admitted that this new policy was more consistent with Brown's multicultural mission. He stated that this involved "having programs in general that are open to all students."[17] I was more inclined to just eliminate the TWTP altogether, but this seemed like a good step in the right direction.

Officially opening TWTP doors to incoming white students wasn't the end of the issue, however. For some reason, the administration decided not to publicize the decision, or even send out invitations to incoming white students. Kind of like not inviting the bride to the wedding if you ask me.

However, this was a difficult time for Karen McLaurin-Chesson, director of the TWC. There were many who didn't want white students to attend TWTP, and believed tainting the program with the inclusion of whites was a bad idea. A 2004 *Herald* article on the restructuring of TWTP stated, "...a number of current students who attended TWTP say they thought the program successfully created a 'safe space' for students of color to discuss diversity issues."[18] One of the minority peer counselors explained, "The positive of only inviting minorities is that it lets people be very open with one another—they can share their experiences as people of color."[19] Another minority student told the campus, "Sometimes you guard yourself if white students are there." This same student also said, "White students could significantly impact TWTP. Students might be less likely to address 'touchy' racial issues if the comfort of the program were compromised."[20] Comfort. Comfort. Comfort. This was the liberal solution to our racial barriers; to restrict speech; to prohibit pluralism; to actually cool the "melting pot;" to curb openness; to restrain honest dialogue; to create comfort with homogeneity. Comfort at the expense of truth. These were the enlightened, open-minded champions of diversity and progressive-minded thinking that I was privileged to spend four years of my life with.

The priorities of liberalism were on display, and so was its treachery. TWTP had put students under the pretense that only incoming minority students suffer feelings of anxiety, nervousness, and uncertainty when arriving at an unfamiliar institution. Suddenly, their emotions trumped any unhealthy environment that may result from a program that promoted segregation. And it was becoming difficult not to suspect that certain people didn't desire the presence of whites because TWTP was an efficient mechanism for breeding future campus activists, a vital component of the perpetuation of minority victim-hood, operated under the guise of emotional support.

The foundation of Brown's student activist groups was consumed by false premises and intellectual dishonesty—dishonesty spawned by the University itself. It is no wonder that Brown's administrators never seemed to be there to express their disapproval of my classmates' indecency. *They were responsible for it!* The administration would surrender to my classmates' demands for reform, and never condemn the deceit that stemmed from their cries and protests. Brown's pupils were being taught that this type of propaganda-slinging was acceptable and justified, even though the basis for their existence was based on lies, deception, and prejudice. And to me, their behavior began to look strikingly familiar to liberal groups existing in the outside world. Yes, students take their political tactics with them after graduation. They recycle themselves back into the intellectual arenas, writing books, columns, editorials. Some run for public office, while some become professors themselves. They *have* to do this. The world needs them because they are smarter than everyone else. These were not my classmates' glory days of political activism. These were people who considered themselves the saviors of tomorrow. They are our irrefutable, intellectual elites—cast with the duty of protecting the rest of us from our own stupidity.

CHAPTER 9
Black, White, and Brown

Every year during my college experience there was a racial face-off that furiously shook the grounds of College Hill. Brown's campus was so race-sensitive that the mere mention of anything that had to do with race caused the campus' ears to perk. Just during my four years at Brown, this uneasy setting set the stage for several heated racial encounters.

I always imagined Brown's administration shaking their heads in utter confusion every time racial disputes occurred on their diverse campus where ethnic tension after years of multiculturalism should have been nonexistent. Weren't we all supposed to be getting along by now?

(The following sentence should be read in a high-pitched and whiny voice)

But our diversity is supposed to solve all of these problems! Why does this keep happening on our culturally rich campus?!

My black classmates had most certainly fallen victim to the liberal mindset. This was not inconsistent with the outside world as a large majority of African-Americans are devoted constituents to the liberal-led Democratic Party. I always felt that of all the minority groups that allowed liberalism to structure their thoughts and actions, the most unfortunate group to allow this was the black students. Of all American social conflicts and controversies, the mistrust between white and black Americans has caused the most pain, suffering, and injustice (not to mention what African-Americans have gone through).

But I don't blame Brown's racial atmosphere on my black classmates. I blame everything on liberalism, that disease of the mind that places the protection of feelings at the head of the line, before principles of freedom, fairness, and truth. Like all of the other liberal activist groups at Brown, the black community's activism was consumed with dishonesty, and was driven by unfounded mistrust for their white classmates. White students, who admittedly shared some blame in campus disputes, could not be blamed, however, for their eventual indifference (or opposition) to the attitude and demeanor of Brown's students of color. After much thought and observation, however, I realized that it was not blacks who should have been blamed. And it was not whites who were at fault either. It was Brown's conspiratorial relationship with leftist theory, infecting the minds of anyone in its path, indiscriminate from race, gender, or levels of intellect.

I had a little apprehension when it came to writing racial commentary at Brown, just because I knew the charges that would surely follow. Liberalism had actually succeeded in redefining racism. The meaning had been broadened to include any opposing viewpoints to those of the liberal mainstream. The new definition saw opposing perspectives that gave discomfort to vocal minorities as cause for censorship and public apologies. If that was Webster's definition, then I would have fully adhered to my racism. But somehow, I knew better.

Just because I "knew better" doesn't mean that I wasn't afraid. In fact, the most powerful evidence I am in possession of that exhibits the campus left's careful control over words and ideas is the fact that I couldn't sleep the night before the release of a column I wrote pertaining to a racial event on Brown's campus. Not one hour did I sleep. I spent the entire night getting up from bed, and going to my computer to preview over-and-over my opinion that everyone would be reading in the morning. I read every sentence carefully to reassure myself that it was not bigoted in any way. Still, I couldn't sleep. What were people going to say? How many friends was I about to lose? What about my black teammates? What were they going to think? Damn! It was too late to retract my column.

That one sleepless and worrisome night makes me resent Brown University. My fears were realized. To this day I unfortunately (but not regrettably) do not share the bond with some of my black friends as I once did. I can't help but blame Brown for this.

The Ebony Thompson Case

Like any college community, simple assaults would frequent Brown's campus, and most went unnoticed by the eyes of the public. They were seen as reoccurring, and no-big-deal (at least to the point where they didn't need to be publicly reported). Some of these unreported instances were large brawls while some "assaults" actually inferred the tiniest of offenses, such as verbal attacks. The Brown administration had their methods of dealing with these instances swiftly, and with as little pain as possible. However, one incident my sophomore year received special attention because campus activists, with only hearsay and rumors to base their opinions on, found this incident of exceptional concern.

When Ebony Thompson (a black female student) claimed that she was assaulted by Adam Santee, Bradley Groover, and Jesse Savage, there were many students (largely from the black community) who felt that it should have been reported to the public, and accused the Brown administration of covering up the incident.(1) With only a couple of days for rumors to circulate, the campus left called for the removal of three white students from campus, and received what they demanded despite conflicting accounts of what had actually occurred. Without adhering to burden of proof or any judiciary process, the administration appeased the rallying activists in order to quell the heated protest. In the process, three Brown students of the wrong skin color were subject to an unjust removal from Brown's campus. Historical precedents of campus assault, a judicial process, or any type of procedure marked by fairness did not determine the outcome of a highly debated incident. Rather, the wrath of a relatively small group of protesters determined the fate of the accused students.

I was outraged as I followed the facts of the case on a daily basis. I was even more outraged at the hasty opinions formed, expressed, and ultimately accepted as truth before the details of the case were publicly revealed. It seemed to me that an opinion being conveyed by an animated rally was determining the outcome of an incident that was becoming increasingly hazy every time more of it was unfolded. But I was a mere insignificant, intimidated, and insecure sophomore. There was not much I could have done, and I never became directly involved in the case. I hadn't begun writing for *The Herald*, but the Ebony Thompson Case was a major reason for my decision to finally confront my classmates the following year.

In order to understand the Ebony Thompson case I only needed to look at the hard facts. It is from that vantage point where my opinion was formed. Others, you will see, decided to hastily form opinion based on their political agendas while ignoring the facts altogether. Liberalism in action.

The Facts

One Early Monday morning around 1:30am Ebony Thompson, a black female student, was walking into a Brown dormitory and did not hold the door open for three white male students. All of the male students admitted to being intoxicated at the time, and one of them made a comment to Thompson for her refusal to hold the door open for them. Ms. Thompson lashed back with some words of her own, and a physical altercation between all four subjects ensued. It has never been determined as to who initiated the first physical act of violence.(2)

Ms. Thompson called the campus police and charged the three men with assault. The police showed up and arrested Santee and Savage. Groover would turn himself in soon after. Santee admitted to drinking seven beers. Groover admitted to five to six beers, and Savage said he drank seven to eight.(3)

Ms. Thompson reported that during the argument one of the boys said to her that she was only at Brown "because of a quota and because my parents were rich and that I didn't belong here." She also reported that another one of the boys then "kicked me in my arm and caused me to drop my CD player and bags. I started swinging my arms in defense and the second male described grabbed me and pulled me off of him."(4)

It did not take long for rumors to circulate around campus that three white students had attacked a black female student merely for being black. Thompson's version of the story was accepted as absolute truth, and on Friday of that week more than 150 students (mostly minority) rallied on the Main Green and in front of the Office of Student Life. News publications reported that a hate crime had been committed. A front-page *Herald* article covered the rally with a picture of protesters holding a sign that asked, *"Are We Safe At Brown."* Protest leaders said that their top reason for rallying was because Brown had allowed the students to remain on campus until a decision had been made as to the outcome of the case. This upset many of the protesters, but Brown's handling speed was not out of ordinary for a campus assault case. Still, one student declared that they "had organized the rally in response to what they saw as inaction by the University."(5) Brown liberals defined "inaction" as others not seeing how important it was to take advantage of any incident that could advance their cause.

The protesters also claimed that they were upset that a formal announcement to the community wasn't made about the incident, and that the "University would have moved more swiftly if the victim had been white and her assailants black."(6) Colonel Verrecchia of the Brown University Police Department (BUPD) refuted that charge by telling the community that crime alerts have *never* been issued unless suspects "remain at large."(7) Colonel Verrecchia just didn't understand. Ms. Thompson was a *black* student, not some ordinary white kid.

Outside of Robin Rose's (dean of student life) office on that same day, students chanted in the rain, "If she was white and they were black, Brown never would have let them back" and "Ho ho, hey hey, kick them out today."(8) I always loved how my classmates cleverly rhymed their chants. Ms. Thompson also gave a speech in front of the protesters that day, recalling her account of what had happened. Someone told me that much of her speech also rhymed.

Concern for the way the University was handling the alleged assault caused more than 300 students to organize a forum in Brown's Sayles Hall later that same day. At the forum, where the three males were not represented, student leaders offered a list of demands to Brown's administration including the "immediate removal of the suspects from on-campus housing." They also stressed the importance of the "continuation of the Women Peer Counseling and Minority Peer Counseling programs."(9) Yes, those counseling programs were needed now more than ever.

Dean Rose made a public statement at the forum declaring, "I'd like to apologize. In my office, it seems that members of my staff and I may have misperceived the level of pain and distress of one of our students and that we did not respond quickly enough or sensitively enough to that situation."(10)

Sensitively.

On Sunday Brown removed Santee and Savage from the University. They would not be allowed to stay in their dorm or attend classes, but somehow retained "their rights and responsibilities as students and were expected to keep up with their course work."(11) Yeah, that makes a lot of sense.

I don't believe Dean Rose could have been more openly dishonest. The decision to hasten any disciplinary action had nothing to do with the "pain and distress" of just "one" student. It had to do with the fiery protests outside of her office. I never found out if Dean Rose regretted her decision to alter Brown's disciplinary procedure after what ensued when more of this story was revealed to the public.

During the weeks following the incident, rumors began to circulate about Ms. Thompson's role in starting the entire incident. And the campus split over whether the punishment was made fairly, justly, or too quickly. Official reports were released stating that the males had informed administrators that Thompson punched Groover first after Groover had only called her a "bitch."(12) It was also discovered that Ms. Thompson's initial statement to the BUPD said nothing about a "quota" comment. She would later include it in a report to the Office of Student Life.(13) The administration knew that the three males had always denied saying any of the racial comments that Thompson accused them of. But most interesting was the fact that there weren't even any witnesses who were able to report any kind of racial slurs made by the accused. In fact, the witness statements overwhelmingly incriminated Ms. Thompson. One witness stated, "I didn't hear any racial comments except when she said something like 'what the fuck do you three niggers think you're going to do?" and "I'm going to fucking shoot you."(14)

The controversy became more and more intense as the males' defense became public to the Brown community. Two of the accused and several witnesses recalled Ms. Thompson threatening the male students, and Santee had told administrators that Thompson screamed, "I'm gonna fuckin' kill you with a fuckin' gun."(15)

Another witness said that, "Thompson had accused the males of breaking her 'shit.'" Then, the males responded by saying, "That's after you punched [Groover] in the head." Thompson replied to that by saying, "I'm gonna get a fuckin' gun and fuckin' kill you."(16)

A witness who had only heard the altercation said all he could hear was Thompson saying, "What the fuck you gonna do?" repeatedly for 4-5 minutes. She also stated "I'm gonna fuck you up" repeatedly for about 30 seconds.(17)

Ms. Thompson's medical reports revealed disturbing facts about her "injuries." She told her first health care provider that she had been kicked in the right arm (the physical contact that had supposedly started the fight) and only had other body aches. But she then told a different examiner 15 minutes later that it was her left elbow that was kicked, and also her right leg. One day after the incident (Tuesday) Thompson visited Brown's Health Services. She complained of pain in her right elbow. The provider wrote in the records that Thompson "states there is no swelling or bruising of the elbow, but [she] doesn't want to come out of [the] sling for [an] exam." The X-rays of the right elbow didn't show any serious injury to it.(18) Then, Thompson's neighbor, who shared a bathroom with her, reported to the administration that Ms. Thompson seemed to have full use of both arms, and frequently would walk around the dorm without her sling, but would put it on to walk around campus.(19) Yeah, my arms also begin to swell when I'm outdoors.

On March 22nd a formal hearing resulted in the expulsion of Groover, the one-year suspension of Santee, and a University sanction for Savage. Unofficial reports disclosed confidential information that Ms. Thompson was rewarded $5000 from each of her alleged attackers in a settlement.(20) Thompson got 15 Grand, and all Groover lost was an Ivy League diploma. This was all justified according to Brown's liberals.

As the facts came out, and the story unfolded, it seemed to me that there was the possibility that a grave injustice may have been committed as a result of campus hysteria over the possibility of racial motives. I thought that the incident might have been better described as just a simple case of students of different ethnicity bickering with one another, and it got out of hand. However, this was the first incident teaching me that nothing clinging to common sense mattered at Brown. The campus left had what they needed, merely an accusation.

Like many others, I followed what came to be known as the "Ebony Thompson Case" very closely, and I couldn't help but become confused, irritated, and intrigued by certain parts of the story. For instance, from the beginning of the investigation I noticed that Groover, Santee, and Savage *admitted* to indecently starting the altercation with a comment made to Ms. Thompson about not holding the dorm door for them. Thompson's account of the story said that the comment was, "That was real fucking inconsiderate of you not to hold the door for us." Then, the three males *admitted* to drinking beers prior to the incident. But they also insisted that Ms. Thompson threw the first punch and was responsible for raising the level of aggressiveness from the beginning of the altercation. The physical fight was described as Thompson and one of the male students taking part as the main participants, while the other two males were trying to get in between them. The males had always refuted strongly Thompson's claim that they had made any racial remarks. She made these accusations the day following the incident, and despite the presence of several witnesses, nobody could verify that the racial comments were made by the boys.

The altering of Brown's normal disciplinary procedure really bothered me. Groover, Santee, and Savage may have been mostly responsible for the incident that night. They may have made the racial comments, and even struck Ms. Thompson first (not that the evidence suggested that). However, they were treated with a more prompt and harsher punishment than most students accused of assault, and the concept of innocence before proven guilt was entirely ignored.

There was more to the story that bothered me, however. The underlying reasons for such a rush to judgment, and the cruel means to achieve the depiction of a hate-crime that may not have even existed leaned more toward my interest and curiosity. I also saw a gleaming contradiction with college diversity in regards to the expectations of whites, who were being called on to accept the fact that serious consequences could result from a mere argument with a fellow neighbor who happened to be a minority.

Are Whites Safe At Brown?

I would be the last person to the male students' defense if I believed the three of them to be racists, but there was simply no credible evidence given to me that suggested this. Nevertheless, the Brown community rushed to Thompson's defense without the slightest amount of time offered to gather the necessary information to confirm a racist encounter. As rumors that week circulated that offered conflicting accounts of what actually happened, many sensed that truth and punishment were being formed by propaganda and protest, rather than a process characterized by fairness and facts.

"Are We Safe at Brown?" Who really should have been asking that question? Should it have been black students within the diversity-rich campus where tolerance was praised, and racism was loathed? Or, should it have been white students who were forced to deal with the reality that if they got into an altercation with a minority whose specific race qualified him as a societal victim, then their privilege to reside at Brown could have been stripped away, and their reputations may have been tarnished by an unfounded accusation? This was the campus reality for Brown's white students who—as the story unfolded—could only think, *Wow, that could have easily been me.*

Would it have been fair, after experiencing events like this, to look down at me if, all of a sudden, I didn't share the desired enthusiasm of liberals to live in a diverse community? Did I just have more common sense enabling me to realize that whomever I was living among, there would always be disagreements and fights that would occur? At Brown, I was being told that if I got into a fight with a minority, then my classmates could bring an avalanche of trouble down on me. These double standards of justice would continue to impede the positive effects of multicultural learning. How could I become an *ally* to minorities? All I could think to do was be honest, and reveal to blacks how many whites really viewed their campus demeanor.

A drink, anyone?

It was uncanny. I couldn't help but notice that nobody ever seemed to want to draw attention to the fact that the three males accused of assault were intoxicated at the time of the incident. At first, I thought that the activists would want to continuously expose that fact. One would think that it would have been important to winning the debate concerning their guilt—to suggest to the public that Groover, Santee, and Savage not only were racists, but were irresponsible drunks as well. Wouldn't that have helped in getting them thrown off campus? Wasn't that what they wanted? Didn't they want to be *"Safe at Brown?"*

Much later I would understand why my classmates ignored the presence of alcohol. They wanted no excuse other than racism to appear as a factor in the alleged attack on Ms. Thompson. It would have been harmful to their purpose of blowing up the incident into something it was not. Savage, Santee, and Groover could not be punished on the grounds of irresponsible drinking habits that caused a disruptive altercation resulting in an injured female student. A drunken act would have taken something away from racist intent, and the last thing their agenda called for was the downplaying of racist motives.

If the activists wanted the three white males thrown off campus so badly, then why wouldn't they expose the fact that all of them admitted to drinking at least five beers that night? It was because even they knew that when they drink five beers they could find themselves acting slightly inappropriately as well. The leadership of the liberal black community did not want the alcohol to have anything to do with the outcome of the incident. They did not want its presence even discussed. They wanted another flimsy example of racism to push their own agenda. The alcohol that the boys were under the influence of seemed like a relevant point to me, but not a word from the protesters was ever intended to bring attention to it. When the fact that the male students were intoxicated was mentioned at their forum, however, one student lashed out, "I came here expecting a unified Brown community, and I'm disappointed. I think the drug is racism, not necessarily alcohol."(21) I thought it was alcohol, not necessarily racism.

The cold shoulder that the protesters gave to the presence of the alcohol only suggested to me that they didn't really care if Santee, Savage, and Groover were thrown off campus, that they actually looked forward to incidents that could thrust their cause into the spotlight. My classmates were always placing their politics before truth, and my *higher* education was telling me that this was acceptable and justified.

You Skinny Prick!

While I was trying to figure out why this entire incident was aggravating me so much, I remembered pondering the actual charge. Ms. Thompson accused the boys of declaring that she was only accepted to Brown because of her skin color. Well, Brown *does* offer racial preferences in its admissions process. To Brown liberals, Affirmative Action is not racism, but to guess that a black student may have been a recipient of such a policy is.

Ms. Thompson was only at Brown "because of a quota," one of the males allegedly said to her. How fierce, huh? Yet, this certainly would have shattered my alma mater's speech code regulations that, according to the Principles of the Brown University Community, forbid anyone to *"subject{ing} another person or group to abusive, threatening, intimidating, or harassing actions, including, but not limited to, those based on race, religion, gender, disability, age, economic status, ethnicity, national origin, sexual orientation, gender identity, or gender expression."*(22)

But the only person who claimed that a racist comment was made by the three boys was Ms. Thompson. No witnesses testified to hearing the boys say anything referring to race, and Ms. Thompson only decided to make the accusation the following day. That's not to say that it didn't happen. However, even Thompson's version of the account showed that the comment was made after a scuffle had begun and tensions were raised. It seemed to me that if race did play a part in the incident, then it came as an unfortunate side-dish, not the main course. An angry comment that belittled Thompson based on her race may not have suggested racism, but it was rather an ignorant comment that sputtered out in a moment of drunkenness and levels of high adrenaline.

If someone gets into a fight with a person who is overweight, and during the course of it yells out "you fat bastard!"—would that prove on any level that he is prejudice towards people who are overweight? Or, is it a meaningless insult meant solely for retaliation during a heightened period of drunken anger and excitement? I wasn't so sure that the alleged comment called for a charge of racism, or a protest demanding their expulsion from Brown. Little attention would be paid to this point, however, because on Brown's campus a *charge* of bigotry was equal to a *conviction* of bigotry, flexibility of justice under the conditions of ethnicity. An accusation was made, and the administration sided with the minority community—a decision based on sensitivity to their feelings, and teaching white students to pick their battles carefully when their opponent was a minority. That lesson hardly had the propensity to bring whites and blacks closer together.

It was not a simple task for an opinionated white student to pass through four years of unchecked liberalism at Brown University. Leaders of the campus left had little interest in actually achieving the goals of fairness, equality, and color blindness. I was being called on to live in peace and harmony with minorities, but I also had to accept the fear of public scorn when doing so. The secret comments I heard from my white friends and classmates made me realize that many of them were nauseated by the actions taken by their black classmates, actions that were teaching all of us to keep our mouths shut. Many white students were simply becoming indifferent to minority causes, and a quiet rift built between the two sides, and only a false peace was accomplished through this stifling of speech. This was the reality that I thought had to break through the barriers of silence, so that true peace and understanding could exist between all ethnicities. There was no doubt in my mind that racial harmony was attainable. It's just that the liberals didn't really want it.

The Racial Profiling Case

If after reading this section about an accusation made against the Brown Police Department doesn't convince you of the campus left's hidden agenda, their desperate search for bigotry, and their cruel willingness to silence those who may confront their lunacy, then I might submit that I will never convince you of the methods and true intentions of university liberals. Myself and others weren't fooled by them, and neither should you be.

I often received harassing emails and phone calls after a column of mine was published. But after I defended a group of Brown police officers from an onslaught of campus opinion that claimed that the character of the Brown University Police Department (BUPD) was one colored with racism, I received a personal warning from one of my black classmates instructing me to "watch my back."

The day my column was printed I was in the Brown weight room pumping some iron. Huge. A friend of mine, who happened to be black, came up to me and offered me some caution. Without a "hello" he said to me, "You better watch your back. A lot of people I know are pissed at you. They're not happy." I suddenly started lifting more weight so he would tell his friends how strong I was. I thought it might scare them off.

I would have thanked him, but he wasn't coming over to give me a friendly forewarning. He was visibly angry with me as well, and was sort of taking pleasure in the fact that I would have to suffer some paranoia. He was a former teammate of mine, and someone that I had previously gotten along with. I have had to suffer quite a few of these strained relationships due to my campus candor. These relationship rifts are unfortunate, but by this time I was a senior, and was out to accomplish something that I felt superceded the peace.

"Yeah, well tell your friends that this is the first criticism that I've heard about my column, but I've already had a bunch of people tell me how much they love what I wrote. Then let me know what they had to say to that." He walked away a little upset, and I haven't spoken to him since.

There were other incidents resulting from my column as well. Emails from certain students demanded that I feel stupid and remorseful, and then apologize to the community. And a few anonymous emails sought to make me fear for my safety. There was one harassing phone-call to my apartment in which I argued with the caller for a good minute and a half before I hung up the phone. Another episode occurred inside a place called *Max's Upstairs*. *Max's* was a popular off-campus bar located on Thayer Street, a frequently traveled road that cuts through the heart of Brown's campus. The night after my column was printed I entered *Max's* and was immediately greeted with a demeaning comment from a table occupied by several male black students, one of which was a former teammate of mine. Him and I had always gotten along, but he had quit the football team the previous year, so we had seen less of each other since then. When I approached his table he stood up and advised me to just ignore the comment and walk away. It was difficult to take his advice as one of his friends was furiously giving me a piece of his mind from across the table of half-emptied pitchers of beer. It pained me to back down so easily, but I was clear on the right thing to do. I walked away.

A few days later another former teammate of mine refused to shake my hand before a pick-up basketball game inside Brown's athletic center. This occurred several days past the printing of my column, and he had acknowledged me every one of those days up until this point, without one mention of what I had written. It was not difficult to understand why his attitude had shifted. We were standing on the basketball court, and he was accompanied by several of his black friends, and they were watching as I offered him my hand. In return I received a dirty look, a roll of the eyes, and the turn of his back. Right then I knew for sure—I had become the topic and target of Brown's black community. Late at night with my white friends, we spoke openly about issues of race, the latest dispute on campus, and my column. Apparently, black students were having the same discussion, only in reverse. At dawn, after nocturnal segregation, we once again became a diverse student body inside the classrooms and the courtyards, on the basketball courts and the pages of *The Herald*. Those were the places of intellectual limitation, and I had crossed the line.

There is no other way to look at these occurrences other than methods of intimidation. It's not that I believe all of my black classmates held a meeting, and conspired to frighten me into submission and apology. It wasn't that at all. These happenings were the result of years of leftist temperament passed on from graduating class to graduating class, finally being confronted by a student who had simply had enough. Directly in my face was Brown's repugnant and institutionalized culture of intolerance, strategically placed in the hands of a fanatical student body.

Below I outline Brown's Racial Profiling case that will lead you up to the reason for some campus members' disdain for what I had written, and their horrible example of how far Brown's campus left would go to make sure opposition to their agendas wouldn't be graced with the opportunity to be heard.

I became heavily involved in the Racial Profiling case as I publicly defended the Brown police officers under attack for trying their best to safeguard the University. Similarly to the Ebony Thompson case, the charge of racial profiling made against the Brown Police Department was entirely absurd, and based on the blind vigor of campus leftists. I was more attached to this incident, and am more passionate about it now because I took a more active role in its controversy than I did with the Ebony Thompson case, where I served merely as a spectator. The Ebony Thompson case upset me, and inspired me to write. The Racial Profiling case personally served as my chance to speak my mind on the injustice that both instances served to the Brown community. I achieved a little redemption for not being able to comment on the Ebony Thompson case as I compared the two incidents in my column.

My classmates' malicious motivation to silence political opponents, and smear the reputations of decent campus citizens was too much for me to handle. When the campus rallied behind two students who had assaulted several Brown police officers only a few hours after they had been arrested for acting disorderly, and began to make public claims that there were racist police officers within the BUPD, I decided to defend Brown's police force.

I entered into the controversy a little biased. By the time I was a senior at Brown I had learned to be a skeptic first, rather than an immediate believer in accusations concerning bigotry. I can only hope that my readers have begun to understand why. Perhaps it wasn't cordial to go in with that bias, but my instinct was affirmed. The platform on which they made their accusations was entirely groundless, and I couldn't help but recognize the similarity in their behavior from the students who were in support of Ebony Thompson just a couple of years earlier. This time the campus activists were just as in a rush to jump to conclusions. This incident occurred on a Friday afternoon, and by 8pm that night, only several hours after the incident, I heard the rumors and accusations being thrown around campus that the Brown Police had assaulted two black students on the Main Green. Apparently, a few hours was more than enough time for false rumors to circulate, and for the campus left to pounce on the dispute, publicly portray it as a hate crime, and use it as their annual example of campus racism. *Yay! We found one! We found one! We can finally protest again!*

Someone had told me that night that the Brown police officers were stopping black students all day, and that the police had yelled racial slurs at the two students they arrested. Those rumors turned out to be entirely false, and all I could think was, "Oh man, here we go again."

Hope High School

Hope High School resides adjacent to Brown University, and its student body is an 85% minority make-up.(23) Every day their students were dismissed from school around 3pm, and they headed toward Brown's campus. It had never been expressed by anybody that Hope High School students weren't welcome at Brown. They were simply a part of the outer rim of the campus, and for the most part the two parties were friendly neighbors. Then, some recent vandalism to Brown's Faunce House (the building that often served as Brown's rally spot on the Main Green) called for a watchful eye around that area. The vandalism had been reoccurring around 3pm, and therefore turned Hope High school students into suspects, rather than visitors.

I thought Hope students were logical suspects. Vandalism tends to be an immature act that high school kids take part in (I know I did). Anyway, between the two sets of students present (Brown and Hope High) it was more likely that Brown students were innocent of the vandalism. So, Brown police officers were set on patrol to watch for suspicious characters around 3pm near Faunce House.

Two Brown students, Michael Smith and David Williams, were walking by Faunce House around this time. They were also Brown freshmen, so they appeared as having the possibility of being high school students straying from Hope High. Because of the high alert the officers were put on near Faunce House, the time of day, and the appearance of the students (meaning age) a Brown police officer decided to ask Smith and Williams to present their Brown IDs. It went against the codes of student conduct to refuse to do this when a Brown officer asked you to. The officer reported that the students kept walking and said, "Why do you need to know?" The officer requested a second time for the students to stop and present their IDs. One of them shouted back to the officer, "I don't need to show you shit!"(24) These types of responses, I thought, could have been described as "high-school-like."

Eventually, when the incident had moved further into the Main Green for about 50 witnesses to view, there were now several officers who had responded to a request for back-up, and they were arguing with the students and making repeated attempts to get them to reveal their Brown IDs.

Various witnesses reported Williams as saying, "Fuck the police, get off of me" and "until you ask everyone here for their IDs I don't have to show you mine!" Witnesses also reported Williams as saying, "You're just doing this because I'm black" and "I pay money to go here, you can't fucking do this to me." Another witness stated that "everything was just escalating out of control at that point." According to the reports, Smith seemed to remain calm until the officers decided to handcuff and arrest Williams. That's when Smith tried to help Williams by jumping on one officer's back. "Smith tried to get some of the police officers off of Williams" one witness said.(25)

Witness Statements

Despite what seemed to be an event highly escalated to physical force by the two students, Brown students who witnessed the account *after* the initial onset of it sided with the two students, and their opinions were printed in *The Herald* for me to follow.

One student sympathetically stated, "They roughly tackled them to the ground and cuffed them. I was pretty appalled by the whole thing."(26)

The Herald reported that many witnesses also thought that Smith and Williams were stopped because they were black. Oh, big surprise. Well, that's what Williams was yelling out, and why wouldn't they believe him? The witnesses didn't need to see the entire incident, or have a full understanding of how and why the rumble started to form an opinion, and then deliver it to the public. Besides, aren't all cops racist? I'm sorry, aren't all *white* cops racist?

A white female student who saw the incident said, "I think it's ridiculous that [the police] were after their IDs. If I was walking across the Main Green, I wouldn't have been stopped."(27) That's because you don't look like a Hope High school student, you bimbo! Sorry.

Another witness stated, "It was clear that they were being picked on because they were black."(28) *Why was it "clear,"* I thought to myself. Because the students were black and the officers were white? All of these student statements were made immediately after the incident. How much could anybody who *partially* witnessed the altercation really know *clearly*? I could only see this opinion as racism in reverse. Reverse-racism, a foreign and laughable concept to an Ivy League intellectual. If there was any racism aimed at whites, Brown liberals found it insignificant, or simply justified. My classmates were hastily assuming the racism of Brown's white police officers. Only self-righteous, agenda-driven individuals could blind themselves to the insult.

Other witnesses, and Colonel Verreccia of the BUPD, reported that Williams pushed and chest-bumped a BUPD sergeant. "[Williams] definitely pushed one of the cops," one spectator observed.(29) No student or faculty outrage resulted.

Many of my classmates objected to the way the police handled the incident, complaining that there were too many officers there to justify handling a couple of freshman students. They also didn't agree with the force that was used in order to get the two students detained. As I was reading the commentary that week in *The Herald* about the occurrence, it *at first* seemed to me that my bratty classmates had no concept or appreciation for realistic police protocol. I knew that police activity calls for certain types of action that best ensures their safety, and also the safety of the community they protect. That protocol includes calling to potential crime scenes as many officers as possible. Obviously, strength-in-numbers is very important. It also includes a forceful handling of suspects when arrest is necessary. It *seemed* my classmates were completely unaware of how much danger police have to assume they are in when confronting anyone they don't know. But that wasn't the case.

My classmates were not stupid. This lack of common sense could only be the result of one thing, the will to believe that racism had something to do with this incident. My classmates were doing everything in their power to demonize the BUPD, criticizing them for their actions that were found later to be in total agreement with police procedure. That didn't matter, though. The only things that mattered were the impulsive opinions of punk students, who the Brown police should have had no interest in protecting after being treated as they were. The campus left was desperately trying to portray the racially paranoid students as two modern-day "Rosa Parks," and the Brown officers as members of the Ku Klux Klan.

Campus Commentary In the Days that Followed

These are all statements made by campus members in the week following the incident. Most of the comments were printed in *The Herald.* As I was reading them it became clear to me that, once again, my classmates had succeeded in twisting the truth.

"The University claims the officers stopped the students on the basis of time of day, apparent age, walking patterns, and behavior. This vague methodology is suspect. We wonder why students aren't stopped everyday."—*Herald* Op-ed$_{(30)}$

"Before the administration dismisses the possibility that Friday's events had something to do with race, it must seriously study the possibility that BUPS officers may engage in racial profiling."—*Herald* Op-ed$_{(31)}$

"Whatever one may say about the students arrested on the Main Green last Friday, one should not pretend that racial profiling does not occur on campus. I had been walking with an African American faculty member one night, and was stopped by a BUPS person who gently and briefly questioned my colleague, the well-dressed black woman, and not me, the blue-jeaned, scruffy-haired white guy. This event, of course, does not mean BUPS did anything wrong last week, or the students were in any way in the right. But it does suggest to me that racial profiling, at least of faculty, can take place here."—J. William Suggs , Associate Professor, Chemistry and Biochemistry$_{(32)}$

"This has exposed what is wrong with arming the Brown police...these issues are intimately connected."—Shaun Joseph '02 concerning a campus dispute of arming the Brown Police(33)

"I think that the incident on the Main Green on Friday proves without a shadow of a doubt that the Brown Police should not, under any circumstances, be armed. The police officers were barbaric in their handling of the situation and the incident would have been exponentially worse if they were armed. Instead of reading an article about two first-years being arrested on the Main Green, I would probably be reading their obituaries...It is very difficult to respect a police force whose main agenda is racial profiling...Instead of obtaining weapons, Brown Police should instead receive lessons on cultural sensitivity and on how to respect human beings, especially the people of color who walk through this campus, regardless of whether or not they attend Brown or Hope High School. Maybe then, I would have a tiny bit of respect for those who claim to protect and serve me.—Onyeka Iloabachie '03(34)

"I believe that this is a clear case of racial profiling on behalf of BUPS. Racial profiling occurs every day in shopping malls, on the highways, in the courtroom and countless other places. What keeps it from happening at Brown? Apparently nothing."—Op-Ed from *The Herald*(35)

"It is very clear that this was a case of racial profiling and that there are racist policies practiced by the Brown Police" and "If (Williams) was cursing, then that is a morally justified response to an act of racism."—Brian Rainey '04(36)

"People came to this meeting pretty upset, and we need to have a plan of action...we need to demand very soon and very publicly that no charges be filed against the students."—Alden Eagle '03 at a campus meeting to discuss the affair(37)

"The Brown police are not making the best impression on students of color on this campus. If anything, they are making me think

twice about walking across this campus at a certain time—day or night."—Joel Payne '05(38)

"Cops love it when their suspicions turn out to be correct—it's the egomaniacal basis behind wanting to be a cop. They become excited because they get to flex their pistol-whipping muscles on you. In Friday's situation, the two students chose to become beasts...out of principle."—Tom Van Buskirk '04(39)

The campus was flooded with the opinions of those who believed (or just wanted to believe) that this was an incident of racism and racial profiling. All of these comments were made in the week following the event, and all of the commentators refused to acknowledge the fact that the Brown police denied the accusation that race was a factor in stopping the students. Why didn't any of my classmates believe them? Why didn't they say, *Oh, we're sorry we acted so impulsively. We understand now that you were on the temporary look-out for students who Smith and Williams fit the description of. Sorry. Our bad.* Why did they refuse to believe the police force that is present daily on the most diverse campus in the world, a police force that experiences the civil and lawful behavior of whites *and* minorities every day? I'm telling you right now that it's because they *wanted* this to be an incident of racism. They *needed* it to be. The end of the school year was arriving, and they hadn't protested yet.

Remember Ebony?

You might want to note this before you read my column.

"I feel their violent actions should be the cause for expulsion from this university...I feel three drunk males fighting one woman should not be tolerated at this university and besides criminally charging them to the fullest, I believe the university should not allow people like this to remain on campus."

—EbonyThompson's Police Report(40)

I had had enough. I got sick every time I picked up *The Herald* and read what the majority of the vocal opinions were. Someone needed to put these people back in their place. Only, despite the fact that the BUPD denied that race had anything to do with their questioning of Smith and Williams, I took the debate to a whole new level when I suggested that racial profiling was a necessary method of crime fighting, an opinion that nobody had dared to speak yet. Here's what I submitted to *The Herald*:

A Normal Point of View by Travis Rowley

Racial Profiling a Necessary Tool of Law Enforcement
Students Deserve Expulsion

I have one word for the Brown administration: expulsion. It's the only punishment for students who assault a police officer, challenging the authority of a campus police force. Too harsh? I seem to remember an incident several years ago when three white male Brown students were accused by a female black student of assault. Despite very different views of what had occurred, the accused were asked to leave the Brown community…I wonder if Brown will follow its own historical precedent and expel those who are accused of assault. Somehow, I doubt it. For some reason, the overwhelming feeling on this campus is that these two delinquents are victims rather than perpetrators.

Police officers obtain and are aware of more information than us, and we must give them the benefit of the doubt rather than make assumptions regarding their character… The Brown Police have explained their reasons for stopping the two students, and they claim that race had nothing to do with it. The only reason for not believing this claim would be due to a lack of trust in the police…

There are many people on this campus who object to police officers using their personal discretion when deciding to question suspicious minorities on the East Side, where 90 percent of the crime is committed by minorities…Police

> officers are already extremely discouraged from these acts out of fear of being accused of being racist, or practicing unjust racial profiling.
>
> It's also time we accept the fact that racial profiling is a necessary tool of security and law enforcement, because, after all, race is a physical characteristic just as height, weight and age are...Hundreds of minority high school students leave Hope High every day and walk straight towards the Main Green. Race should never be the sole determinant in deciding whether to make someone a suspect, but we can't pretend to be blind to people's skin color when it could help in counteracting crime...[Racial profiling] is a necessity that we must all deal with to provide safer communities for everyone...Police officers must be allowed to use discretion, and we have to trust their discretion in order to maintain an un-intimidated society.
>
> Smith and Williams deserve no support or sympathy. All that will do is teach others that not cooperating with authority is acceptable depending on one's race. These students acted impulsively, ignorantly, irresponsibly and illegally March 8, and they should receive the penalty that fits their crime.(41)

———

These words represented my honest opinion, and yet I couldn't sleep the night before its publication. I sat up all night with feelings of anxiety. Today, it's comical to me. I didn't know it as a Brown senior, but my column was tame in comparison to the well-articulated arguments others have made supporting racial profiling—found nowhere near Brown's campus, where I was only allowed to intellectually operate from the premise that racial profiling was inarguably an evil. I decided to operate off of common sense instead.

Without defending my column too much, let me explain my position a little further. I was just playing the odds. 85% of Hope High students were minorities. That meant that any high school student walking through campus at 3pm when Hope dismissed its students had an 85% chance of being a minority. So, when the police were on the lookout for high school students around Faunce, and they were having trouble telling the difference between Brown freshmen and high school students, I thought they needed to be afforded a little latitude, and be allowed to practice sound police work. The Brown police were on the lookout for Hope High students that day, and no opinion on the matter could change the fact that Hope High students were minorities. If a Brown police officer saw a "high-school-aged" black male walk through campus that day and did not stop him, then I would suggest that he be fired for incompetence and negligence. I would ask the same for the airport security guard that allows Bin Laden look-alikes to skip onto jetliners. This was my foundation of logic that set the campus aflame.

I didn't see my definition of racial profiling the same as an officer pulling more black people over on the highway without any other reasons for doing so. The BUPD was looking for certain things, things that the public had no knowledge of. I never stated that the Brown police should have been stopping more black students randomly without reason for doing so, but the angry and determined minds of my classmates wouldn't even recognize that a line in my column stated, "Race should *never* be the sole determinant in deciding whether to make someone a suspect" (emphasis added). Their eyes seemed to skip right over that line. I wonder why. Actually, no I don't. It was because they had learned to see any view that contradicted their own as stemmed from racist intent, and to stifle that opposition before it could catch the current of common sense.

License and Registration, Please

During my four years at Brown I was pulled over in my car three times by the police. Two out of those three occasions I had been doing nothing wrong, and seemed to be pulled over randomly. During one of those stops the officer was very polite and respectful. He only asked me where I was going, and where I had been. I offered him the same respect back, and he said "good night." The second incident, however, the officer who pulled me over was more abrasive, treating me as if I had done something wrong. I still responded humbly and respectfully, and was allowed to continue on.

Others decided not to handle their run-ins with the police as I did.

They preferred to act as if they were in the Deep South in the 1950s, fighting the power! *There's no way racism had anything to do with this incident*, I kept thinking. But where was the administration? Who was going to put these students, who were insulting every white member of the Brown community, back in their place? Wasn't this getting out-of-hand on our campus, all of these absurd accusations of racism? I was sick of this political irresponsibility. This political dishonesty. This injustice. This racism! And this administration, so fearful of offending some of their students that they wouldn't even defend their own police force. Brown was embittering me, just as many others became scornful toward the University's most vocal. But I elected not to take the passive and silent road through my four years of liberal indoctrination.

Stories such as the Ebony Thompson case and the Racial Profiling case were always hastily reported as hate crimes before facts were able to reveal the lunacy of the charges. I witnessed how this compounded collection of accusations multiplied the mistrust of on-looking blacks, and built white resentment for the unfounded anger, hatred and extremism of the liberal black agenda. I couldn't help but put most of the blame on the activist sect of the black community for Brown's racial tension. I could only blame whites when I saw racism. I just never saw a legitimate occurrence of it.

Thanks For the Support, Pal!

One of the more humorous stories I took from the debates I was involved in on campus was one that involved a friend of mine who was enrolled in a course that dealt primarily with today's racial issues. Even though I got a good laugh out of the incident, it still served as another sad portrayal of the campus left's political aggression.

In the midst of the racial profiling controversy surrounding the Brown Police Department, and a couple of days after my opinion had been printed on the matter, I received a phone call in the afternoon from my friend, Jeff. Jeff had stepped out of class to call me. He informed me that the professor had printed copies of my article on racial profiling for everyone in the class, and they were discussing it.

"You should get down here, buddy. They're really trashing you," he told me.

"Why? What are they saying?"

"Well, there isn't one kid in there that agrees with what you said. That's for sure. They're saying some pretty nasty stuff about you too."

"Like what?" I asked.

"They're calling you a racist and stuff like that."

"Okay, I'm coming down there now," I told him.

Now, I knew exactly what I was walking into. I had actually attended this class at the beginning of the semester during Brown's "shopping period" when students were allowed to sample a number of courses before settling on the four or five they wished to take. The course description for this class interested me, and not only was I interested in the topic, but I also thought I could offer a lot to the class as well. The class was mostly filled with minority students, and the professor allowed the class to involve open discussion. It seemed like just my sort of thing, but after only a few classes I dropped the course. It was my last semester at Brown, and judging from the dialogue that occurred during those first few meetings, the class was going to cause more stress in my life than I wanted during my last semester before graduation. I didn't say much for the first couple of classes as my classmates expressed their opinions on racial issues. I just sat back and listened to them.

During the last class that I attended for this course, the professor started a discussion about American norms. "What are some American norms?" he asked us.

A black female student raised her hand and listed some, "Fairness, equality, justice" she told him.

"Okay. Any more?" the professor asked the class.

A male black student raised his hand in protest to the previous girl and said, "I wouldn't call those norms, but rather ideals."

As I looked around I noticed that the class quietly agreed with him. Of course they did. His comment was ordinary. No doubt about it. Our nation is so awful that we are unable to call *fairness*, *equality*, and *justice* norms. That statement found solace among many others just like it on Brown's campus, where the language of victim-hood was spoken with unrelenting regularity. Minorities are oppressed victims of a cruel country—racially profiled, battered, and discriminated against; taught to forever simmer in exaggerated misery while being pampered as often as possible by compassionate liberals.

His comment was exactly the type of anti-American statement that had begun to irritate my conservatism. I must have been having an off day, because rather than pick a fight with thirty other students, I walked out of class and dropped the course from my schedule. I never thought I would return to the same classroom a couple of months later.

My plan was to only go into the classroom and listen to what they had to say about me. I wasn't going to say a word. I brought a pad and pencil to take notes because I was already thinking about writing another article on what their opinions may have been. *Spying on Liberals*, I would have called my latest column. I just hoped that nobody would recognize me, but someone did.

The class must have been between 70 and 90 percent minority-based, and I felt slightly uncomfortable, especially after reading what so many had said about me after my column was printed. Oh yeah, and also because of the threats of violence.

I walked into the class that was already in the middle of a discussion about me. Sure enough, everyone was holding a printout of my column. There was even one on the empty seat that I took directly behind Jeff. I offered him only a simple head-nod so nobody would know that we were friends, and that he had called me down to the class. I felt like James Bond on an undercover assignment. I sat there for about five minutes and listened to the professor and the students discuss why my brain works as it does. *How could he possibly hold these opinions?*

They were shocked at the content of my column. And they would never have believed me if I told them how many pats on the back I received after it was printed. They would never have believed me if I told them about the emails I received from alumni telling me how much they loved what I had written, and how much they agreed with me. Instead, they were awe-struck to the point where they actually dedicated an hour of educational time that focused on my "unique" viewpoints, and what they could do about it. Slightly out of touch with reality, I always thought.

After several minutes of listening to their discussion a female student raised her hand and said pointing to me, "I'd just like to know how Mr. Rowley feels about all of this." I was exposed.

"Huh? What do you mean?" the professor asked.

"Well, that's him right there" she explained (still pointing at me). Now the entire class looked my way.

"Mr. Rowley?" the professor asked if it was really me.

"Yes" I responded.

"What are you doing here?" he asked with bewilderment.

I had to think quickly. "Well, uh, I heard that you might be discussing my article in class today. So I thought I might come down and see what everyone had to say." I was scared out of my mind.

"Oh...well...uh" He was still surprised to find out I had been sitting there all along. He may have even been a little embarrassed.

I offered to leave, "If I'm a big distraction, professor, I'll leave. I didn't mean for anyone to know I was here." I was doing my best to exude confidence, but the truth is: I wanted OUT of that classroom. Immediately.

"No. We're happy to have you with us," he assumed for the rest of the students in the class. "Is there something you wanted to say?"

I took his offer to speak as a dare. Still trying to appear unafraid, I felt I had to say something. And, in fact, there were a million things I wanted to say. I started with this: "Well, first of all I'd like to say that I'm not a white supremacist, and..." All of a sudden I was interrupted by a black female student at the head of the class.

"Excuse me. I don't feel like he should be able to take part in our discussion. Frankly, I can't even look at him right now." She pointed at me, but spoke in the direction of the professor. She *really* couldn't look at me.

Another black female student offered her support from across the room. "I agree! He shouldn't be here!" she shouted angrily. And suddenly, I was calm. Not so nervous, and my heart was settling. For some reason, an active and hostile fight is what I preferred.

The professor was still in shock that I was in his classroom. He fumbled for the right thing to do and told the class, "Well I guess we'll just put it to a vote. If anyone thinks that Travis should be able to take part in discussion today, raise your hand?"

A vote? How about sticking up for the principle of open debate, Professor? Besides, wouldn't the clarification of some of my misunderstood points have been beneficial to the purpose of the dialogue? The professor probably didn't want to make it appear as if he was siding with me because that would have offended his already-offended students. God forbid! So, I didn't object. Besides, a vote would be fun. I knew that I would have at least one vote as my good buddy, Jeff, who had called me to suggest I come down to the class to defend myself, sat directly in front of me. So, I sat there knowing that when one hand went up to defend my right to participate, a few others might follow that courage.

After the professor called for the vote I looked around the room expecting to see a few hands raised in support, but none went up. I was a little surprised, but it was like a punch to my chin when I looked in front of me and saw Jeff's hands tightly folded on his desk, cowering from the majority's intimidation. At the time it didn't make me smile, but later on back at my room there was a chorus of laughter as Jeff and I re-told the story to everyone else. "Did you see how angry those kids were? I wasn't going to raise my hand," was Jeff's candid explanation.

As it turned out, the professor decided that it was okay for me to stay in the room, but I was *not* allowed to speak. A brilliant compromise.

Like most things in my life I was able to find the humor within this story, but a more significant observation to this occurrence was the proof it provided to the existence of dissenting thought on Brown's campus. By the time I was a senior I knew I wasn't alone. Not by a long-shot. I began to recognize hints of conservatism, and frustration with campus intolerance being quietly expressed at the dining tables and late-night drunken conversations. For the most part, yes, it lied dormant in the mind of the Ivy League conservative. But there were others in that room who agreed with what I had written. There were others in that room who believed I should at least have been allowed to speak. But Brown no longer offered its students an intellectual frontier. Rather, the University on nearly every matter acutely limited appropriate discourse. I began to find this unacceptable within an Ivy League academic setting, where a regulated exchange of ideas had the worst of consequences—a loss of history, the distortion of reality, and the theft of the intellect.

CHAPTER 10

David Horowitz and A Racial Eruption

Advanced Liberalism: When you can't discredit the thought, discredit the source.

In 2001, Rhode Island College professor, Richard Lobban, visited College Hill to speak about Brown University's involvement in the American slave trade, and also offered his opinions on Reparations for Slavery, the idea that hands out government cash to black Americans who descended from former slaves. Professor Lobban's lecture was sponsored by Brown's Organization of United African Peoples and Third World ACTION. His oration painted a historical picture of the United States that suggested that our nation's past is only one that can be described as racist and treacherous. By the time I was a senior I began to be able to recognize lectures that sought to ensure that my classmates and I would graduate believing that our nation was one that was established by grave injustices.

The Herald printed an article entitled, "In talk, RIC professor calls slavery 'part of the American pedigree.'" It stated:

> "According to Lobban, 'we need to have a sense of national apology.' Slavery went on for longer and killed more people than the Holocaust, he said, and its victims are just as deserving of compensation."
>
> "All we have done so far is the Emancipation Proclamation,' Lobban said, although he dismissed even that as 'political warfare.'"(1)

Sweeping and loony remarks from guest lecturers were typical at

Brown because speakers knew there would be nobody there to challenge their irresponsible comments. The only thing the United States has ever done for black Americans was when President Lincoln passed the Emancipation Proclamation?

Professor Lobban's invitation to College Hill was actually a component of the campus left's response to an incident that had occurred several months earlier on Brown's campus.

David Horowitz

David Horowitz, the former 1960s anti-war Marxist turned conservative writer, tried to comment on modern issues of race on Brown's campus that year as well, but it wasn't in the form of a self-hateful lecture, and his commentary wasn't so well-received. *The Herald* published an advertisement by David Horowitz that contested the idea of slavery reparations. The ad was meant to promote Mr. Horowitz's book, *The Death of the Civil Rights Movement.* When another opinion surfaced that didn't run parallel with Professor Lobban's notion that we need a "sense of national apology" for slavery, Brown's underground racial mistrust surfaced with so much anger and emotion that the nation could not help but notice the turmoil. Campus protesters reacted to the ad by making certain demands to *The Herald*, and when those demands were not met, the student activists seized 5000 copies of the March 16th edition of the school newspaper. The incident brought to question Brown's devotion to our most basic freedoms, and served as a national warning of just how intolerant our campuses are.

The Horowitz controversy occurred soon after I had decided to begin writing for *The Herald*, and it was undoubtedly the turning point for my own personal political development. It turned Brown's campus into an ideological battlefield, pitting students against one another, and even revealing a distinct philosophical division amongst the faculty. I couldn't help but be attracted to the turbulence Horowitz had created, and when it was all over I found myself entirely captured by conservative thought, further emboldened to continue battling Brown University's most radical progressives because—if for no other reason—I suddenly realized how many secret "allies" I actually had on campus.

Mr. Horowitz submitted his ad to 73 American college newspapers. Forty-three immediately refused to print it, many conceding that their rejection of the ad was due to its content. Of those who did run Horowitz's ad, most editors published editorials next to it that ridiculed its argument. Others later surrendered to "campus correctness," and apologized for running the ad.(2)

The Herald received Horowitz's ad on Monday, March 12th, 2001, and decided to print it. Jahred Adelman '02, one of four *Herald* editors, said that after they received the ad, "We [the editors] discussed it very briefly. We thought it might upset some of our readers, but we also thought it's not our responsibility to censor this conservative opinion."(3)

The editors also said that they didn't want to set the precedent of rejecting ads based on their political content, or also start a trend of including counter-editorials every time they printed something that might be considered offensive. Brooks King '02, another one of the editors, told reporters, "To us that didn't seem like a good idea. For one thing, we thought it would be a very difficult precedent to keep up. It also seemed like a slippery slope."(4)

I had never heard of David Horowitz, or the notion of slavery reparations until Brown's "Horowitz controversy." The first time I was exposed to the issue was when I picked up my copy of *The Herald* on March 13, 2001, and read David Horowitz's advertisement, "Ten Reasons Why Reparations for Slavery is a Bad Idea—and Racist Too." It was a full-page ad, and at the top of the page the editors included a box that read, "Paid Advertisement." At the bottom of the page was an order form for Mr. Horowitz's book, *The Death of the Civil Rights Movement*, that explains how Martin Luther King Jr.'s ideas and intentions are being injured by today's civil rights leaders such as Al Sharpton, Jesse Jackson, and Louis Farrakhan.

Among Horowitz' ten points were:

"There were 3000 black slave-owners in the ante-bellum United States. Are reparations to be paid by their descendants too? There were white slaves in colonial America. Are their descendants going to receive payments?"

"The claim for reparations is premised on the false assumption that only whites have benefited from slavery. If slave labor has created wealth for Americans, then obviously it has created wealth for black Americans as well, including the descendants of slaves."

"Only a tiny minority of Americans ever owned slaves. This is true even for those who lived in the ante-bellum South where only one white in five was a slaveholder...What about the 350,000 Union soldiers who died to free the slaves? They gave their lives. What morality would ask their descendants to pay again?"

"Two great waves of American immigration occurred after 1880, and then after 1960. What logic would require Vietnamese boat people, Russian refuseniks, Iranian refugees, Armenian victims of the Turkish persecution, Jews, Mexicans, Greeks, or Polish, Hungarian, Cambodian and Korean victims of Communism, to pay reparations to American blacks?

"The black middle-class in America is a prosperous community that is now larger in absolute terms than the black underclass. Its existence suggests that present economic adversity is the result of failures of individual character rather than the lingering after-effects of racial discrimination or a slave system that ceased to exist well over a century ago."

"The reparations claim is one more attempt to turn African-Americans into victims. It sends a damaging message to the African-American community and to others...To focus social passions of African-Americans on what some other Americans may have done to their ancestors fifty or a hundred-and-fifty years ago is to burden them with a crippling sense of victim-hood."

"Reparations to African Americans have already been paid...Since the passage of the Civil Rights Acts and the advent of the Great Society in 1965, trillions of dollars in transfer payments have been made to African-Americans in the form of welfare benefits and racial preferences."

"What about the debt blacks owe to America?...Slavery existed for thousands of years before the Atlantic slave trade, and in all societies. But in the thousand years of slavery's existence, there never was an anti-slavery movement until white Anglo-Saxon Christians

created one. If not for the sacrifices of white soldiers and a white American President who gave his life to sign the Emancipation Proclamation, blacks in America would still be slaves."(5)

Mr. Horowitz's advertisement was interesting to me. Professor Lobban, in typical campus fashion, had made Brown students feel ashamed for being American, but Horowitz raised some points that actually commended the United States for its national slavery revolt, and self-condemnation for its participation in human bondage. His ad raised questions and thoughts that never would have entered my mind without the spark of his claims. There were white slaves? Blacks owned slaves too? There had never been a movement to rid the world of slavery until the one that ended up freeing the American slaves? Was this true? Were these lies? I wasn't sure, but judging from the reaction of many Brown members, I had to conclude that Mr. Horowitz was telling the truth, and they despised him for it.

The above arguments were several of Horowitz's points that campus liberals had a tough time swallowing. To me, there seemed to be nothing racist within the ad. In fact, Horowitz's entire commentary had a familiar tone. It was the exact type of talk that I had heard for four years behind the Ivy curtain, only among close friends at private lunch tables and soundproof dorm rooms.

After I read the advertisement I turned the page and skimmed through the rest of *The Herald.* I thought nothing more of it until the campus erupted into a frenzy of protesters screaming "racism" on the part of Horowitz and *The Herald.* What happened in the weeks to come exemplified Brown's political correctness, and resulted in the most national publicity Brown received while I was a student there.

Nothing To Read

Rather than even try to dispute Horowitz's points, Brown liberals denounced Horowitz, his ad, and *The Herald* editors as racists. The left's ideological bullies had failed in blocking an alternative perspective from reaching the campus ears, and they were pissed. So what did they do? On the day the ad was printed student activists started a petition that listed two demands: (1) that *The Herald* contribute the money it received ($580) to the *Third World Center*, and (2) that they provide room for a free, one-page, student-written article on reparations.(6)

The campus movement began to pick up steam. By Wednesday (the following day) the group of students had a name, *The Coalition of Concerned Brown Students.* They had collected over 200 signatures, and had been endorsed by at least eight campus student-groups. The night after the printing of the ad about 60 students marched to *The Herald* office building making their demands to the editors. Brooks King '02 told *The Coalition* that they would not meet the demands, but would meet with them the following night in a more relaxed atmosphere to discuss the situation further.(7)

In a predetermined Brown building the following night (Thursday) the two parties met again, and leaders of *The Coalition* made the same demands as the night before, and the editors again refused to concur with their terms. The meeting ended without a peaceful compromise, and one member of *The Coalition* said as he was leaving, "If you don't give in to our demands by the middle of next week, no one's going to read your papers. We're going to ensure that your papers aren't read on campus."(8)

The Coalition didn't give the editors the time they had promised to think about conceding to their demands. I walked into the cafeteria the next morning to find nothing to read as I ate my English muffins and tater-tots. Where was my *Brown DAILY Herald?!*

That afternoon I was informed that about 5000 copies of the *The Herald* were stolen from the normal distribution points, and the literal act of speech denial became a front-page story in Saturday's *Boston Globe.* The national attention that the issue received didn't allow Brown to sweep this latest incident under the rug, and *The Coalition* underwent harsh questioning and criticism for their actions. *The Herald* editors, representatives of *The Coalition*, and Brown faculty members who sympathized with *The Coalition* became guests of cable talk shows over the weekend as well. Brooks King '02 (*Herald* editor) faced off against Shaun Joseph '02 (International Socialist Organization) on Sunday morning's Weekend Today show on NBC. The controversy would become more and more heated and highly emotional, characterized by name-calling, threats of violence, campus disunity, and a watchful national eye. Even several years past the incident, passions would escalate when you mentioned the name "Horowitz" on Brown's campus.

I'm not sure if Mr. Horowitz foresaw his ad's repercussions. If so, he got exactly what he wanted, and more. Brown went to a national extent to verify the school's lack of concern for First Amendment principles, and duties as an institution of higher learning. Horowitz dedicated an entire chapter in his new book, *Uncivil Wars: The Controversy Over Reparations For Slavery*, to what happened at Brown as a result of his ad.

Many Brown students began to shout "racism" after the publication of Horowitz's ad, and the entire liberal community followed suit. But who would be the one to stand up and define the racism? Who would tell me, the interested and uninformed white kid, why the ad was racist and should be considered harassment? Nobody.

$$$$$$$$$

The dishonesty with which *The Coalition* approached the situation was troubling, but not out of the ordinary. They claimed that their main problem was that they didn't have the money to be on a fair playing field with Horowitz because he was able to afford a full-page ad, while they could not. Asmara Ghebremichael '01, the female student who was primarily responsible for creating *The Coalition*'s movement, wrote a column entitled, *Free Speech Is Only For Those Who Can Afford to Pay*, and *The Herald* printed it two days after the Horowitz ad. Ghebremichael, an Afro-American studies concentrator, wrote:

> **"Are you going to protect the free speech of the rich or the poor? Horowitz is saying that as long as you can back your words with money, anything goes: lies, harassment and hate included. He could have sent his commentary as a letter or a guest column, but no, he sent it as a paid advertisement. There was an exchange of money. Thus, the issue is not what was actually written, but the money that went into getting it printed."** (9)

This "money" issue wouldn't go away. When *The Coalition* stole the papers, they also left behind leaflets that said:

> **"We are wholly unconcerned with David Horowitz and**

his political games...He has the money to play such games, we do not. Therefore, we are using this action as an opportunity to show our community at Brown that our newspaper is not accountable to its supposed constituents." (10)

Come on! Who did these students think they were kidding? I found it laughable that a student-group was pretending to be out-gunned when it came to political debate on Brown's campus, as if they didn't have the resources, the strength in numbers, or the support of educated faculty to fight off one opinion that countered their own. To many (including myself) it only appeared that they were unable to dispute Horowitz's ten points, so they needed another way to justify their silencing of him. They decided to focus the campus' vision on the fact that *The Herald* was paid to print the ad, and somehow that tilted Brown's political scales in conservative favor—a principled position of poverty versus wealth in the arena of ideas. But since when did liberals become so principled?

Who needed money to refute Horowitz's opinion anyway? Regular opinion columns ran a half-page long. I thought that if only two of the 200 students who signed their petition wrote an opposing column, then all would be fair, right? Hell, write three and take the lead! Or, if money was really the issue that they were concerned with, then they could easily have collected a few bucks each from their 200 supporters and bought an ad space from *The Herald*. How hard would that be? How poor were they that 200 students couldn't come up with $580? Have a bake sale for God's sake!

Their attempt at portraying Horowitz as some deep-pocketed Republican capable of buying more campus ear-shots was as ludicrous as much as it was dishonest. Mr. Horowitz was a nationally known political figure, who had succeeded in presenting his views on a dramatically decorated page within *The Herald*. The campus left needed their response to be in proportion to Horowitz's stardom, all while attempting to portray his ad as an unacceptable spectacle of hate.

Members of *The Coalition* needed to appear slightly more sophisticated than your average college protester, so they tried to take this campus quarrel to some sort of phony intellectual level that could possibly override the charges of censorship that might come their way. What *The Coalition* did not anticipate, however, was the incident's public stage, forcing a more honest and in-depth handling of the dispute. This gave truth the upper hand against political correctness, and virtually nobody bit on *The Coalition's* assertion that *The Herald* had prostituted itself.

The Campus Left: Children Watching Porn

Worse than anything may have been the Brown administration's handling of the incident. At first, though, President Sheila Blumstein criticized *The Coalition*'s act of thievery as a serious breach of freedom of speech. The day after the papers were stolen President Blumstein issued a statement that read, "Consistent with its commitment to the free exchange of ideas, the University recognizes and supports *The Herald*'s right to publish any material it chooses, even if that material is objectionable to members of the campus community." She added, "Discussion, debate, and dialogue are the proper tools for resolving disagreements within an academic community." (11) That's nice, president Blumstein, but words are cheap. We'll see president Blumstein's rollback to the middle ground in a while. For now, though, *The Coalition* had fallen under heavy scrutiny, even by administration officials who usually sided with Brown's mind-manipulators. *The Coalition* had underestimated the will of the Brown community that was tired of putting up with liberal pettiness. They had left the campus with nothing to read one Friday morning, so many Brown students left *The Coalition* with a question: *Who do you guys think you are?*

The Herald stated that they were going to pursue criminal charges for the individuals who had stolen the papers. *The Coalition* was forced to defend their actions, and they were repeatedly calling for sensitivity to the feelings of those minorities who were intertwined with the debate, but they never failed to keep up with their claim that Horowitz's ad was filled with lies, and was blatantly racist.

I picked up a campus flyer that *The Coalition* released. It read:

"Does the BDH Serve You By Profiting Off Of Lies and Racial Hatred?"

On the back of the flyer was a defense and an explanation of their actions, and seemed to be asking the Brown community for a little understanding and sympathy. On the bottom it said: **"It's Time For Dialogue."** To me, this seemed to be an attempt to eradicate the image they had created for themselves as a bunch of leftist intimidators, as if they were interested in any dialogue at all. All they were interested in was collecting campus compassion, a little leeway due to their hurt feelings, so that their actions would be overlooked. The rest of the flyer began:

> "The removal of the March 16th issue of the Brown Daily Herald from on-campus distribution points was a legitimate act of civil disobedience. This one-time symbolic removal was undertaken to protest the paper's decision to run the paid advertisement "Why Reparations for Slavery are a Bad Idea—and Racist Too," thereby endorsing and profiting from an overtly racist political project...Furthermore, the Coalition has never opposed free speech, and has never protested offensive student editorials or letters...The March 16th actions were taken to initiate a fair and even dialogue on race, representation, and reparations in a manner that does not disenfranchise communities of color...The Herald's announcement that it would pursue criminal charges in reaction to this legitimate act of civil disobedience is regrettable, unwise, disappointing, and entirely out of proportion."(12)

The Coalition, all along, wanted to "initiate a fair and even dialogue on race, representation, and reparations"? As someone with some political experience now under my belt, it seemed pretty clear to me that the theft of the papers was done out of revenge, and to teach the entire campus some sort of lesson, not to initiate a dialogue. *The Coalition*'s initial action after their formation was to make demands to *The Herald* offices, not to sit down and talk peacefully about what had been printed. When the editors refused their terms, it wasn't peace talks *The Coalition* was interested in then either, but rather revenge. Their vindictive act came in the form of making as many people as possible believe that the ad was racist. So, they stole the papers and left behind leaflets to the community that assaulted the character of Horowitz and the editors, entirely consistent with Brown's political heritage.

And while *The Coalition* was attempting to explain themselves, they were constantly reminding the campus of the racism that existed within Horowitz's ad. Fine, but tell me *why* it was racist, please! This is where any objective spectator was offered box seats to the type of political games Brown students were taught to play. My classmates' impulse for activism was grossly dishonest, only driven by spirited emotion, and downright lacking in due thought.

If they wanted me to believe that this latest campus disturbance was different from any of their other protests, then I needed to hear them explain *why* the ad was racist. If this was a "one-time" "symbolic" event of "civil disobedience" that I should have tolerated, then I needed just one member of *The Coalition* to tell me *why* the ad was "overtly racist." Otherwise, in my eyes, it was they who had acted "entirely out of proportion."

The Coalition was searching for support, and was having trouble finding it. They looked like a bunch of teenagers who had lost the remote control while watching a pornographic movie, and could all of a sudden hear an adult walking toward the living room while they frantically searched for the device that would save them. Where were the bleeding-heart liberals that helped maintain their intellectual dominance on Brown's campus for so many years? *The Coalition* seemed to have walked right into a wall of defiance that hadn't been there before. However, Brown's liberals were a feisty bunch, and wouldn't give up that easily. They would never apologize for the theft of the papers. Rather, they continued to stubbornly shout *racism, racism, racism*! How obvious it became that this was the only approach they knew of when it came to campus debate. On both sides, the passions that escalated enflamed a bitter campus, and it was too early to tell if the Horowitz controversy would become what I hoped for, a momentous movement to rid Brown of political tyranny.

Brown's True Ethnic Atmosphere

The secretary of the Afro-American studies program checked the department's voicemail on the Monday morning following the theft of the papers, and listened to this:

> **"Hello. Is this the asshole that ripped off all those papers because of that slavery article? What a bunch of chickenshit bullshit. I mean, you're proving that you're**

> **inferior. You're proving it more and more all the time. And wait 'til you get out in the real fucking world. You'll find out really how useless you are..."**(13)

The same man left another message following that one...

> **"Gimme an N. Gimme an I. Gimme a G...And you know what that spells? Or maybe you don't. It's actually got six letters, so it's probably a little bit beyond you...(sings) N—,n—,n—...N—,n—,n—..."**(14)

I also read a report that told me professor Lewis Gordon, the Afro-American studies professor who helped lead and support *The Coalition*'s movement, received hate e-mail within the week following the ad. It read:

> **"Why are niggers so criminally oriented? Just look at the Niggers biggest 'Hero,' MLK, he plagarized (sic) his doctoral thesis and committed adultry (sic), in other words he was a thief and a whore like all niggers are."**(15)

I could have blamed these statements on the high emotion that characterized Brown during this time period. I could have blamed them on a mindless few who actually held racist feelings. I just wasn't sure what was fueling the actions of the morons who left these messages, but I still felt the same way about the incident, no matter how vicious the debate became. And I refused to abandon my honest thoughts on the Horowitz affair, even though I knew the campus left would attempt to group anyone on the "wrong" side of this issue with the people who delivered these messages.

Plus, I knew this: There were many others, besides these people, basking in the glory of seeing the politically correct liberals finally fall under the scrutiny that they deserved. Maybe those who had made these racist comments actually were racists, not just people who were taking their satisfaction with the incident much too far. But there were many non-racists who were enjoying the sight of their squirming liberal counterparts finally falling under the knife of social justice. The Horowitz controversy exposed the racial uptightness that brewed behind the campus exterior, and showed the true level of racial harmony that was a result of Brown's mishandling of multiculturalism, the end game of a diverse student body under the spell of liberalism.

These statements began to damage the conservative uprising that was smashing down Brown's history of political correctness, and a *Coalition* of students searching for an avenue toward campus sensitivity that would veil their fanaticism. Horowitz's ideas were suddenly being muddled with the racist statements made by a few extremists hiding amongst the Brown community. These hostile messages served for *The Coalition* as faulty evidence for the uninviting culture that Brown presents to all minorities. Despite harassing phone calls and emails to *The Herald* offices serving as the same type of intimidation during a time of heightened emotion, *The Herald* personnel decided to brush them aside quietly, rather than publicly expose them as *The Coalition* did theirs.

President Blumstein pulled back her reigns of Americanism, and issued a second statement on March 20th saying, "Even as we uphold our principles, we cannot deny the impact the publication of this advertisement has had on the Brown community as a whole. It was written to be inflammatory. In addition, it was deliberately and deeply hurtful."(16) President Blumstein also failed to explain to me how the ad was "hurtful," and I couldn't fail to notice the compromise of thought that she was heading toward, and that she had just placed all the blame for the entire ordeal on the lap of David Horowitz.

President Blumstein then described the two values that were clashing: "the principle of freedom of the press and freedom of expression, and the value placed on having a diverse community where people of all races and ethnicities can feel free to live and learn."(17) Yes, the principles of freedom were colliding with the values of diversity. Guess which side Brown stood on. We were again going to learn the Ivy lesson, that truth is not something of discovery, but is something we must mold ourselves while always keeping in mind the two most important factors: Ethnicity and Sensitivity.

There's a fight to life. And Brown said, "run."

Brown's campus split into two factions. One side defended their opinions using American standards of free speech, and the other side relied on sympathy for their damaged mentality. Associate Professor of American Civilization, Afro-American studies, and History, James Campbell said:

> **"On these issues, I am a lot closer to a First Amendment absolutist than most of my colleagues, but we need a more nuanced understanding of the First Amendment. We need to recognize, for example, that Brown, like any institution, imposes certain kinds of responsibilities on those who voluntarily choose to participate in it. A person does not have the right to stand up after someone speaks in my classroom and say, 'You're stupid because you're black.' The right to say that is protected in the wider society, but not in a Brown classroom. We need sensitivity there, not to restrict the reasoned exchange of ideas, but to make it possible."**(18)

To me, Professor Campbell seemed to be saying that Brown should be willing to teach its students that it's okay to compromise our nation's most basic freedoms for the sake of not offending anyone. But wouldn't my classmates and I take that lesson with us into "the wider society?" What about the University's civic responsibility to teach their students the code of conduct in the outside world? And who was to decide what should be considered "the reasoned exchange of ideas?" Who was in charge of framing what should be considered decent political speech? Brown administrators and professors preferred not to make a stand and say, *Hey, this is how our University is. If you can't handle educational honesty, then don't come here.* Rather, they would say, *Well, some of our students have special interests and concerns, so we can't allow for certain opinions to be heard.* Professor William Keach said, "his [Horowitz] well-funded racist assault on the reparations movement warranted intense, angry denunciation and did not deserve our usual customs of respectful debate."(19)

Brown liberals didn't seek truth. Rather, they considered truth a fortunate byproduct of a diverse campus. Professor Campbell may have been "closer" to being a First Amendment "absolutist" than other Brown professors, but he wasn't nearly as close as he should have been, especially within an educational setting. Brown had created intellectual boundaries, and liberals justified their thought-restriction as morally justified, that the thoughts they were prohibiting were just plain mean. And the lines they had drawn to frame acceptable dialogue were non-negotiable.

As you might expect, I couldn't have disagreed more with Professor Campbell. I didn't see the First Amendment as something that should ever be compromised for the sake of sensitivity. Did that make me a jerk? I thought it made me American. I thought that compassion should be a way of life, not something mandated by government, or societal restrictions of political correctness. Some part of me just knew that we can't make people be nice. You know, the whole "sticks and stones" thing.

I remember finding Professor Campbell's "nuanced" position on the First Amendment a cowardly one, and was keeping students disconnected from the outside world. Campbell's personal outlook was precisely the cause of Brown's ethnic friction that resulted in one of the most painful campus controversies in Brown's long history.

I argued with some of my friends and classmates about this. I told them that a white student who actually believed another black student was stupid "because you're black" should be allowed to get up and pronounce his bigotry. *Shocked! Stupefied! Angry!* These were the reactions of those I argued with. "I would love for you to be a minority for just one day, so you could see what it's like," one of my *white* classmates told me.

As much as my classmates didn't understand me, I also had a tough time understanding them. Did they believe that there would be a large number of students who would get up and actually assert racism if Brown cut their speech codes from the student handbook? What were they afraid of? Wouldn't someone with that type of ignorance in his heart be shot down with overwhelming reason, ultimately creating a prejudice-free society? I thought that this was a basic American principle, that the result of honest discussion was the discovery of what is right and truthful. After all, doesn't American democracy allow us to practice self-reflection, and then self-improvement? And wasn't it American democracy, overwhelmed with good-natured Christian humanitarians, that caused the ultimate destruction of the American slave-system? But Brown liberals seemed to have not only lost faith in Americanism, but also their faith in the goodness of people.

The Horowitz controversy reminded me to go through life not fearing evil thought, but always confronting it. I thought that an educational atmosphere would have also desired the outright expression of bigotry, rather than allow it to dwell in an Ivy underworld. At Brown, this would have revealed the contrast between true bigotry, and those incidents that often got confused with racism and prejudice, and set whites and blacks further apart. To have allowed space for bigotry would have dared the holders of it to reveal themselves from their hidden bunkers. That self-exposure was not only protected by principles of free speech, but was also the only path that would have led to bigotry's breakdown. Above all other things, an *honest* education is what Brown should have been striving for, because true peace is never realized with the denial of evil, only its defeat. My alma mater should not have been forcing compassionate speech, because in order to truly learn virtue, my classmates and I needed to experience transgressions.

One had to understand the deceit of liberalism to realize why my particular mentality was restricted from students' ears. Brown liberals were simply unable to agree with me, or to allow bigotry to be clearly defined for the Brown community. To do so would mean their ruin. They kept the evil of prejudice unmarked, always insisting it was heavily abound to validate their activism. They actually craved discrimination, prejudice, hate-speech, gay-bashing, and ethnic division. Or any episode they could twist into appearing so. This ensured the survival of the campus left. After all, what is a liberal if there is no more bigotry to battle?

Here Comes the Faculty

While a few professors chimed in on behalf of free speech, much of the faculty threw their support behind *The Coalition*. The students sought help in Lewis Gordon, an Afro-American studies professor, and he defended The *Coalition* by saying, "This is not a free speech issue. It is a hate speech issue."(20) Even when liberals seemed to abandon their tactics of silencing and tried to actually argue, they were still making the same point. *Racism! Hate speech!* No, Professor Gordon. This was a free speech issue.

Kenneth Knies from the same department as Professor Gordon

searched for sympathy by telling reporters, "I have talked to students who told me that they can't perform basic functions like walking or sleeping because of this ad."(21) 57 faculty members signed a letter to President Blumstein requesting that no disciplinary action be taken against the students responsible for the theft of the papers, and that she officially condemn Horowitz's ad as "harassment." *Racism! Harassment!* The professors declared to Blumstein that the theft of the papers was a "symbolic protest over both the publication of Horowitz's commercial ad, and the *Brown Daily Herald*'s refusal to provide the students with equal space, free of charge, for response to the ad's racist and assaultive statements." *Racism! Assault!* I'm still waiting for the faculty to explain to me how the ad was "racist" or "assaultive." And also how the theft and destruction of property was "symbolic." The Coalition hadn't *symbolically* burned the editors in effigy, they *literally* stole the outlet that was conveying ideas they disagreed with. Literal literary larceny.

The Coalition was no longer a rabble of confused students. They now had an army, supporters within the student body, faculty, and administration. Concerning a meeting that consisted of members/representatives of *The Herald,* the faculty, *The Coalition*, and the administration the week after the Horowitz ad, Patrick Moos '02 (*Herald* editor) stated, "We were very disappointed in that meeting. We thought we were coming in to sit down and talk rationally, but the conversation was very one-sided. All the administrators—including people I really respect—were acting like we were clearly in the wrong. No one stood up for us."(22)

More than failing to refute any portion of Horowitz's ad, the faculty also stood in silence on points that they knew represented historical truth. Horowitz made in one of his "ten reasons" what many saw as an outrageous claim, that blacks owe a debt to America because if not for white Americans' involvement in the abolitionist movement, blacks would still be slaves in America. His reasoning behind this notion was that while history had seen many slave revolts by those who were enslaved themselves, the movement starting in the late 1700s was the first time a movement was formed that was "dedicated to the belief that the institution of slavery was itself immoral," and that movement was started by white Anglo-Saxons.(23)

It seemed to me that this line of reasoning gave whites and blacks a reason to be proud of America, that it was our nation that, while slavery came across the Atlantic with us, took a large part in abolishing the practice of slavery that had always achieved global existence. Horowitz had something to say about the professors who refused to educate their rallying students.

> "Every professor of American history within range of the ad who knew anything about slavery—and there were surely thousands—knew precisely what I was referring to, and knew that the point I had made in the ad was historically accurate. But not one of them came forward to defend it. Instead they allowed black students, like Asmara Ghebremichael, to remain comfortable in their ignorance of facts that were central to the understanding of their own history. That was what the specter of fear that now haunts our campuses had accomplished."(24)

While Brown's African-American students were livid from Horowitz's ad, a monthly contributor to the *Providence Journal* offered the words of black conservative columnist Thomas Sowell:

> "Nothing we can do in the 21st Century can redress the wrongs done by people long dead against other people long dead. So we might as well put away these sweeping definitions of 'whites' and 'blacks' that extend back through history and talk about those particular whites, blacks and others who are alive today. As one of those black Americans, I consider it as ridiculous as it would be phony to pretend that I am worse off than if my ancestors had remained in West Africa and I had been born there. They themselves might well have been better off remaining in Africa, but they are not the ones who would get any reparations."(25)

A black conservative! I had no idea.

Here I was able to see an African-American expressing contrasting opinions from my black classmates. My classmates, for some reason, couldn't tolerate the fact that Horowitz had raised the question of why black students were being discouraged from feeling proud of being American, or even some gratitude for their ancestors' sacrifices, and also the sacrifices of white Americans who died so they may be free.

I was beginning to be able to answer this question for Mr. Horowitz. The upheaval over that thought, that all Americans (even black Americans) should feel proud of their nation, and be grateful for the opportunity it presents to all of us, simply undermined the victimization of African-Americans. Others may not have viewed them as the "unjustly wounded" anymore, but rather individuals provided with ample opportunity by a great country—the wretched antithesis of the University's pampering message of self-pity. Brown had made my minority classmates so dependent on a victim's mentality, that when it became threatened they would actually lose their ability to "walk" and "sleep." The University had given them their campus itch, forcing them to scratch and claw in order to retain victim status. Leftist political strategy had turned my classmates into their own worst enemy. Now, pain and pessimism was necessary to achieve their end. This compelled them to act with dishonesty, prohibiting honest debate. Now they had to continually express negativity, painting every pittance of conservatism as reason for outrage, driving others further away from them.

Why Are Black People Fighting With One Another?

Significant time had passed since the printing of the ad, and *The Coalition* had grown strong. Many had forgotten the actual content of the ad. I had only read it once, and many others had never even received the chance to read it. *The Coalition*'s claim that the ad was racist was beginning to be accepted as undeniable truth. The debate began to evolve into whether *The Herald* should be allowed to print hate speech or not at a diverse educational setting such as Brown, when it was never even concluded that Horowitz had written hate speech. I guess if you say something enough times it starts to take some form of truth.

After the incident that had shed light on the problems Brown has, President Blumstein came to the University's defense. "Is Brown politically correct?" she asked herself. "Look at what happened. We are one of the few places that published the ad. Sure, there was a reaction—the taking of the newspapers—but there has also been a strong reaction against the taking. I think it's unfair to label an entire community as politically correct when all the values society speaks to are clearly alive and well here."(26)

Does "alive and well" mean having to deal with an eruption of theft and intimidation every time there's an utterance of conservatism? Is harassment the justified consequence for students who want to speak their minds? It wasn't going to matter who won this battle of persuasion. My classmates and I were learning a clear lesson. From this point forward, how many students would dare offer an honest opinion on racial subjects after the example that was being made out of *The Herald*'s editors? When asked if *The Herald* would run the ad again, editor Jahred Adelman responded, "Ideally...we've been telling people that what we did was right, and we would do it again under the same circumstances. If Horowitz came to our door and said, 'I want to run it again,' I'm not sure we would. Not after all that hate mail and those racist messages."(27) Perhaps President Blumstein was either a little disillusioned about Brown's state of political correctness, or was just being slightly dishonest as she felt it was her duty as president to defend the University no-matter-what.

About a month after the printing of the advertisement, Brown leftists organized a forum where Professor Gordon and Brother Everett Muhammad, the Black Muslim, were members of the panel. The forum began to show just how flimsy and dishonest *The Coalition*'s movement was, and how easily it could fall apart. At the forum one senior admitted that members of *The Coalition* weren't equipped with the knowledge to rebut Mr. Horowitz. I wondered why they had been rebutting him all that time if they didn't know if what Horowitz had said was true or not. Anyway, due to their now-confessed ignorance, this student "condemned Brown as a racist institution with no interest in African-Americans."(28) After all of the controversy and vicious debate, this student had the audacity to say that Brown didn't care about its black students!

Professor Gordon was also upset with the comment, and seemingly let out some suppressed frustration with the leaders of *The Coalition* that had been depending on him for his counsel. A *Providence Journal* story reported Professor Gordon's words:

> **"I'm Brown University, too. Black people at Brown have taken 'a lot of heat' over the years to make the University what it is, Gordon said, and the students' 'politically immature' actions and 'anti-intellectualism' are damaging to all."**(29)

Well put, Professor. But Brother Everett disagreed with Gordon, and came to the student's defense. The same *Providence Journal* report stated:

> **"Brother Everett 'Muhammad expressed anger about the tone of Gordon's admonitions, and they argued loudly. A student started crying and shouted, 'Why are black people arguing with each other!?'"**(30)

As a freshman, Brown's racial uptightness confused me. But by the time I was a senior I had come to fully understand why the University had become so segregated. Liberalism had created a troubling and erroneous "us-against-them" mentality for all types of minorities, as if siding with a person of identical skin color was more important than siding with truth. My classmates were always acting as if there was a war going on. And perhaps there *was* a remaining struggle for justice, some remnants of bigotry that needed to be demolished. But the separatist attitude of the campus left had blown any remaining levels of racism out of proportion, and had motivated willing students to scowl at anyone who didn't see the level of bigotry that Brown liberals insisted was plentiful, and often accused those students as being racist themselves. *You're either with us, or against us*, they demanded, causing bitter ethnic divide.

Why were blacks fighting amongst themselves? It was because people of the same skin tone were never meant to unconditionally agree with one another. The color of the mind is not black or white. But Brown had long abandoned individualism, and had created collective racial consciousness, unopposed within the minds of its members. This black classmate of mine was actually under the impression that something was wrong if blacks disagreed on an issue concerning race. Being a certain color should not have resigned her to one mode of opinion, but that was Brown's designed indoctrination. Why were blacks arguing with each other? It's because Professor Gordon decided to express his own individual thoughts, rather than the anticipated collective liberalism that had been stemming from his mouth for the past month. One of Brown's African-American professors was trying to be honest about Brown's political thuggery, and it confused my classmates.

I was grasping the reality that a Brown education would never allow this student to realize that there were other minorities out there who agreed wholeheartedly with David Horowitz. A Brown education would only keep that student immersed in a tub of pessimism, distrust, and isolation. Not only detached from reality, but also infected with the negative outlook of leftism.

This classmate of mine was just another Ivy tragedy, a victim of a modern-day college education. She had been trained to think of herself as a member of the black community first, and an individual second. Brown failed her. The University enslaved her. From day-one she was placed in her respective ethnic box, and was told that her thinking may not extend beyond its walls. An open-minded education? Yeah, right. Perhaps it is Brown who should be offering reparations. They could start by refunding tuition payments to all of those students who did not receive the open-minded, and intellectually diverse education that they were promised.

A call for a color-blind campus was perhaps the most disingenuous appeal from the campus left. The University could not have been more obsessed with the color of people's skin. Cornel West, the widely disputed, leftist, African-American, Ivy League professor gave a lecture to the Brown community in 2004 saying that he would "rather be seen as a black man than just as a man."(31) That's fine, but he and professors of his ilk shouldn't be dragging the entire black community down with them.

Threats of Violence

Remaining consistent with the values of education, my alma mater's recently revived College Republicans invited David Horowitz to speak to the Brown community about his views on slavery reparations, and possibly clarify some of his points. Maybe his visit would help heal some psychological wounds that the campus had suffered, and also help to truly unify the Brown community. Mr. Horowitz accepted, but the invitation was retracted when rumors of likely violence were made known by certain campus leftists.(32) My classmates needed time to cool down, but David Horowitz would eventually make his way onto campus.

In the meantime Brown's liberals invited Sam Anderson, a founder of the Harlem Branch of the Black Panther Party, to speak to the Ivy League community, and re-deliver a feeling of victim-hood to my black classmates. "The people here who have taken up the struggle against a man named 'Horror-itz' have done a great thing," Anderson pronounced.(33) During his talk he denounced capitalism for creating an attitude of white supremacy, and made at least one vague reference to an "enemy." When a student in the audience asked who this "enemy" was that he had referred to, Anderson replied, "The enemy I'm talking about is predominantly the white class and their Negro lackeys." I remember wishing that Anderson owned his own campus newspaper. You know, so I could steal all of them.

Horowitz Arrives

In October of 2003, nearly two years after the controversy over his ad, David Horowitz was again invited to speak on Brown's campus by a better-organized (and committed) College Republicans. This time, with the help of a new University president seemingly dedicated to the principles of academic freedom, and also several years of controversy that had been making fools out of Brown's most intolerant, Horowitz was allowed to speak his mind on Providence's College Hill. It was sure to be a dramatic occasion. The Herald reported that some students were still "not emotionally prepared."(34)

An especially insulting notation to this occasion was the fact that Brown's Undergraduate Finance Board would only pay Mr. Horowitz barely more than a tenth of his normal speaking fee. Devoted to his cause of academic freedom, Mr. Horowitz ignored the indignity of the Finance Board, and arrived anyway.

Of course, still residing in the area, I wouldn't miss the opportunity to attend. I was running late to the event as I had to come straight from work, so I arranged for a friend of mine to open the side door minutes before "show-time" while dozens of other students were rejected in an orderly line at the front door. Hey, I would have climbed down the chimney to see this event.

With the presence of the police to ensure civility, Mr. Horowitz met a toned-down version of Brown's typical defiance. During his oration he was interrupted several times. I was sitting toward the front of Salomon Auditorium only three rows back. I remember hearing a disruption from the back of the room while Horowitz was in the middle of his talk. I looked back and a visibly angry white man (not a student) took a final look at Mr. Horowitz, pointed at him, and said, "You wrote a racist article. That's it." The man then stormed out of the room. A white female student was continually interrupting Mr. Horowitz, and was told by the audience to "shut up." The emotions of the incident were still vivid, and I could understand that. I mean, I still held strong opinions about the incident as well.

Besides only a few interruptions, the demeanor of the students was commendable (if you can commend someone for having common decency). For Brown students, however, it was respectable. Their politeness may have been because Dean of the College Paul Armstrong, and President Ruth Simmons were also at the event. Dean Armstrong was acting as the curator (on stage with Horowitz), and President Simmons sat in the crowd, directly to my left.

Horowitz's lecture, focusing more on educational freedom than it did on slavery reparations, reminded Brown students that it had taken two years for him to be invited onto the campus. Then he said, "You can't get a good education if they're only telling you one half of the story." That statement made so much sense to me, and I began to think of Professor Lobban who had visited Brown in 2001 to tell Brown students that we need to have a sense of national apology for the slavery that America sacrificed the lives of 350,000 men, and one President to eradicate.

Like myself, Horowitz had also noticed that there hadn't been any real debate over slavery reparations yet. "Nobody has made an argument against my ad yet. Not even tonight has anyone stood up and argued against one of my 'ten reasons.'" Even after that dare, not one person stood up and attempted to refute one of the points in his ad. They seemed to have just shown up under the impression that this guy had written something racist two years ago, and sent it to *The Herald* for publication.

At the end of his lecture, Mr. Horowitz took questions from the crowd of mostly left-minded Brown students. Each question wasn't really a question, but rather a rebuttal framed as a question. And they would always receive applause from the crowd before Horowitz could reply. It got pretty annoying listening to students make points that I thought Horowitz had already pre-argued during his lecture, and then receive an applause for not paying attention. One black male student stood up and began his question by reminding Horowitz that he had said that "blacks should be grateful that they were brought to America on slave ships." Horowitz cut him off and said, "I never, ever said that." Later he would say, "Look, I'm not a racist. Conservatives and liberals merely disagree as to the correct, and most effective way to help black Americans."

Don't think for a second that Brown students were cured of their misconception of a true education just because they maintained a level of politeness during Horowitz's lecture. Students had hung flyers all over campus that promoted the denial of Horowitz's presence on campus. Focusing his lecture on academic freedom, Horowitz and the College Republicans found it appropriate to make copies of this flyer and hand them out to the crowd to help prove Horowitz's point about Brown's one-sided education, and the bullying of the campus left. The flyer (exactly as printed) read:

Right Wing Ideologues are trying to bring
David Horowitz
A CONSERVATIVE RACIST to College Hill

Colleges are liberal institutions where liberal ideas flourish. Ultrapowerful figures like Paul Wolfowitz, David Horowitz, Ehud Barak and others have made a concerted effort to bring their propaganda-ideology to American universities.

THIS DISSENT IS AN ASSAULT ON OUR FREEDOM OF SPEECH

Even Brown professors agree: SILENCE DAVID HOROWITZ in order to save democracy or else there will be NO OPEN MINDED LEADERS IN THE FUTURE OF AMERICA.

--- (35)

They just didn't get it.

CHAPTER 11
Death of the All-American

Then strip, lads, and to it, though
sharp be the weather,
And if, by mischance, you should
happen to fall,
There are worse things in life
than a tumble on heather,
And life is itself but
a game at football.

Sir Walter Scott,
The Lord of the Isles, "Song," 1815

The Ivy League was established in 1945 to distinguish a handful of eastern college football programs from the rest of the nation by upholding high academic standards. A decade later, these standards were applied to all other sports. Common academic eligibility requirements and the forbiddance of athletic scholarships had officially created our nation's most prestigious collegiate conference. However, these were decisions that had the potential to drastically lower the standards of play. But this was also a move that would attract a special form of young athlete. Those who would accept this new collegiate contract now had to be of a special breed, those who were as serious about academics as they were about athletics, those of a daring mentality and high competitive nature. Ivy League athletes would now enter into an agreement that they knew would challenge them; a rigorous athletic schedule combined with the highest academic competition in the country, absent of financial support for athletic prowess. A true student-athlete. This would become the all-American figure, a person of athletic heroism, with an equally admirable intellectual side. And those with the talent, brains, and fortitude to enter into such an agreement have kept Ivy League athletics at a shockingly high level of Division I competition, exhibiting a rare ability to compete successfully against even those who still offer athletic scholarships.

In 1945, sustaining an esteemed athletic reputation was important to the Ivy League community. But by the time I had arrived at Brown, everything had been flipped upside down. Despite the long love affair between athletics and the Ivy League, Brown's athletes now held a shameful campus reputation. One didn't have to look very far to discover the reason for others' contempt for us. We made up a large portion of the conservatives on campus, and there was a direct correlation between their contempt, and our conservatism.

Evidence to my assertion that Brown athletes were not appreciated to a normal degree was the pathetic amount of student support that accompanied our sporting events. Brown athletics was a great community within itself, but it wasn't as large a part of student life as it is on most other college campuses. Believe me, the last thing you'll find on Brown's campus is a pep-rally, and the majority of students that attended athletic events were often members of other Brown teams. Brown men's and women's basketball teams were provided with a gym that was slightly larger than most high school gymnasiums simply because a larger one wasn't needed. I think if they tried really hard, the Brown Feminists could have drawn more students to a pro-choice rally than one of Brown's football games. I'm not bitter, but I'm not wrong either.

Even beyond the lack of student support for athletics, Brown athletes couldn't help but feel a scornful glare, and the hidden comments made by the campus left who stereotyped their athletes as a bunch of meat-headed jocks. Brown athletes tended to suffer not just from disrespect from the other students, but were also viciously discriminated against. And their nastiness was often proudly pronounced. In a special Freshmen Orientation edition of the *Brown Daily Herald*, designed to familiarize first-years with the campus specifics, the paper declared, "Our football stadium is two miles off campus, and we like to keep it that way."(1) I'm sure this statement made the freshmen football players feel right at home.

There are some who will make the claim that, perhaps at an elite university, we should expect some scorn aimed at the athletes, who are suddenly reaping what they sowed in high school when they were picking on their smaller classmates. Revenge of the Nerds! An interesting thought, but there are a few problems with it. First off, it's stupid. Second, there are plenty of elite institutions across the nation that highly revere their athletic programs. Notre Dame, Duke, Georgetown, Stanford, etc. Why do *their* campuses cultivate a reputable outlook on athletes? Thirdly, by pardoning Brown's non-athletes' disdain for a certain campus group would be to vindicate their bigotry—as if it is justified to scoff at every athlete for the rest of one's life because that person may have had a bad adolescent experience with his high school's all-star shortstop. All of a sudden, we would be excusing prejudice, and admitting that, yes, liberals do stereotype, discriminate, and hate. Any liberal wishing to dispute me on the topic of Ivy athletics may not want to go down this road. For some other reason, the cultural divide between geeks and jocks had been increased to its greatest width at Brown University. And there was much more to the situation than just some brainiacs' irrational resentment.

The Ivy League, born from athletic tradition (particularly of football), seemed to have lost an appreciation for its athletes by the time I had arrived. A once renowned campus lifestyle now had a hideous stigma attached to it. Times had changed.

Conservative Frat Boys

When writing *Out of Ivy* I was forced to reflect back to the beginning of my Brown experience, and wondered *how* and *why* I became such a staunch conservative at the liberal Ivy. If I was as politically inexperienced entering Brown as I have claimed, then I should have been more easily influenced by the campus liberals than most other students.

I think football saved me. One of the main reasons why I never set foot on the path of student activism with my classmates was because I already had an identity. Playing football always provided that for me, and I was never in search of something that could offer me more substance simply because I was already part of something. Therefore, my role in campus politics was initially that of a spectator.

However, I only partially credit my conservatism to the fact that I already had an individuality that served me just fine, even if the majority of students rejected me for it. Another reason for my traditional thought was my athletic upbringing. Regardless of whether or not I had extended my athletic career to the collegiate level, sports had already played a tremendous role in my life. From the time that I was very young, and through high school, my time on the playing fields had shaped my character upon my entrance to Brown University. Sports helped instill in me a set of values that I now believe ultimately deterred me from joining any campus group that promoted liberal ideals.

Sports have always been the most accurate representations of life (especially American life). There's a reason why thousands of people fill stadiums in order to witness "just a game." There's a reason why professional sports in America is a multi-billion dollar industry, and it's not because people just enjoy watching a bunch of guys butt their heads together for a few hours. Athletics closely resemble the human condition. There are ups and downs. Struggles. Victory. Defeat. Comebacks. People have always had an appreciation for athletics, and the lessons they teach us. People love sports because they emulate humanity, and elicit the values that we cherish and admire. Sports dismiss the notion of idealism—there will be a winner and a loser to every contest, and there is no perfect game to be played, only continuously strived for. Athletic events demand respect for rules and authority. They teach us the importance of balance—there are times for risk, and there are times for caution; extremism in either direction is inevitably reckless. Sports remind us of the underdog's chances for triumph, and they teach that victory rightfully goes to the deserving, that success is not an entitlement, but rather a "mind over matter" equation. Success is something that must be earned through work, preparation, and attitude. The prevailing mentality in sports is one that resists the temptation to form excuses, or accept pity from others. Successful teams are saturated with hope and optimism. And while team unity is seen as an indispensable component of athletic success, individuality streamlines all athletic contests. These values found on our playing fields are profoundly conservative ones.

Still, one thing that was undeniable on Brown's campus was a sourness toward normalcy, and a distaste for the all-American student-athlete. And it was no coincidence that the Brown athletes made up a large portion of the conservative thinkers on campus. Brown liberals, who had no concept of competition, perseverance, and the American

Dream were not interested in athletics. Rather, they ignored, mocked, and belittled those who represented the University on the playing fields, and would refuse to add to school spirit at sporting events. They rejected and vilified their athletes, and enjoyed being part of a respected majority of like-minded liberals who now finally shared a campus-identity that was more respected than even the all-American student-athlete.

Frat Boys Without a Sport

One Saturday morning, three friends and I went out for breakfast. Dressed in normal attire (baseball caps, hooded sweatshirts and jeans, etc), we waited about ten minutes for a table in a busy restaurant on Providence's famous Wickenden Street adjacent to Brown's campus. A girl and what seemed to be her boyfriend were right next to us, also waiting for a table. They were dressed quite differently from us as they fashioned shaggier hair and vintage-style clothing. Hippies. I remember that the guy was also wearing big shades over his eyes in an attempt to sport some sort of 70's disco-look. But I only started to study their attire after what happened in the following minutes.

When the waitress called us to our table, and all but one of us had passed the two hippies, the girl said to her boyfriend in an attempt to mock us, "Hey look, it's a bunch of frat boys without a sport."

Now, even though we offered no criticism about *her* lifestyle, *her* clothing, or *her* personal interests, she still felt the need to ridicule us. These were the people I was to believe were the fluffy-hearted heroes of diversity and understanding.

But I guess we were easily recognizable as conservative frat-boys due to the fact that we were not wearing clothes that we had made ourselves out of recycled paper for last year's Earth Day march. Little did this girl know that my third friend, lagging a little further behind, heard her make the comment. My friend and her locked eyes as she realized she was caught making such a discriminatory remark. He decided to ignore her ignorance, as she couldn't have been more wrong with her assessment. *None* of us were members of a fraternity, and *all* of us played a college sport. To this day I still do not fully understand the comment. Without a sport?

Nevertheless, I was still bothered when my friend told us what she had said, simply because it was a derogatory comment aimed at me.

Coincidentally, we all enjoyed a very awkward breakfast as the waitress sat the two of them down right next to us five minutes later. I almost threw my pancakes at her.

Prejudice and victim-hood were the rallying cries of Brown's special-interest student groups. But the student with the only legitimate claim to campus discrimination was the athlete. Strikingly, you didn't find a single grievance or complaint, only a mysterious absence of a touchy-feely support group to compensate for the player's plight and predicament.

Why They Hate

We were the campus idiots. No doubt, we were the Ivy League's "Flyover Country." Noticeably right-wing, and therefore lazily regarded by liberals as stupid; a group unworthy of intellectual engagement. But judging from my own experiences, my classmates never struck me as more intelligent than my teammates. In my eyes, the campus left had miscalculated when they decided that our conservatism was a result of inferior intellect, rather than an athletic lifestyle that taught us to despise leftist ideals.

There is no doubt in my mind of the connection between athletic conservatism, and athletes' vilification. We were a proud and blatant campus minority, wearing Gap and Abercrombie, playing sports, occupying the off-campus bars, dominating fraternity life, and absent from student protests. Oh, how they hated us.

Ironically, Brown's athletes were the most likely to be found implementing the leftist creed of tolerance and diversity. Walk onto Brown's campus and ask where the Ratty is. The Ratty, believe it or not, is what students call the cafeteria. When you enter the Ratty, you will notice the dining tables ethnically divided. Black students sitting with other black students. Whites with other whites. Asians with Asians. Now, this wasn't a strict rule, but it was reliably commonplace. There was one group, however, that you could always catch exercising diversity dining. The athletes.

Jokingly one day, answering one of my black teammates who had just asked me where he could find the fresh apple pie that I had on my food tray, I told him, "Oh, it's over by the silverware. You know, right next to the *black* section," referring to the side of the cafeteria that was occupied by African-American students. Both he and I laughed, not because it was a stunning observation, but because of my insensitive candor toward a previously unspoken truth. In other words, it was the University's speech codes that actually made something so obvious, so funny.

Not that this type of honesty was rare from Brown athletes. As I said before, conservatives were much more comfortable with themselves, unashamed with who they were. We were much less concerned with always saying the "correct" thing.

During the spring of my junior year it came time for the fraternities to elect their officers for the following fall semester. Brown's Greek life was dominated by the athletes, and Theta Delta Chi (Thete, for short) was predominantly occupied by members of the football team. It was the "football house." Well, members of Thete had elected one of their black fraternity brothers as next year's president, and their annual custom was to officially induct that person by putting him through some sort of hazing. While being elected president of anything is always an honor, this tradition almost dissuaded Thete members from wishing it upon themselves. The practical joke that was played on the elected was typically unpleasant. And this spring, my teammates decided to kidnap their new executive, tie him to a chair in the middle of the quad, and paint him...white.

Pause for a second, and think about that.

If more people (or perhaps certain people) had seen this episode, then you can be sure that there would have either been expulsions, a heated controversy, or some sort of campus upheaval. Certainly, someone would have had some explaining to do. Fortunately, this politically incorrect event, for the most part, slipped under the campus radar. I had only heard about it because *my* friends had organized and conducted the "paint incident." Although, one black female student happened to walk by, and witnessed the horror. Later on she made her repulsion known to my teammates as she informed them as to just how appalled she was at their insensitivity. Upon learning how upset this girl had become, a few of my teammates approached her later to apologize.

Insensitive? On Brown's campus, the "paint incident" was much more than insensitive. It was a mortal sin. It was exactly the type of thing that could have caused a riot, earning my classmates appearances on national news programs as they protested the atrocity. When I was told what they had done to their new president, I was shocked for only that reason. My teammates had not heeded the warnings of the Ivy social order. They had risked it all for the sake of tradition, laughs, and brotherhood.

Events such as this are how Brown's athletes distinguished themselves from the liberal pack. While most campus conservatives kept quiet, the Brown athletes were more candid and visible. A highly self-confident group more difficult for liberals to gag.

And we were colorblind. If there were any racists on campus, it certainly wasn't us. So confident were my teammates that they were *not* bigoted, that they defied Brown's campus correctness in the middle of the quad for all to see. They stared every speech code, every meeting on diversity, and all of Brown's sensitivity training right in the eyes and said, "This is our friend, our president, our teammate. And we're painting him white."

I don't know if anyone other than another Brown conservative can appreciate how hilarious I found this story to be. At first, I was knocked right off my stool. Stunned! Dazed! But only because I couldn't believe the spectacle they dared to create. But I understood all of it. I knew these guys, and where they were coming from. They just weren't concerned. To them, it was funny and innocent. They had elected their friend as next year's president, and they would do what they had always done. They would play a practical joke that was relevant to their own personal relationship. If the campus left had a problem with it, they could all go to hell.

The defiance of campus correctness. This is why athletes were despised so much. Because we were honest.

As for liberals. Truth meant nothing to them. Diversity meant nothing to them. An assault on all that is traditional was the left's agenda. They worked for a new order. A new religion. But they were the most disingenuous people on campus, actually maligning those who dared to exercise their mantra.

Insignificant Games

It was my senior year, and I received an invitation to attend a meeting in Brown's Pizzitola, one of the University's athletic buildings. I didn't know what the purpose of the meeting was even as I arrived. As I entered the conference room where the meeting was to take place I noticed that I was joined by about twenty of my classmates, all captains of our respective teams. David Roach, Brown's athletic director, began to explain why he had called us to this night's gathering.

The *Council of Ivy Group Presidents* was to assemble very soon to discuss the future of Ivy League athletics, and certain modifications had already been suggested. All of these changes served to further de-emphasize the role of athletics on the eight campuses. Partially responsible for this sudden deliberation was the 2001 printing of the book, *The Game of Life*, a work that raises doubt over the importance of collegiate sports in higher education. The book criticizes the intensification of varsity athletics, advocates only the existence of club-sports with unpaid coaches, and calls for an end to all recruiting and athletic scholarships. One of the book's co-authors is William Bowen, former president of Princeton University.(2) Go figure.

Among the proposed changes the *Council* was to consider were: an allotment of seven weeks in the off-season in which there could be no required athletic activity, no voluntary athletic activity with coaching supervision—and specifically for the sport of football, the reduction in the number of annual recruits, from 35 to 30. Mr. Roach wanted to know, upfront from his athletes, what our opinions were on these potential restrictions put on Ivy League athletic teams.

I was outraged when I heard the news from Mr. Roach, mostly because I couldn't help but be insulted. The Ivy League presidents, it seemed to me at the time, were downsizing the importance of something I deeply believed in. I made my objection vocal in the meeting by asking, "Isn't playing a college sport something that we are able to take credit for later on in life? Isn't it something that most of us will put on a job resume? Isn't it *supposed* to be difficult, something that others highly respect? Why should athletes be distinguished if we make collegiate athletics something that is easy to fulfill?" This, I still believe, is a great point. But I was preaching to the choir. My classmates all made similar comments, telling Mr. Roach that if the coaches were forced to cut down practice time, say by five hours per week, then that would be five hours of time that they would just volunteer back to their team. We were athletes who had come to Brown to compete, but the Ivy League wanted to turn their athletic programs into something as admirable as playing hop-skotch after the bell rang.

There were no athletes at Brown being paid for their athletic ability. So, stepping off of the playing fields wouldn't have cost us a dime in extra tuition cost. Nevertheless, the presidents of the Ivy League felt obligated to instruct their athletes as to what they should do with their spare time. But the presidents were not interfering with the lives of any other students, my classmates who were dedicating all of their time to classical literature, the Brown Democrats, or the Young Communist League. No, the *Council* was only coming to the rescue of their athletes. For some reason we were the only ones being forced to consider other campus lifestyles.

Nobody within the Ivy League athletic community agreed with the further diminishment of their athletic programs. Travis Belden, the captain of the University of Pennsylvania's football team, told others, "Athletics is not just hitting someone. It is an irreplaceable, educational experience."(3) James Jones, Yale's basketball coach, said, "The student-athletes that get accepted to Yale know how important academics are."(4) Yale basketball player, Ime Archibong '03, commented, "I think it is pretty closed-minded…I think that it wasn't the answer to getting athletes a better 'Ivy League experience.'"(5) Steve Bilsky, Penn's athletic director, said, "Making changes in policy may make the Ivy League into more of a Division III program than Division I…I am very concerned about the direction of the Ivy League."(6) And Neil Rose, Harvard's quarterback, declared, "It would be a shame to reduce the number of recruited athletes. I think they are some of the most dynamic people I have ever known…How many prominent citizens, businessmen and leaders out there were Ivy League athletes? Those who think Harvard should limit recruiting probably don't know many athletes very well."(8)

Despite fiery objections from their athletic directors, coaches, and athletes, the Ivy presidents took the actions that we expected from them. This arrogant elitism began to feel so familiar to me. The eight presidents of the Ivy League, claiming to have the best interests of their athletes in mind, were ignoring the will of the majority. That's okay. They knew, much more than we ever could, what was best for us.

The fact that this was even going to be discussed by the heads of the Elite Eight was insulting to all of us in that room. They were treating us as if we needed others to help us decide what was important. They didn't believe that we were true student-athletes, who knew beforehand the time that would have to be devoted to our sport, time that would make it extra-difficult to compete with other Brown students in the classroom. But other Ivy League students had risen to this challenge for years. Brendan Reed '03, a pitcher for Harvard's baseball team said, "I've always made time to do the things I wanted outside of baseball, without sacrificing my commitment to the team and my teammates...Often times it means late nights, early mornings, but we all deal with that."(9) So why, all of a sudden, did Ivy League athletes need to be saved from the "clutches" of their sports?

Well, for one thing, this wasn't something that was happening "all of a sudden." The Ivy League, I came to find out, had been reducing the scope of its athletics for years. In 1980 the presidents began to limit practice and game schedules to downscale demands on Ivy athletes. And in 1991 the number of Ivy League football recruits was reduced to 35 from 50. I had never considered the reasons for my own team's restrictions. Pre-season football camp was only allowed to commence three weeks after most other Division I programs, and we would play 10 games while others played 11 or 12. Our season was forced to end before Thanksgiving while other champions of other conferences were allowed to compete in the National 1-AA Playoffs. I guess the Ivy League presidents wished to remain highly distinguished, never wanting to give the impression that the Ivy League cares as much as other schools do about their sports. So there we remained, with the minimum amount of school spirit, and half-filled stadiums. But this made us smarter. Oh yes, much smarter than everyone else.

I closely followed the decision to, yet again, downsize Ivy League sports. But now I found my initial reaction (to be insulted) rather irrelevant to what I was currently focusing on, the supremacy of liberalism on Brown's campus, and the fact that I found athletic values to conflict sharply with the ideals of the modern left. So, no matter what reasons the *Council* gave for lowering athletic standards, there was no one who could deny that for decades sports were being diminished to a mere hobby on Ivy League campuses, that athletes were viewed as conservative dummies, and that this could only have inferred one thing to Ivy League students: The lessons and values learned through athletics are trivial, and carry no worldly significance.

Now it had become clear to me. The rest of the Ivy League had joined Brown in its quest to redefine the all-American. Nobody in 1945 could have imagined how irrelevant the Ivy League would attempt to portray athletic programs. I am inclined to believe that if not for the power of the alumni dollar, a dollar that is handed to the universities often with the thoughts of gridiron glory attached to it, then the Ivy League would have already shed its campuses of these "insignificant games." Instead, the Ivy League has decided to quietly slaughter perhaps the only vehicle of conservatism on their campuses with all the stealth and steadiness of a crouching tiger.

CHAPTER 12
Conservativephobia and Female Ejaculation

Before coming to Brown I had little experience with homosexuality. As you know, I quickly became accustomed to living in a "dorm of diversity." Brown set me up in a living quarters that contained whites, blacks, girls (yay!), Asians, and homosexuals. Cross-dressers were frequently in sight, and the presence of homosexuality could not be ignored. Of course, freshmen were immediately trained to be very sensitive to this gay presence. Some upperclassmen RCs (*Resident Counselors* within freshmen dorms) found it necessary to instill dorm rules that prohibited students from referring to anyone as a "boyfriend" or "girlfriend." To refer to another person using this terminology did not take into account the lifestyles of certain homosexual factions that did not find these terms accurate when referring to a significant other. Whatever.

But this was how complete and total the homosexual agenda was at Brown. The group primarily responsible for advancing certain word restrictions was the LGBTA (Lesbian, Gay, Bisexual, Transsexual Alliance). *Alliance!* Members of the LGBTA were masters of enforcing political correctness, using their skills to let it be known that particular words were deemed insensitive, and therefore off-limits. And once a limited vocabulary was established for the community, it became strikingly clear to everyone that, for certain, particular opinions were unwelcome as well. The LGBTA forced the Brown community to speak with precision, forbidding the utterance of particular thoughts, allowing only certain words at certain times, and even controlling the tone and manner in which those words could be delivered.

The manner in which the LGBTA controlled the campus chatter was complex, and also pretty remarkable. They were a highly organized group of students that was never out of sight. Again, their most astonishing accomplishment was the creation of their very own campus language. The LGBTA had actually invented their own vocabulary, demonstrating to spectators the surefootedness one should have before speaking of matters concerning homosexuality. Within their very own name the LGBTA specified which types of sexually estranged people they represented, delicately ordering the community to be conscious and sensitive to the fact that they weren't *just* "gay." In fact, some LGBTA sub-groups existed exclusively for specific ethnicities (imagine if I had begun an *all-white* dating group!). I frequently saw the LGBTA's name in subtle variation. Sometimes it was the GLBTA, and other times it was the LGBTQ. Or the GLTBQQ. But then, out of nowhere, they often found it more convenient to just collectively call themselves "queer," or the "Queer Alliance." Was I allowed to do the same? I wasn't sure. The LGBTA would use words such as "queering" and "heteronormative" and "gender normativity." They referred to certain "queers" as "cross gender" and "transgender" and "transgendered" and "gender variant" and "gender non-conforming." But some were "genderqueer" and "gender neutral." The LGBTA spoke of "gender identity" and "sexual identity" and "queer identity." They organized a "Trans Day" and a "Coming Out Week" and a "Pride Month" where they encouraged "queerlings" and other "allied students" to "combat" "homophobia" and "queerphobia" and "heterosexism" and "heterosexual privilege." And also to talk about "queer-related" and "rainbowlicious" issues. Was anyone just "gay" or "lesbian" anymore? Apparently, it was sometimes more appropriate to call some people "bi" or "bisexual" or "trans" or "transsexual" or "trans folks" or "transmen" or "trannyfags" living in "interracial" and "trans communities." Some were "same gender loving" and "two-spirited" and "intersex." Others were just "questioning."(1)

All of the LGBTA's gobbledygook confused the hell out of me. But that was the point, to keep everyone intellectually off-balance. The only thing I knew for sure was that the LGBTA would not be content until every corner of the University agreed to acknowledge their sexual lifestyle as normal and harmless, and also succumb to their claim that gays were unwelcome on College Hill. And of course, they believed that there couldn't be any intelligent reasons for opposing any portion of the gay agenda. Only bigotry. "Homophobia," they called it. So the LGBTA thought their primary aim should be to allow others to *just get to know them a little bit.* Proclaiming it vital to the queer community that they exercise more "verbal recognition of their presence, particularly within Greek organizations," one guest lecturer "used games such as calculating a G.P.A.—Gay Point Average—to quiz straight audience members on 'gay culture,' asking them the color of the gay flag (pink) and the shape used to represent gay activism (the triangle)." (2) Cool.

There was so much wrong with Brown's LGBTA, but all opposition to them was met with the "homophobe lie," that any criticism gays fell under could only be due to homophobia, a hateful condition causing the bigotry of heterosexuals, their fear of homosexuals, or their own inner homosexuality. Therefore, the LGBTA kept the campus saturated with discussions and accusations of "hate crimes." But I just couldn't go along with the LGBTA's campus perception of homophobia. The only reason I had to fear a homosexual on campus was that I had to be very wary of what I said when that particular classmate of mine was around. I had to be certain not to get into an altercation with a homosexual, or say the word "boyfriend" around him/her/person. And certainly, I could never have offered a conservative political opinion concerning queer issues, such as gay marriage. These were things that could easily ignite a charge of homophobia, and cause an entire campus to scowl at me as they portrayed me as a hateful and homophobic Christian. This was Brown's *actual* homophobia. Nevertheless, the LGBTA successfully achieved their desired campus outlook, a University that was failing to offer homosexual students a safe refuge. But the truth was this; at Brown it was easier for a homosexual to come out of the closet, than for a conservative to do the same. The LGBTA would likely call this "conservativephobia."

EVERYTHING was About Their Agenda

Brown's homosexuals, individually, did not bother me. Their presence did not disgust me, even after several inappropriate encounters with a few of them. Early in my freshman year one of my male classmates called me on the phone only to describe what sexual acts he wished to perform with me. Click. And I *know* another classmate of mine crossed the decency line when he tried to kiss me at a dark late-night party. Twice! With more class than should have been expected from me, I brushed these instances aside quietly. So, I had to reject the charges of homophobia that always came my way after I criticized the LGBTA. It was neither hatred nor fear that prompted me to criticize the LGBTA, but rather it was their attempts to exalt homosexuality, their public displays of indecency, and their effort to sustain the campus image of a "Gay vs. Straight" heavyweight bout.

My column concerning the protest at President Bush's Inauguration had nothing to do with race, gender, or sexual orientations. It was merely a commentary on my classmates' willingness to protest no-matter-what. During my claim that many of the protesters only went down to Washington to discharge some youthful zeal, I said that Brown students only protested at the Inauguration so they could say someday, "Oh yes son, I protested at George W.'s Inauguration. I even flipped him the bird."(3) And somehow one of my classmates, who probably hadn't protested in *at least* a couple of weeks, managed to turn this line into a discussion about homophobia:

> "Hetero-Sexist!
>
> Travis Rowley claims that all Brown students went to protest the inauguration just so that they could say that they were there. 'Oh, yes son, I protested at George W's inauguration. I even flipped him the bird.' As someone who did partake in the expression of free speech during the midst of a racist coup, I would like to say that Rowley's statement is extremely homophobic. Although many GLBT (Gay, Lesbian, Bisexual, Transsexual) and Queer people do adopt or have biological children, many Queer people and families do not have the same institutional and cultural privilege to form such families. As a result of the blatant heterosexist language used in the racist article, Travis' article loses all its legitimacy in my eyes."(4)

Another objector to my Inauguration column, and someone who attended the protest, stated, "As the Black Panthers who took over a bleacher near me on Inaug[uration] Day shouted, 'Racist, sexist, anti-gay, Travis Rowley go away!'"(5) At Brown, anything that defied any portion of the total liberal mantra was instantly considered a bigoted assault, and was an opportunity for all campus groups to attain recognition. This compelled all components of the campus left to rush to an offensive position, crying bigotry while also achieving the silence of any other potential critics.

This type of context-twisting was common, and was especially overused by the LGBTA. Their cause, their agenda, and their minority status were always at the forefront of their minds. Overly blatant was their top priority—to keep their victim-hood visible in order to normalize their sexual lifestyles. "Images of gay sexuality need to be put out in public because people like Rowley need to get themselves used to it," one of my classmates told the Brown community after a column of mine attacked the LGBTA.(6) On Valentine's Day the LGBTA recruited homosexuals to participate in a public, homosexual make-out session on what they considered "the most heteronormative day of the year."(7) According to the LGBTA, the make-out session was being done to "combat" sexual normalcy "for the sake of queer visibility and activism." To liberals, "queer visibility" was the answer to conservative bigotry. If they could "promote desensitization to gay romantic imagery,"(8) then they would win the battle of the minds against those "conservatives who hate gay people."(9)

Tagged with much irony, the lifestyle the LGBTA was promoting and glorifying was the same one they always claimed was nobody's business but the person practicing it.

Sex, Power, and God

Every year the LGBTA hosted a couple of large parties in an attempt to familiarize the rest of the students with their sexual lifestyles. The two most popular ones were called *Sex, Power, God* and *Starf*ck.* These parties were advertised for a couple of weeks before the event, and the advertisements were as much about homosexuality as they were about the party itself. The LGBTA used large posters to promote these events, and they slung them up all over Brown's campus so that they were not only visible to students, but also to Brown visitors and neighbors. They would also place table-slips on Brown's cafeteria tables to advertise their parties. Table-slips were notecard-sized advertisements that were always scattered throughout the cafeteria in order to publicize upcoming events, or to promote some student-group's agenda.

It wasn't that the LGBTA posters were large and visible so that people could see that the gay community was hosting a party. I didn't mind that people were aware that gays were in abundance on Brown's campus. It was the fact that images of naked men licking each other's nipples, two naked women groping one another, and four men having group sex were staring the campus in the face. And I knew I was forbidden to disapprove. One of these posters literally portrayed four naked men lined up in a shower-room, each having anal sex with the man in front of him. Yes, some of the pictures were tactful, portraying clothed men pecking one another, and women doing likewise. But the LGBTA always cleverly pushed the limits, never missing an opportunity to create at least a couple of offensive images that would hopefully ignite an objection. They were always crossing the line of common decency to reel in bigots, but I never thought their extremism was a valid hook.

Since the administration never found it necessary or worthwhile to forbid, or merely criticize, the LGBTA's posters, I took it upon myself to do so.

A NORMAL POINT OF VIEW
by Travis Rowley

LGBTA'S SEX POSTERS INTENDED TO GENERATE CONTROVERSY

> While eating lunch one day last week I had a disturbing thing happen to me. I slid my tray over to make room for a friend, and much to my surprise I was suddenly staring at one of the Ratty's famous table-slips with a picture of two men having anal sex in a shower. Needless to say, I couldn't finish that second hotdog.
>
> [T]he advertisements for these events...are meant to get a negative reaction from just one student who is appalled. That is all the LGBTA needs to start a riot on campus, and there is nothing they would love more...They can't just put up signs that read "Party Hosted by Gay Community." No way, not extreme enough to reel in a homophobe nowadays. They need to take the fight to the next level by posting porn all over our campus...because they have ulterior motives other than just the promotion of a party...They put up those posters and asked, "What are ya gonna do about it, huh?"...These actions are too over-active for the environment they are in. I suggest

other means of finishing your mission of equality besides throwing gasoline on the spark by showing a bunch of men "starf*cking" in the shower.

Tagline: Travis Rowley is from Narragansett, RI. He admits that he may be wrong about this entire issue, but he doesn't think so.

Travis, the Mind-Reader

To me, it was blatantly obvious that the LGBTA was more concerned with justifying the existence of a student-group than actually acquiring equality, or any other respectable foundation for activism. Their persistent attempts to spin every incident into a case of homophobia were evident, but also unspeakable. Of course, I met the natural resistance to my claim. There were some who had a problem with me accusing the LGBTA of having an ulterior motive that drove them to create their offensive posters. How could I possibly know the minds and intentions of others? My column was "unsubstantiated," some declared.

Well, what else could I conclude? As someone coming from a gay-less background, I could only draw two conclusions. Either the LGBTA's posters were meant to trigger a response, or they were an accurate reflection of gays' overly promiscuous lifestyles, a reputation I found the homosexual community consistently calling a bigoted stereotype. Imagine the repercussions if I had offered the latter conclusion, telling the entire campus that the posters were proof of homosexuals' crudeness and immorality. No, these posters were an annual opportunity for an uproar, not the result of one person's bad taste, but rather the result of a learned political strategy. And along with other examples of their consistent campus zealotry, I reached my final opinion on the LGBTA.

Keep in mind that I was attacking the LGBTA, not Brown's gay community. One thing I became aware of was that the LGBTA was not an entirely accurate representation of all homosexuals. Some homosexuals at Brown wanted nothing to do with the extremism and spotlight brought on by these radicals. One gay student told the campus:

"Starf*ck posters have a direct effect on me and any other gay persons' relationship with the larger community. These

> misrepresentations are problematic because their images are so closely aligned with widespread misconceptions that consistently act as barriers to gay rights. They portray gays as hypersexual and irresponsible...How can we hope to advance gay rights if those who claim to represent the gay community consistently misrepresent us in a manner that is no different from the way the most right-winged, anti-gay bigot would choose to slander us?"(10)

I could have done without the "right-winged, anti-gay bigot" line, but the writer was making a valid point. Nevertheless, another student who represented the majority opinion told the campus, "I hope [Travis] never goes to Europe, where depictions of sex and sexuality are far more common—he'd discover that his repulsion about 'pornography' is not much more than parochial American narrow-mindedness."(11) (This notion that Europe is some sort of "beacon of enlightenment" was something I came to notice more and more on Brown's campus).

Others didn't blame my opinions on "narrow-mindedness." In typical Brown fashion, they labeled me a bigot. Such turbulence occurred after my column. So many charges of homophobia and intolerance on my part. "Chill [Travis] and don't deny people civil rights because a few are enthusiastic," one member of the Brown community wrote.(12) Another said, "Don't play the homophobe card, warns Rowley...? Of course it's homophobia! Duh!"(13) And another told the Brown community, "His homophobia seems obvious and I think he needs to deal with it rather than deny it."(14) Yes, I will work on it. I promise.

Strange, though. So many members of the Brown community were calling me a homophobe. Yet, the following years I noticed that the *Starf*ck* and *Sex, Power, God* posters were much more tame, certainly void of the graphic depictions from previous years. Why would the LGBTA demonize me as an anti-gay homophobe, but then take action that seemed to suggest that they agreed with what I had said?

Sex, Sex, Sex, Sex, Sex, Sex.........Sex!

Besides the LGBTA's radical political activity, there was one more reason for my disapproval of their campus activism, their unabashed encouragement of reckless promiscuity. While college campuses are renowned for sexual discovery, my alma mater was shameless with its glorification of sexual adventurism. The LGBTA's political tactics only added to a horrific lack of modesty concerning sexual behavior.

Now, I am, in fact, a product of our nation's sexual revolution, entirely unflinching to homosexuality, pornography and sexual exploration. However, I found absolutely *nothing* sacred about sexual behavior on Brown's campus. And while this openness was something that I youthfully enjoyed, and thought was more hysterical than offensive, I was raised to believe in the sanctity of intercourse, and some sort of moral compos that guides sexual behavior. But the LGBTA, like all campus forces, was training me to reconsider my upbringing.

Remember, Brown liberals considered opposition to their desires as a result of hatred, or an irrational clinging to unenlightened Christian values. As they assumed my bigotry (after all, I was a straight, white, male Catholic), liberals believed that all they had to do to convert me into an "ally" was show me how nice they were, and then numb my eyes to the sight of anything hypersexual. If their pornographic posters didn't do the trick, and if I was unable to attend Starf*ck, then I could go to some of their other functions. For instance, the LGBTA frequently sponsored lectures by infamous pornographers. They organized "drag shows" and "porn parties." And they conducted oral-sex and anal-sex "workshops." These were not quiet happenings, but rather open and advertised to a campus where nobody dared to question the LGBTA's unapologetic efforts to sexually radicalize the student body.

There may have been only one other campus sect that outmatched the LGBTA when it came to the University's decline of sexual morality—Brown women.

Boobie Traps

My female classmates were intelligent, highly confident, capable, and actually outnumbered the males in Brown's undergraduate student body. None of their qualities shocked me, however. I did not walk onto campus and say, *Wow, these girls are smart! I don't believe it!* I was aware of the capabilities of women before arriving at Brown, and I was never threatened by women who were smarter or more equipped for success than myself. But that's what my opponents always said.

"You just have no respect for women! That's your problem!" one of my female classmates shouted at me during a party on the deck of my own off-campus apartment senior year. My reply: "What are you talking about? I love girls! I think they're hot!" You'll have to forgive my sarcasm. I was slightly tired of my classmates harassing me at bars and keg parties.

I grew up in a time where boys were ordered to respect girls as equals, that women were just as capable beings as men. And for the most part, I had learned that girls *were* of equal status in terms of intelligence and capability. However, my experiences often fused with my common sense telling me that there were also significant and fundamental differences between the sexes. Still, people at Brown just didn't agree with my traditional views when it came to women, and they searched for the origin of what they referred to as my "sexism" and "Neanderthal" viewpoints.

I was unfamiliar with feminism. Well, the type of feminism that existed on Brown's campus, that is. However, I was able to recognize similarities between Brown's feminists and other campus activist groups. Some parallels that could always be drawn between them were a claim to victimization, and a radical political strategy to achieve that reputation. And there was a history.

In the early 1990s Brown was the setting of an infamous, high-profile Title IX court case that helped in the dismantling of men's athletic programs throughout the country when one of Brown's female athletes sued the University for discrimination. Also in the speech code era of the 1990s, shaky precedents of sexual harassment and rape allegations afforded Brown seats on national media outlets showing the nation that Brown women were holding significant power over their male classmates. Brown also has a large lesbian population, and the LGBTA was one of the most influential and boisterous groups on campus. It was also reported to me that in 1999, a certain men's magazine had rated Brown University among the worst 10 colleges/universities for a male student to attend. A major criteria for the ratings was the degree of feminist fervor found at the universities. I found it notable that even outsiders could recognize the intense feminism that emulated off of the Ivy League campus.

Years of feminist attempts at increasing female empowerment had caused Brown's definition of sexual harassment to evolve into a pro-female definition. Brown's *Office of Equal Employment and Affirmative Action declares:*

> **"Sexual harassment need not be intentional. Under Brown's sexual harassment policies, the intent of the person who is alleged to have behaved improperly is not relevant to determining whether a violation of Brown's policy has occurred. The relevant determination is whether a reasonable person could have interpreted the alleged behavior to be sexual."**

I guess Brown men were safe because one thing was for sure—my female classmates were not "reasonable."

VAGINA

As a junior I began to see how the radical feminist outlook, one that sought to alter the course of nature, and blame women's societal position on men, could have negative affects on our society. Like most special-interest groups on campus, I began to sense something wrong with the feminist movement, something amiss that was at least slightly affecting the minds of most members of the Brown community.

The she-pimp from Chapter 3 gave me a glimpse of the type of liberal feminism that I would witness throughout my career at Brown. One of my later encounters with radical feminism occurred one day during my junior year inside the main campus cafeteria.

There I was again sitting at one of Brown's cafeteria tables getting ready to have my appetite spoiled by disgusting student activism. This time it was not the LGBTA trying to incite a campus riot with one of their table-slips, but the Brown Feminists. There were about a dozen table-slips in front of me advertising various campus events. The most noticeable one was bright-red, and it had a single word written on it in bold capital letters. **VAGINA**. Nothing else was written on the table slip. Just **VAGINA**. My intuition told me that it was the Brown Feminists who had placed these monstrosities all over the cafeteria tables. I couldn't say that for sure, though, because no organization had signed its name to these vagina-slips.

I was confused, but also very interested. I mean, I liked vagina, but I wondered why the feminists felt a need to remind me of female genitalia as I ate my lunch. I was quite vexed, so I asked several people about the slips. They told me that the purpose of the vagina-slips was to make people comfortable with the word "vagina." Feminist theory was that people are comfortable referring to a penis in a variety of ways, but explicit references to female sexuality make people cringe. Oh. Alright.

The following day I went back to the cafeteria for lunch (I don't know why I kept eating there). Anyway, this time I found what appeared to be the same exact table-slip on my table. It too was bright-red and had the word "vagina" on it. The fems pulled a fast one on the rest of the campus, however. They put out a batch of new-and-improved vagina-slips in the middle of the night while others slept. This time they issued double-sided table-slips. One side had the forbidden V-word on it. But when I turned my new vagina-slip over and read what they had printed on the back, it said: **HOW DOES IT SMELL?**

Well, I guess it depended on the vagina that they were talking about. I thought back to the supposed purpose of these vagina-slips: normalization of the word "vagina." I hadn't wholeheartedly agreed with the assumption that a table-slip that said "penis" on it was more appetizing to people than one that said "vagina." Now, my classmates seemed to be suggesting that people would actually be pleased to see a table-slip that read: *Penis, how does it taste?*

Besides my bewilderment with feminist logic, was it appropriate to put things like vagina-slips on the cafeteria tables? Was the anonymous feminist organization going to be allowed to do so without impunity? Yes, they were. Nobody on campus even flinched.

But how could anyone flinch? The vagina-slips were nothing compared to other productions of the Brown feminists. For instance, their campus sex-toy workshops. That's right. Sex-toy "workshops." But perhaps the most unforgettable feminist event was the airing of the female ejaculation video, which featured four disturbed women masturbating to the point of ejaculation. Awesome. Just awesome.

I heard about the female ejaculation video from yet another public campus advertisement. *Come see women ejaculate! Salomon Hall, Wednesday 4pm.* Of course, I wouldn't miss it. I actually arrived early to grab a seat in the front row with my two roommates. We laughed our asses off.

It may not surprise the reader by now to learn that the female ejaculation video was not something that was aired in an off-campus dwelling. This was not something that was intended to be hidden from University administrators. Rather, this was an event inside a Brown educational facility, approved by the University. After some time, this is what I found most disturbing, the fact that administrators were never present to chastise radical feminists, or other sexual extremists, for turning the campus into one big Hustler Magazine.

Again, here was the administration using the energy and verve of their students to create a haven for anything liberal. If serious criticism ever came, the administration had an easy out. *Hey, it wasn't us. I didn't know what was going on. But we'll be sure to solve this problem right away.* Yeah, right. Concerning instances of campus pornography, whether it was the LGBTA posters or the fems' masturbation video, Brown's administration never saw a need to oppose their indecency. This refusal to oppose my classmates, and the fact that they were allowed to use Brown's facilities for their purposes, could only suggest that the administration was actually endorsing their behavior. Or, if you're still not comfortable incriminating the administration for student activity, then consider the fact that the administration-run Sarah Doyle Women's Center hosts and conducts "female orgasm workshops" for all Brown women. It's a well-known fact that more females apply to Brown each year than young men. Geez, now I know why.

I must admit, as a student, I found this sexual openness as funny as it was repulsive. Perhaps my attendance at the female ejaculation video was motivated by a little more than my need for opposition research. But where were the adults who should have been in charge of the University? Shouldn't they have been concerned with a campus environment in which students had about as much sexual restraint as dogs in heat? Did I find Brown's sexual immorality humorous? Of course. Would I send my *own* son or daughter to Brown? Absolutely not.

At Brown, the message was clearly this: *Have sex. Lots of it. And with as many partners as possible. Gay sex with five other men in a shower if you prefer.* And I couldn't help but notice it again, liberalism was not asking people to do better, or to be better. Instead the message was: *Just do whatever feels good right now, young ones. Nothing of sacrifice, discipline, or responsibility matters. And don't go worrying about any "consequences." Especially pregnancy. There's an easy way out of that.*

Abortion

After a Republican President was elected in 2000, the campus fems began to push the importance of women's right to *choose*. Discussions, forums, and invited guest speakers were frequent occurrences, and I attended quite a few of them. Abortion became an issue that I formed a passionate opinion about, and it was pro-choice arguments that I felt epitomized leftist thought.

I found Brown's pro-choicers demanding compassion for women who become pregnant. A very *liberal* thing to do. The pregnancy will cause HER to drop out of school. The pregnancy will cause HER to leave her job. The pregnancy will cause HER embarrassment. The pregnancy will make HER poor. The pregnancy will cause HER mental and physical stress. And the insignificant sperm-donor will likely abandon HER. And, he'll probably beat HER up before he leaves. That's the thought-process I witnessed from those pushing the abortion agenda.

I also began to see the feminist movement laced with an unhealthy man-hating sentiment. This was understandable. In order for feminists to convince others of their second-class citizenship, and their claim to victim-hood, eventually they would have to point their fingers toward their persecutors. Women's History Month was usually accompanied by a ceremonial march for rape victims, sponsored by a national organization called *Take Back the Night*. Every year the Brown Feminists made sure that ludicrous statistics were reported in *The Herald* that revealed that an astonishingly high percentage of female college students had either been raped or sexually harassed while on campus. I needed no political experience to wince at the annual reports that told me that 90% of my female classmates would be sexually harassed before they graduated, and that one out of three would be raped.

We must now bring a Brown education to its wide-screen format. Young male students arrive on campus and are offered an unlimited supply of dormitory condoms. With the help of a banana, they are shown how to use them. Then, they are invited to oral sex workshops, sex-toy workshops, female ejaculation videos, and countless lectures on pornography. They are then blamed for viewing women only as sexual objects as they are washed through the liberal rhetoric of male insensitivity. While trying to live a normal college life that includes dating, and eventual sexual encounters, they are immersed in a crowd of young female students who are encouraged by influential campus forces to think of themselves as oppressed victims of rape, sexual harassment, and a "glass ceiling." As long as a female student wishing to levy charges against a male student can be perceived as a "reasonable person" she can proceed to ruin the life of any male student wishing to court her. The boy's "intent" is seen as irrelevant. This was the scheme of sexual divisiveness. And this wretched backwardness eventually came into focus for me.

The distrustful division Brown feminists attempted to create between men and women was visible primarily by paying attention to the feminists' opinions on the abortion issue. Brown's feminists didn't believe that *couples* became pregnant. They believed that only women reaped the consequences of intercourse. They would insist that all men desert the women they impregnate, a notion that I found not only ludicrous, but another attempt to pit women against their *oppressors*. Then, the fems would always declare that the few men who did "stick around" should have no say in whether an abortion will take place or not. The man should have no input at all, even if the insignificant sperm-guy objects to the abortion on moral grounds. Then, campus feminists ensured that men's opinions would have no bearing on pregnancy decisions by discrediting their rationale on abortion. They did this by declaring that a man's opinion was one that was hopelessly insensitive because...well... he's a man! All men do is discriminate against women, rape women, and then abandon women when they're pregnant. If a woman is lucky, the man will be late for work, and therefore won't have the time to give her one last beating. These insulting and disrespectful views for men I could only see as hateful, or were opinions that showed no regard for the feelings or opinions of men. So, I decided to label the feminist movement as "man-hating."

I submitted a column on feminism to *The Herald* that dealt with the abortion issue, and a few days after it was printed, I attended a pro-choice play. It was written and directed by one of my classmates, who requested my presence (I guess she wanted me to learn something). The play was made up of short skits portraying young women coping with unwanted pregnancies, and glorifying the act of abortion by showing the heavy load that was lifted from their shoulders after their abortions. At the end, a panel of "professionals" took questions from the crowd. I waited a while, and toward the end of the discussion session I stood up and asked the writer/director a question. "All of these stories within your play make an appeal to the sensitivity of this crowd. So, where do you think pro-lifers are coming from? Are they people of less compassion? Why would they still be opposed to legalized abortion after seeing your play?"

One of the panelists answered for her, "The problem *is* that we have a bunch of Neanderthal men with no respect for women. I don't know if anyone read *The Herald* a few days ago, but...." He was cut off as everyone else began to laugh, knowing exactly who I was. That's okay. Just keep saying stuff that proves my point.

The panelist's comment was telling. At Brown, all liberals had to do to validate their message was associate alternative perspectives with bigotry, stupidity, or Neanderthals. This tactic discredited conservatism right off the bat, impressing upon students the notion that investigating traditional thought would be a painful waste of time. If they were going to listen to a conservative, then they might as well read Hitler's *Mein Kampf* while they're at it.

These were the types of opinions that began to get under my skin, so when Patricia Ireland, the president of NOW (National Organization for Women), visited Brown during *Women's History Month* to re-emphasize the feminist outlook, I replied to her visit with my own feelings on feminism. Below is the column that made me a Neanderthal. Argh.

A NORMAL POINT OF VIEW—Travis Rowley
Despite What Feminists Say, Women Still Need Men

> Radical feminists lead an anti-men movement that teaches young women not to trust men, that men are their enemies...For instance, feminists make the constant claim that men (the enemy) do everything in their power to keep women out of high positions in the business world. They call it "sexual discrimination," and the enemy faces it everyday. The truth is that men aren't holding women down at all, nature is. Women bear children, and when they do their careers come in second...Women have tried for so long to break into the corporate world just as the fems ordered...What really is driving the fems up the wall is that more and more women are giving up their careers

for their motherhood, proving that there are fundamental differences between men and women...Housewives don't exist because of sexism. They exist because it is what women naturally choose to become...It doesn't have to do with women being naturally better at cooking and cleaning, but when you're home all day you eventually find your way to the kitchen.

The fems tell them that this is a bad thing; that women should not give up their careers for their children...[and] the fems have convinced women that it's okay to have a child without a father figure, that women do not need the enemy to be successful. As a result, the illegitimacy rate in this country has increased dramatically...[women] are now raising their kids without the help of a male partner. The fems will have you believe that this is because men are jerks who abandon the women they impregnate. The real reason is because women today are told to give men the impression that they are not needed. Did men all of a sudden become less sensitive than before? No, women became militant...Now, in order for women to succeed at the workplace they must abandon their children. Most choose day care or babysitters to replace the role of the parents. Without the presence of parents children just don't learn basic American family values. Then we have more children with discipline problems, drug problems, alcohol problems...

Patricia Ireland told us that she hopes women can "begin the 21st century by taking real power." Ireland realizes that in order for women to have a chance to succeed in the workplace they need abortion to remain legal.

Tagline: Ladies, Travis is a junior from Narragansett,

RI. He enjoys candlelight dinners and long walks on the beach. Shall we start the bidding?(16)

I Just Wanted Some Ketchup

Well, I probably should have known better than to have shown my face that day. My column had prompted furious anger within some of my classmates. One of them actually informed the Brown community that my column was "border[ing] on hate speech against women," and another student roared, "I'd buy Mr. Rowley...and then castrate him, dress him in a french maid costume, and make him serve my girlfriend and I on his hands and knees. Women don't "need" men, Mr. Rowley. Thousands of us do just fine without you, thank you."(17)

I was in the crowded cafeteria again, and I needed some ketchup for my French fries. I was at the condiment dispenser watching the ketchup poor out onto my plate. While I was pumping the handle that dispensed the ketchup I heard a woman's voice yell out with insult, "Hey Rowley! Great article this morning!" I looked up to see one of my female classmates standing by the ice cream machine, glaring at me. She finished off her attack, "Yeah, real nice!" I didn't know what to say, and there was an audience. I just smiled and returned to my table. What is it with distressed girls and ice cream?

At Brown, this was the consequence I was forced to accept if I wished to stress the importance of the family unit, family values, and a pro-life position. Not that I cared all that much, or that I was bothered by being yelled at in front of a bunch of people. In fact, I expected such a reaction. Besides, I was beginning to be under the impression that if my classmates became upset with something I wrote, then I was probably saying something right.

Travis is a Man's Name

Every year Spring would arrive with *Women's History Month* on its back, a free piggy-back ride aimed at reminding everyone of what female genitalia smells like, and what men are *really* good for—rape, oppression, and sperm donations.

Again, one leftist point of view on abortion that I could never stomach was the notion that abortion is a "men vs. women" issue. A female classmate of mine said after my first column, "The suggestion that the increase in single-parent families is a result of feminism is absurd. Rather, this is a result of fathers who don't stay around to take responsibility for their children because of their sexist beliefs (apparently shared by Mr. Rowley) that only women are responsible for their children."(18) **Translation:** Rowley is a sexist.

Brown's pro-choicers always suggested that a man's opinion on the abortion debate was not valid. Apparently, a man could not have a legitimate opinion on the matter because he was not the one who became physically pregnant. A man was simply unable to understand, or truly grasp the anguish a woman feels by acquiring an unwanted pregnancy. This was true unless the man was pro-choice. In this case, his opinion held water because this man had proven himself as one of those new-age hipsters in touch with his feminine side, rather than the "Neanderthal" hunting-type unable to understand the hardship of pregnancy. I usually heard this point made vocally within spoken debate, but in a letter-to-the-editor in *The Herald* after my column on abortion, one female student made the opinion public voicing that, "Rowley will never have to make a decision about abortion, nor will he ever have to face anti-female discrimination."(19) **Translation:** Rowley is a sexist.

I guess I can never understand what being discriminated against feels like, or ever feel what it's like to be desperate, isolated, trapped, or terrified. My life is just honky-dory because I was born with a penis, and the validity of my opinion is, therefore, discredited. It was that particular point that was cleverly submitted into my column by someone at *The Herald* before it was printed.

The last column I ever wrote for *The Herald* was another one on the topic of abortion. It had to be my last one because of the fight I got into with *The Herald* editors for the action they decided to take after I submitted my column on this controversial issue. They certainly would never print anything I submitted to them after the argument we engaged in the day my column was printed. I said some nasty things.

The "men-just-don't-understand" argument was used against me at Brown every time I debated the issue with my classmates. It was their fail-safe line of reasoning pulled out of their arsenal whenever they were painted into a corner. I was a man incapable of understanding. I never expected someone to be so offended by my article, and to feel so compelled to discredit me, that they would distort the content of my column to make their own political points. But that's exactly what happened, and in my anger I made sure they realized the error of their ways. Before I go any further you need to hear the argument that I used to defend my position:

A NORMAL POINT OF VIEW by Travis Rowley

If Abortion Is Not Murder, Then Nothing Is

Empathy and Female Empowerment Are No Excuse For the Murder of the Innocent

> Sarah Weddington, a leader of the nonsensical feminist movement who successfully argued Roe v. Wade before the U.S. Supreme Court, lectured at Brown on April 14, and she shrieked all of the typical pro-choice arguments, exhibiting the fact that the lunacy of the feminist movement starts right at the top.
>
> Forget all the scientific studies from both sides of the abortion argument that try to show when life may begin or not. Both sides show different results, and leave us with much doubt as to the validity of the studies. However, it is this doubt that proves the immorality of abortion. Ask yourself this: When a child has just exited a vagina, can you kill it? No. How about one minute before the birth? I wouldn't think so. How about one hour before the birth? One day? One week? One month? So, keep going backwards through time and tell me when it is okay to terminate the life of the child. Believe it or not, there are those out there who will be so arrogant as to tell you when.

Nobody knows when life begins. So, shouldn't we give life, our most precious gift, the benefit of the doubt? You would think so, but instead we have millions of selfish people who support the disgusting act of abortion. They believe in terminating the life they started for their own selfish reasons. These reasons include preserving the way of life they always envisioned for themselves, financial status, fear of losing the respect of friends and family, and being able to keep their jobs or stay in school.

The most selfish and ridiculous reason for believing in the justification of abortion is to achieve the empowerment of women in our society. Weddington, in her lecture, seemed to want to prove that women use abortion as a tool for gaining power over men when she said that before abortion was legalized "women who became pregnant had no choice but to leave college and their jobs." She also remarked, "Nothing is more important to a woman's liberty than the ability to make such decisions regarding her pregnancy."

These are typical comments from a radical feminist. When Patricia Ireland, the president of the National Organization for Women, visited Brown last year, she told her crowd that she hoped women could "begin the 21st-century by taking real power." It's important to realize that these types of radical feminists will go to ridiculous measures to achieve this power. Weddington also seemed to exhibit the typical feminist bitterness towards men when she relived her glory days by telling the crowd that men used to cry, "Women cannot do what a man can." And how proudly she added, "we would ask why."

Tagline: Travis Rowley is a *male* senior from Narragansett,

Rhode Island. He has never killed anybody. And he is sure of that because he has never had an abortion.(20)

There were some within *The Herald* that did not appreciate my column, and it infuriated those people so much that they had the audacity to believe that they could edit the content of my column to advance their own personal values.

You see, the taglines at the end of every column were often used for satire or to describe where the writer of the column was from. I always liked to also use it to arrogantly reiterate the point I had made within my column. Notice the word "male" within my tagline. I didn't put that word in. My submitted tagline read "Travis Rowley is a senior from Narragansett, Rhode Island." I didn't feel my gender had anything to do with my opinion, or that it was necessary to tell Brown students that "Travis" is a man's name.

I had been writing for *The Herald* for almost two years, and any everyday reader of the newspaper was familiar with me. There was no need to clarify what my gender was. Besides, I referred to myself as "he" three times within my tagline. Didn't that lead people to believe that the writer must have been a male? I mean, besides Brown's transsexuals, what female writer preferred to call herself "he"?

I made a point to inspect every tagline in every column printed for the next few weeks. Not one defined the gender of the writer. So you see, there was only one possible reason why someone would slip the word "male" into my column—to make their *own* political point, and to discredit *my* opinion while doing so. This is what Brown's culture of intolerance taught students to do in the face of political opposition. Simply don't allow room for it.

I wouldn't say I flipped out right away. It took a few minutes. I may have been in shock. It was difficult for me to believe that an *opinions* editor of a newspaper would get his/her duties of editing for space and material confused with editing *actual opinions*. So before I did anything I went back to my computer (where I had my column saved) just to make sure that I really didn't write the word "male" in my tagline. Just as I thought, I hadn't.

There's not much to tell from there. I called *The Herald* once or twice and was given the runaround. My phone calls weren't returned.

I then harshly emailed one of the editors who I initially suspected was responsible for tampering with my column's message. She (female) fought back viciously with some emails of her own. She placed the blame on someone else, who I then contacted. He (male) denied it. Nobody knew anything. Then, all contact with me ceased. Nobody would return my phone calls or email me back. They just shut up and prayed that I wouldn't make a bigger deal out of this than I already had. And I didn't. I was too busy that week. I had an intramural softball game and a hot date (female). So, I couldn't deal with those little pea-brains running around *The Herald.*

Obstructionists, Not Thinkers

Even my closest friends at Brown didn't understand me. *But Travis, your tagline was so insensitive. What about those Brown students who have had an abortion? You just told them that they may have killed a person!*

Liberalism was all about feelings, and now I realize that that is what was bothering me the most. I have stated it in earlier chapters—leftists took the fight out of everything. For some reason, I took serious issue with a shrinking aptitude to tolerate mental anguish. It was the feminization of our overall mentality, and the willingness to distort reality in order to save people from insult that bothered me the most. For me, the abortion issue was only a side-dish to a larger meal—the University's diminishing ability to discover truth.

No doubt, Brown's culture of intolerance is what prompted the editors' actions. An atmosphere of elitism and narrow-mindedness had only the capacity to offer one lesson, one that taught students that their political fury caused by foreign opinion justifies the obstruction of fair dialogue, and academic freedom. Ivy League doctrine was telling students that the abuse of power will be socially accepted if that abuse is to push an agenda that one finds important enough. The ruthless game of politics was being taught to be played at the most dishonest levels, and our nation's brightest young liberals were bringing that lesson to America's infrastructure.

My altercation with *The Herald* demonstrated liberals' preparedness to distort public argument, to betray freedom. This was instruction to be carried beyond the Ivy borders. We are sadly mistaken if we believe this ethic was not taken into the outside world, that an isolated incident concerning a tiny campus newspaper was not a microcosm of what was happening inside the walls of Brown University, that students were not becoming the people they would be for the rest of their lives during their college years. Suddenly I was waking up next to a frightening reality—liberty was not entirely protected. Some sort of morality had to guide our freedom. Could anyone have felt safe knowing that the person responsible for tampering with my column could some day be the chief editor for the *New York Times*? A Supreme Court Justice? A U.S. President? If such a renowned and prestigious place of scholarship could be morphed into an intolerable chamber of intellectual imbalance, then why not the halls of Congress?

My frustration with Brown University was at an all-time high. Yes, the word "male" probably went unnoticed by most readers, and I'm sure the point I was trying to make in my tagline is what really sunk in to most readers' heads. But at this point it had been four years of my ideas being publicly distorted, four years of stomaching the hypocrisy from the "open-minded" campus left, and four years of being made to feel stupid and bigoted. And I now found myself clinging to defined principles that were giving me the strength to confront all dishonest acts of intolerance, an intolerance I now saw stemming from an immoral mentality that I now called "liberalism."

I was not inspired to let everyone know what had happened inside *The Herald* offices. Perhaps I thought that it might have seemed too trivial of a topic to most people. It may even seem trivial to you. However, I hope by now you realize what I was attempting to do by the time I was a senior at Brown, the narrow-mindedness I was trying to eradicate. I remember feeling vengeful during this incident. I wanted the people/person responsible to know that I knew what *The Herald* had done. I wanted them to feel stupid for having done it, and for them to feel ashamed. I wanted them to see my point about Brown University, how fanatical and bigoted a place it really is, and how *The Herald* (despite the heroics of a few of them during the Horowitz controversy) just may be a part of the problem. This is how seriously I had begun to view Brown's atmosphere of silence, and the danger college campuses present when they remain philosophically sealed. In four years, Brown had amazingly taken a politically disinterested teenager, and developed him into a passionately conservative student of the Ivy League.

CHAPTER 13
Smart People Hate America

By its nature, treason needs a secret refuge, and it has chosen the university.

"This country was founded on racism, genocide, and theft."—member of the Brown Green Party(1)

"The people who want to go to war are these white trash who will follow whatever the government says."—member of the Brown Communist Party(2)

"1,2,3,4 We don't want a racist war!"—anti-war rally chant(3)
"I consider myself a patriot. I think this country does wonderful things for its citizens, but we must acknowledge the terrible things it often does to the citizens of other countries."—Brown University student activist(4)

"The unfortunate fact is that terrorism is carried out by the U.S. and carried out routinely by its allies."—Anthony Arnove, author at Brown's Anti-War Panel(5)

"By understanding America's history of imperialism in places such as Honduras, Venezuela, Haiti, and Iraq, future terrorist attacks on America can be prevented."—Anthony Arnove, author at Brown's Anti-War Panel(6)

"Instead of rushing to judgment and seeking vengeance against those responsible for the terror...understand the more difficult question of 'why did they do it?'"—Brown Professor William Beeman(7)

"We don't have a President, we have a cowboy-in-chief. There are millions of people in this country who are tired of militarism, but it still stands at the core of what this country stands for."—Greg Gerrit, Green Party's candidate for Mayor of Providence at Brown's Anti-War Panel (8)

"We cannot simply go on with our daily routines as our country prosecutes an unjust war. Students are walking out in solidarity with the people of Afghanistan who must now suffer the double burden of a dictatorial regime and American bombs."—Shaun Joseph '02 (9)

"Shaun Joseph '02, another organizer of the event, said he would like to see a 'truth commission' investigate all incidents of terrorism, including those committed by the United States, which he referred to as the largest terrorist state in the world."—Brown Daily Herald report 10/9/01 (10)

"What happened on September 11th was terrorism, but what happened during the Gulf War was also terrorism."—Professor of English, William Keach (11)

"In theory, this war can end only to the extent that we relinquish our role as world leader, overhaul our lifestyle and achieve political neutrality...Many wonder if we are paying an accumulated debt for centuries of dominance and intervention far from home, retribution for our culture of consumption and exploitation...Let's start by revising the physics of political power in the world, in which even the most magnificent of nations can be paralyzed by one misguided renegade act, in which no one power is superior to others...We must come to terms with the reality that we cannot utterly control the powers of all peoples, re-examine our place in the world, and begin to imagine a world without superpowers."—Brown Professor, Kevin Lourie (12)

"They just stand behind the flag no matter what, and it seems they will blindly follow the government."—Leah Neuhauser '03 (13)

"To call this a just war is to ignore the mountain of injustice it is based on."—Brian Rainey '04(14)

"Patriotism can very quickly lead into this kind of zealotism."—Brown Professor of English, Maria Josefina Saldana(15)

"Since the Cold War the American mentality has been 'we can have it all.' We will be having to sacrifice in the future."—Assistant Professor of International Relations, Nina Tannenwald(16)

"I was cheering when the Pentagon got hit because I know about the brutality of the military. The American flag is nothing but a symbol of hate and should be used for toilet paper for all I care."—Peter Zedrin, Brown visitor(17)

"A member of Third World ACTION said on a recent trip she saw "many American flags flying, and that scared me."—BDH report of anti-war protest(18)

These are quotes from members of the Brown community concerning the events and controversy surrounding the 9/11 Terrorist Attacks.

My 9/11

Like most Americans, I suppose, I will never forget where I was when television first delivered to me the frightening image of two smoldering towers.

It was about 9am on a Tuesday morning, and I walked into the Brown football office expecting to prepare for our opening game that week in San Diego (a game that was canceled due to the closing of airports after the attacks). My coaches were gathered in one room watching the terrible news, and brought me up-to-date. A second plane, moments before I arrived, had hit the second tower.

The moment reeked of uncertainty. Planes had embedded themselves into the face of the World Trade Center. Breaking news was informing us of similar happenings in Washington and Pennsylvania. We watched and waited. Would there be any more destruction? Terrorism and national security had never been my concern. Now, I watched two buildings burn, and witnessed fellow Americans leap to their deaths to escape the flames. Soon, the first tower fell. "I wonder if the other one will fall," I thought to myself.

Confusion. Wasn't that what everyone was feeling that day? How serious was this? A plane flew into the Pentagon too? Terrorists? Osama who? Who could make heads or tails of any of it? And there was stuff to do. Work. Class. Practice. We couldn't watch the news *all* day, right? Or should we? At Brown, the first campus dispute after the attacks was over whether professors should cancel classes or not. *We should just go on with our regular routines right now. How can you say that? People are dead!*

As for the football team, we held practice at the regular time. From 3pm to 6pm I had to go on with my daily routine, and put the confusion from that morning's events aside for a while. I guess I was okay with that. I couldn't make sense out of anything anyway. Besides, we had a government, a military, and a President to handle all this stuff. I trusted they would do the right thing. America is the greatest nation in the world. Everything would be okay.

Little did I know that my faith in our government, my loyalty to the President, and even my patriotism would not be entirely welcome on Brown's campus.

The Subtlety of Sedition

This was pretty new to me, all of this hatred for our homeland. I didn't recognize it as hatred at first. Much of the scorn for America that Brown members would attempt to spread wasn't in such obvious form as the quotes presented at the beginning of this chapter. Intolerance for American follies, and opinions that undermined the United States had always pervaded Brown's campus, but within the confines of campus life treason had disguised itself as progressive thought and multicultural learning.

Anti-Americanism came in subtle form so to not reveal the true character of the campus left, a bunch of American seditionists, and their pack of followers who found it trendy and intelligent to exert an anti-American perspective. *American slavery. American genocide. American imperialism. American greed. American cruelty.* This uninterrupted propaganda was telling me that the only way to escape American shame was to join the rabble of pacifists and apologists. This would have put me above the bigoted fray, excluded from the label "American." That's what the indoctrination of guilt was out to accomplish.

Then, September 11th. No other event could have better exposed the treachery of the left, and its campus mission to turn all young Americans against their home. Anti-war activism took place on many campuses across the country, but Brown took a leadership role as the campus invited famed intellectuals to come speak against the war, sponsored regional discussions, and coordinated national rallies as well. To the campus left, the terrorist attacks were a golden opportunity to bring even more students to the anti-American scene. But after 9/11, the passions of Brown leftists couldn't be entirely contained by the barriers of subtlety any longer.

Disgraceful

Without a doubt, the most embarrassed I had ever been of being associated with Brown University was during this time period. Yes, I was embarrassed to be associated with the Brown students who had acted with the utmost disrespect at President Bush's first Inauguration, but their behavior after September 11th embarrassed me to the point of wanting to disassociate myself with all things Brown. During this period I was able to see up-close-and-personal the utter lack of patriotism our freedom allows, and campus liberalism takes advantage of.

Only a week after the devastating attacks on New York City and the Pentagon, my classmates and professors began their nationwide leadership of a movement that called on the U.S. to refrain from defending itself with any use of force against the terrorist groups that targeted our country. This mindless opinion was undoubtedly a reason for my embarrassment, but the contempt for the United States that the holders of that opinion expressed was a much larger cause for it. It wouldn't have been so bad for me, but the need for some Brown students to appear more enlightened, more sophisticated, more progressive, more compassionate, and smarter than the rest of America, compelled the local and national media to capture my classmates as they led their glorious charge against the evil United States.

What could have been done to overtake the campus's domineering sentiments of anti-Americanism? Not much. The viciousness of the campus left was well-documented by those who may have wished to defy them. Fierce character assassination would have certainly been the consequence of dissent, and the liberals offered soft warning to anyone who may have been considering it. Just look at some of the declarations at the beginning of the chapter. One student called anyone in support of a war effort "white trash." Others were saying that the United States was itself a terrorist state, delicately suggesting that anyone supporting the U.S. could also be considered a terrorist. More of their comments suggested that anyone who was pro-war should be considered racist, zealous, and unaware that their own nation is an evil participant of imperialism and genocide. "They just stand behind the flag no matter what, and it seems they will blindly follow the government," declared one of my elitist classmates, suggesting the ignorance of those young students who never found it necessary to justify their patriotism or will to defend their home. These authoritarian statements persuaded many students to believe in the enlightenment of the left, and kept others who defied this self-hatred silent. So many of us just sat back and waited for the eventual end to another disturbing protest.

Providence Journal
Take Your Student Protest to Afghanistan
Michael Carbone, Lincoln, RI

While America and the world continued to reel from the unspeakable evil that was perpetrated in this country on Sept. 11, good people around the world rose up to protest the atrocity. Meanwhile, the students at Brown University chose to protest what they perceive this country might do in retaliation.

If they wished to be truly effective, the students should not have held their protest in an enclave of like-minded individuals, where their rhetoric simply reached the ears of those who would nod their head in silent agreement.

Instead, the students should have taken their protest to the still smoldering ruins of New York's ground zero—to the rescue workers who continue to labor tirelessly, to former World Trade Center employees who will have nightmares

> the rest of their lives, and to the nearby residents who have known a fear no one in America should ever have to know. Here, they could have preached their convincing arguments to the firemen who lost a buddy, or to the cop who lost his brother, or to the wife who lost her husband, or to the man who lost his sister, or the children who lost parents.
>
> Once finished in New York, they should have all hopped a plane to Afghanistan and met with its leaders. Then they could have showed the world how to reach a peaceful solution with hate-demanded zealots.(19)

There were many who rightfully held this opinion of Brown University students during the times surrounding September 11th. I won't pretend to be able to express my opinion on my classmates any better than Mr. Carbone, but I will elaborate a bit more on what exactly went on at Brown during the events surrounding the terrorist attacks of September 11, 2001.

The Quiet of Unpatriotic Adults

The professors got the ball rolling, and their lack of national loyalty helped spark the massive student anti-retaliation protests. On September 17, 2001, just six days after the attacks, *The Herald* printed a story entitled *"Brown Profs See Need For Restraint in U.S. Response."* Here we go.

The article highlighted Brown professors suggesting that there is likely a better alternative than using military retaliation against the terrorists of 9/11. More nauseating, however, was the turncoatedness that trickled from the faculty remarks. (I know "turncoatedness" is not a word. I made it up. It means "hidden treason by arrogant elitists that makes you want to vomit").

"Professor of History Abbott Gleason described the current mentality of many Americans as 'we are going to whip these people'...What might be wiser, Gleason suggested, would be to put aside an initial desire for revenge and instead consider more calculated responses."(20) Of course, only university elites have this ability to weather their natural urges. Most Americans are mindless barbarians.

Not that it was uncommon for professors to separate themselves from the peasants. The "inclination" to "seek revenge" was only "natural," they explained.

Being older and wiser, the professorate was much more careful with their sedition, and their public word-choice than were the students. They often walked the fine line between traitorous rhetoric and other comments that weren't *necessarily* unpatriotic. But they still made you want to punch them.

"The attack 'was a crime against humanity—it is not a war,' said Professor Philip Terrance Hopmann." A crime. Not a war. Today I wonder if this was a purposeful diminishment of the terrorists' deeds. Hopmann "frowned upon an all-out attack on a possible perpetrator" out of concern for innocent civilians of Middle Eastern nations. So did Nina Tannenwald, assistant professor of international relations. It seemed to hurt her when she said it, but she admitted, "A military attack may be necessary, but there needs to be a variety of responses." Oh, so we may need the commoners' "inclination" to "seek revenge" after all.

"Likewise, Tannenwald said, any attack should not strike at civilians and should not escalate the level of violence from last week." Professor Tannenwald thought we should have made sure that we didn't kill any more than 3000 terrorists, and should have only destroyed three of their buildings and four of their planes. Even Steven.

The faculty spoke as if all other Americans wanted to nuke the Eastern Hemisphere. Professor Hopmann warned that our retaliation should be "precise" and not include "randomly bombing Afghanistan and killing more innocent people...The military response should be to get the people who perpetrated the act." Wow. How many years of school did Professor Hopmann have to attend to acquire the brainpower to formulate that idea? I wanted to bomb Tokyo.

The professors were so distraught over racial profiling, too. The article stated, "The natural reaction of any group of people to such an attack is 'anger, outrage, horror, fear,' Hopmann said, and 'some have directed this fear and anger at people who are different from the majority—particularly people from Arab countries." *Um, yeah!* The article continued: "[Professor of History Engin] Akarli said although he understands the tendency to look for a scapegoat, such racial profiling should not go without notice." And Professor Gleason said, "It is important to realize we are not at war with Islamic or Muslim people." To this day, in the midst of the Terror War, Brown professors are the only ones who show no "fear" when boarding a plane with a Muslim. They are an astonishing people.

Racial profiling and civilian casualties. These were the top concerns for my professors in the days that followed September 11th. Liberal treachery always disguised itself with a veil of tenderness. Liberals care, and conservatives "randomly" drop bombs. The campus left never missed an opportunity to prove their monopoly over the compassion industry. But it was all a farce. Brown professors may have been concerned for Arab-Americans and foreign civilians, but no more than anyone else. They only held a special place in their heart for these two groups because they were convenient victims for America's campus enemies, being used as rationale for withholding our retaliation. Sympathy for brown-skinned Americans, and concern for innocent Arabs standing beneath "random" U.S. bombings served as reasons *not* to defend ourselves. The professors, like all members of the anti-American crowd, didn't want America to strike back after 9/11. "A military response may be necessary, but..."

It *may* be necessary?!

When Professor Tannenwald was done voicing her concern for Arabs being searched in airports, and painfully admitted that we "may" have to go to war, she also told *The Herald*, "Since the Cold War the American mentality has been 'we can have it all'...We will be having to sacrifice in the future." On that dreadful day, we got what we deserved.

From the Brown University News Service, Professor Kevin Lourie resounded similar sentiments. "We cannot wage a successful war without a definable, visible enemy." Professor Lourie's solution, then, was to throw in the towel. "Now we have concrete evidence that the more powerful we are, the more formidable the dangers we face...In theory, this war can end only to the extent that we relinquish our role as world leader, overhaul our lifestyle and achieve political neutrality." But Professor, where do we begin? "Let's start by revising the physics of political power in the world, in which even the most magnificent of nations can be paralyzed by one misguided renegade act, in which no one power is superior to others." Brilliant. Someone hits us with a stick, and the wise thing to do is give up our pistol.

Professor Lourie didn't stop there. As many after him would do, he asked the Brown community to consider how the death toll of 3000

Americans was the fault of the United States. "Perhaps our best options now are to search for the origins of this new war...and make changes within ourselves and within our relationships to others...Many wonder if we are paying an accumulated debt for centuries of dominance and intervention far from home, retribution for our culture of consumption and exploitation."

So slight and cunning were the intentions of certain faculty members. "Many wonder" was Professor Lourie's way of saying, *This is what I think.* This is how Brown used the leftist impulse of the students to push the agendas of those making up the administration and faculty. It's no secret that their weapon was the classroom, where they could manipulate the minds of students who were anxious to act on what they were told. You will notice that during my classmates' blatant anti-American upheaval, there were no professors who spoke out against them. The overly-opinionated campus adults were suddenly quiet. This is simply because the students were doing their dirty work.

The Peace Vigil

After professors had over a week to spread their philosophy inside Brown classrooms and media outlets, a new student activist group was formed calling themselves *Not Another Victim Anywhere* (NAVA). This group was dedicated to resisting the eventual military strikes on terrorist organizations, but not dedicated to suggesting any other credible alternative responses. Their unpopular opinion was rejected by most Americans as a poll at this time found that 92% of Americans backed the use of military force against those who were responsible for the attacks.(21)

One day walking through campus I noticed some writing on Brown's cement walkways that extend through campus. In colored chalk, the markings read "Not Another Victim Anywhere," "Peace," "No More War" and other related phrases that discouraged military action. There were also postings that informed everyone of the planned events for that night on Brown's campus.

That night the International Socialist Organization (ISO), one of Brown's more vocal student activist groups, sponsored a "vigil for peace" where the 100 people that attended for over an hour held candles showing their disapproval of military action. They could call it a "vigil" if they wanted to, but it was just a fancy word for another one of their protests.

More than ten campus activist groups were present including the typical players: the International Socialist Organization, Green Party, Arab-American Anti-discrimination Committee, Communist Party USA, Young Communist League, Brown International Organization, Third World ACTION, etc. Unfortunately, I was unable to attend the vigil and had to settle for reading about it the next morning in *The Herald.*

As I ate my breakfast I read in *The Herald* about how the peace vigil was to express opposition to a potential war triggered by the terrorist attacks, and an open mic allowed for comments. Student after student got on the mic to express their disagreement with the idea of retaliation. A member of the Green Party proudly stood up during his turn to make an ass out of himself and told the crowd, "This country was founded on racism, genocide, and theft!" Yeah! And don't forget about what Americans do to the ozone layer either, maaaan!

Another classmate of mine, who was a member of Brown's Communist Party, stood up soon after and told everyone that, "the people who want to go to war are these white trash who will follow whatever the government says." No other statement could have more perfectly exhibited Brown's prevalent national outlook. 92% of Americans approved of military retaliation, but as far as the campus left was concerned, 92% of Americans were brainwashed by the government. It was up to the campus elites to save their countrymen from their own stupidity. And there was no possible way a *minority* would be willing to go to war for America, the nation that oppresses him! Only "white trash" would ever want to wage war on terrorism!

A University of Rhode Island student decided to attend the ISO's vigil (or protest) as well. He complained about his own university's lack of activism, and had heard about this event, and decided to attend. He claimed that he came for the "free exchange of ideas with people who are as concerned as I am." Oh man, this poor kid didn't know what he was in for. Despite what he had heard about Brown's openness to ideas, these America-hating students at the vigil were not concerned with exchanging any ideas unless they were echoes of their own thoughts. After the vigil the URI student expressed disappointment with what he found on Brown's campus. "There was no real discussion. This seemed to be a symbolic meeting rather than an activist one."(22) No real discussion? At Brown? Nooooo.

200 Students Rally on Faunce

Just a couple of days after the vigil student activists doubled the amount of campus support for their nonviolent solution to end terrorism when 200 campus members came together for another Anti-American... oh I'm sorry...I mean Anti-war rally. All across the nation (at 145 other campuses) members of a new national student-group called Peaceful Justice were sponsoring individual rallies on this very same day at 12pm on the dot. I guess the precise coordination, and the simultaneous acts of buffoonery were supposed to send a message to the other 92% of Americans.

This rally would have been tolerable, and less unsettling if the opinion of non-violent response to the attacks was the only distasteful thing present at the rally. Unfortunately, there were other things present, such as members of the media who couldn't wait to broadcast the collegiate feelings on how to bring the terrorists to justice. Some of them were so anxious that they were broadcasting live from the Main Green.

The Peace Rally was being held, again, on Brown's Main Green on the steps of a building called Faunce House. The spot was used as an outside study area, but often served as the stage for my classmates' protests. I'm surprised the steps haven't collapsed yet.

At the Peaceful Justice Peace Rally "students performed musical acts and interpretive dance routines to show their support for peace." Protesting in the old-fashioned way by chanting slogans and holding picket signs must get old very quickly when you do it on such a regular basis. So, most likely just to amuse themselves, they decided to protest in more of an artsy way this time. Good for them.

Deciding to join the fun was professor of English, Maria Josefina Saldana. She grabbed the microphone and spoke to the crowd about the possibility of war, and the recent harassment of Arab-Americans. "Nationalism, especially at times of war, is always tinged with 'otherism,'" and "Patriotism can very quickly lead into this kind of zealotism." Yes, being patriotic isn't as cool as one might think.

The Anti-War Panel

Within the next few weeks I watched as Brown continued its leadership of the anti-war movement. NAVA sponsored a panel called "Why You Should Oppose The Upcoming War." As you might expect, there were no panelists invited who believed military action was necessary. The discussion focused on "American imperialism," "how the media does a poor job spreading actual truth," and "how to organize against the upcoming war" against terrorism. The professionals that spoke at the panel were author, Anthony Arnove, Associate Professor of Modern Culture and Media, Lynne Joyrich, and Greg Gerritt, the co-chair of the Rhode Island Green Party.

The panelists, before a gathered group of members of the Brown community, spoke the same "Blame America" speech that had been thrown around campus during the previous weeks. Judging from the article in *The Herald*, Arnove took the reigns of the panel as he told the audience, "By understanding America's history of imperialism in places such as Honduras, Venezuela, Haiti, and Iraq, future terrorist attacks on America can be prevented." He went on to say, "The unfortunate fact is that terrorism is carried out by the U.S. and carried out routinely by its allies."

The Green Party's Greg Gerritt asked the audience to target their anger and frustration against the "appropriate parties." In other words, stop being so upset with Al Qaeda, and redirect that anger toward...the Republican Party? He was most likely suggesting this, judging from what he said about the Republicans' top dog. "We don't have a President, we have a cowboy-in-chief. There are millions of people in this country who are tired of militarism but it still stands at the core of what this country stands for." He added that, "the American military is way bigger than they need to be to protect us, though obviously they weren't very good at it" and "your government, in the goodness of its heart, supplies weapons to everybody."

The Walk-Out

A few days after the anti-war panel NAVA sponsored another campus protest, this time in the form of a synchronized walk-out. An estimated 120 students left their classrooms at 11:30am to show their resistance to America's self-defense. Brown professors remained consistent in their participation as at least two of them dismissed their classes early encouraging their students to join them at the protest. The students who did not support NAVA's cause just had to accept the fact that an hour of class time would not be deducted from their tuition bills.

Professor William Keach dismissed his students early, and took part in the rally on the Main Green. Keach took the microphone briefly, and told the crowd of students that, "what happened on September 11 was terrorism, but what happened during the Gulf War was also terrorism." Then, he gave hope to the students who despised America's retaliation by telling them, "The anti-war movement may seem like a small voice now, but it will continue to grow in the days to come." Professor Keach must have had a lot of experience with leading irrational collegiate movements, because he was right. More and more students would join Brown's activists during the next couple of months as they led a nationwide movement to denounce President Bush as a trigger-happy cowboy, and anyone who supported him as racist white trash.

Finally, some students who could feel the spread of anti-Americanism on their campus decided to denounce the protesters as only a minority of students that did not represent the overall feeling of the University. Ten students stood against the 120 Bin-Laden apologists in a counter-protest. One student was reported as saying, "We feel that the peace protesters are not representative of the greater Brown community. Six thousand students go here, and only 100 showed up, which shows that they reflect the extreme end of the spectrum."(23) That may have been true, but I knew for sure that the voice of the campus left was getting louder, and opposition to it was pretty much nonexistent.

Joining my fellow classmates at their glorious resistance to President Bush was Peter Zedrin, a freelance writer in Providence. Mr. Zedrin wasted no time in exposing his disdain for America when he grabbed the mic and pronounced from the quad that he was "cheering when the Pentagon got hit because I know about the brutality of the military. The American flag is nothing but a symbol of hate and should be used for toilet paper for all I care."

Zedrin's comment spoke volumes about Brown's political atmosphere. For someone to feel comfortable enough to openly pronounce such a hateful comment toward the U.S., he must have felt as if the people who shared his company also shared his opinions. Trust me, many of the protesters did. Zedrin joined Brown students and professors who had called the United States the "largest terrorist state in the world." He stood beside people who had declared that the U.S. was "founded on racism, genocide, and theft." Brown had created a comforting haven for a man who is inarguably an enemy within our own borders. When words such as these were spoken in my own community, pride in my school was the last thing I was able to feel. I only felt embarrassed, and couldn't help but realize that Brown was always accommodating men such as Zedrin, allowing them to come and proclaim that our nation is a black mark on the history of the world. And I had to wonder why my classmates were bound by a gut feeling that told them to assume the responsibility of their own nation at any turn of tragedy.

Solutionless

It may have been my athletic experience that enabled me to recognize the vulnerable position of a dispirited and divided nation. Any athlete will tell you that the best way to bring down a formidable team is from within that team itself, rather than chucking a single stone at Goliath's head. To attack the soul, to discourage and dishearten—that is how you find your opponent's true resolve. And once you see that team bickering among themselves, you know you have them right where you want them. This may have been what I finally saw so clearly from atop College Hill. Whether intentional or unintentional, by all or by some, the campus left was set on bringing America to its knees by ripping us of our moral certainty.

The campus left claimed other objectives, but the sole purpose for their activism was to convince others of the evil that is America. Proof positive of their desire to spread their hate rested in the irritating truth that they never offered any other response to the terrorist attacks (other than Professor Lourie who offered the unclear solution of "relinquish[ing] our role as world leader"). I watched as my classmates, with the faculty in their corner, voiced only opposition to non-violent measures, but never offered any alternatives that would bring Bin Laden to justice for the "crime" he had committed. They only called on Americans to realize that the U.S. was also a terrorist organization, and to consider the fact that we deserved what happened to us on that terrible Tuesday morning. Due to media interest, they achieved the attention of the entire country, and American citizens who vehemently disagreed with them were waiting for their surrogate solution that never came.

You see, the campus left didn't believe that the best way to defeat terrorism was without using the most powerful military the world has ever known. They just didn't believe the terrorists should have been attacked, that the U.S. had instigated 9/11 through terrorism of its own. Professor William Beeman proclaimed to his students, "Instead of rushing to judgment and seeking vengeance against those responsible for the terror...understand the more difficult question of 'why did they do it?'" Brian Rainey '04 said, "To call this a just war is to ignore the mountain of injustice it is based on." Shaun Joseph '02 resounded Rainey's rhetoric when he said, "We cannot simply go on with our daily routines as our country prosecutes an unjust war."

My classmates, just like the faculty, knew they were treading dangerous ground, so they shadowed their true intentions with comments of concern for the victims of the attacks, and also Arab-Americans suffering from harassment and racial profiling. In fact, many of their statements at this time were expressions of support. A Peaceful Justice member told everyone that their peace rally was to show "not only solidarity for the victims but that the best way to honor their memory is to not kill more people." And NAVA made sure their three goals were understood when they reported them to *The Herald*: "[1] opposing retaliatory violence, [2] upholding civil liberties, and [3] considering the underlying causes of violence."(24) I couldn't help but notice that right before NAVA encouraged people to consider how the U.S. actually caused its own fate on 9/11, they wanted to make sure everyone understood that they were concerned for the civil liberties of Arab-Americans. I thought that was very sweet, but I was more intrigued by their third goal. Public expressions of patriotic support for the victims were continuously spoken. But their blatant unpatriotic statements were sparse, only oozing from their rallies incidentally, like the honesty that inevitably drips from the mouth of a drunk.

I slowly discovered the reason why my classmates had created this distraction to their main purpose. They had no other legitimate response to offer America, and they needed to *appear* patriotic. The last thing they needed was their hatred for America to shine through their mask of sensitivity. So they held up candles, called their protests "vigils," expressed concern for our Arab brethren, conveyed support for weeping families, and repetitively referred to their activities as "*Peace* Rallies" and "*Peace* Vigils" as part of some sort of "*Peace* Movement" organized by "*Peaceful* Justice." Nauseating.

My classmates were trying so hard to conceal their intent, but painting "peace" on their forehead didn't entirely convince people that they were of the soft and gentle. People were becoming suspicious of them. After all, concern and compassion are skeptical reasons to protest. *What was the true conscience and character of the anti-war protesters*, many were wondering.

Lynne Cheney (wife of Dick Cheney, VP) and Senator Joseph Lieberman found it important to expose universities' welcoming environment to anti-Americanism in a time when the country needed to be united. In 1995 they had founded the American Council of Trustees and Alumni (ACTA) whose purpose was to combat political intolerance within America's universities. ACTA released a report in November of 2001 that, in its simplest form, could be described as a collection of quotations taken from university newspapers across America. These references proved that anti-Americanism was roaring from institutions of higher learning. The report contained 115 anti-American quotes. Brown and the University of North Carolina shamed themselves by boasting the most citations within the report, with 14 each.

This external criticism caused the campus left to go on the defensive. I heard so many of them screaming *freedom of speech!*, and actually attempted to compare ACTA's report to McCarthyism. And their response to the charge of them being unpatriotic was this: *Just because we have a different opinion doesn't mean we're not patriotic! What's more American than dissent?! And haven't you heard? We support the victims!* Hearing my classmates and professors assert their patriotism couldn't have been more irritating. For them to make the claim, after all of their protests, that their opposition to the war had nothing to do with their level of patriotism, and that they loved America too, was as phony as me saying that I love Brown University. How could I, with a straight face at this point in the book, tell my readers that there's a special place in my heart for Brown? Certainly I hold contempt for Brown! I don't pretend to share the values of my alma mater, and while I enjoyed and appreciated certain aspects of my college years, I would never want to appear so disingenuous as to declare that I loved Brown just as much as, say, a member of the College Democrats! Nevertheless, this line of reasoning didn't stop my classmates from pronouncing how patriotic they were.

My classmates' defensiveness was telling. *It's our American right to speak our minds!* I just loved it whenever they would defend their hatred for America with the rights of freedom that the U.S. afforded them. I came to see that they were absolutely right, however. They could say whatever they wanted, and that's why none of my classmates were rounded up and brought to prison. But what they failed to understand was that while their right to intellectual freedom would be upheld, they would not be free from scrutiny. This latest outcry from my alma mater was given a national stage, stripping the campus left of political immunity. What they were really upset about was that some people were challenging them (something they weren't used to). Suddenly, they were the ones speaking beyond the parameters of political correctness. Outsiders were discovering what they truly were, a bunch of leftist, identity-seeking college students with less respect for the U.S. than Bin Laden, himself. Their sedition was exposed. As much as they tried to disguise their true feelings, some couldn't help but shout out their unpatriotic cry, and *real* Americans were watching.

Diversity Schmersity!

National loyalty was not to be learned on top of College Hill, my vantage point of 9/11. And the lack of patriotism that surrounded me caused me to examine the root of Brown's sedition.

Brown's Dean of the College, Paul Armstrong, outlined the purpose of Brown's open curriculum in his essay, "The American Scholar at Brown: Diversity, the 'Open Curriculum,' and Liberal Education." I read it. The essay offered great insight into the history of American academia, and revolved around Ralph Waldo Emerson's famous speech to Alpha of Massachusetts in 1837 where Emerson defined what the "American scholar" should be. Armstrong's essay made reference to the birth of open curriculums that sprouted in the 1960s as part of a liberal movement to change educational methods.[25] *Relevance* became a popular ideal that meant for education to be connected to each individual student's personal concerns. *Relevance* strayed from the traditional educational mode of ensuring the knowledge of core subjects such as History, Mathematics, Science, and Literature. And thus, Brown followed suit.

Open curriculums have been highly debated and criticized, and Dean Armstrong called on his readers to recognize Brown's diverse student body so they could fully understand the purpose of what Brown calls the *New Curriculum.* Similarly (but in reverse), I feel that to best understand Brown's perception of diversity, and why anti-Americanism propagated so heavily on my alma mater's campus, then we should understand the

New Curriculum that has characterized Brown University for the past several decades.

It is diversity that defends Brown's method of scholarship, the open curriculum that allows students to discriminate from any educational subjects that they feel disinterested in. Students take on the full responsibility of creating their own education. Brown also allows them to create independent studies (individual or group) in an effort to study specific topics not offered among the course selection. Students may practice this course conception in a full-fledged creation of an academic concentration (more commonly known as a "major"). In other words, students can receive a degree in a concentration that they create themselves. Lastly, Brown students may elect to take courses on a pass/fail basis rather than receiving a letter grade. Brown's curriculum may be better described as WIDE-open. It is an educational process that gives unparalleled autonomy to the students.

If a core curriculum had a stomach, it would vomit from the sight of Brown's academic policy. Many schools have combined the two notions of learning to satisfy both modes of academia. Numerous colleges require that certain courses be taken while they allow the students to choose from a variety of others to fulfill their required studies. Brown has no interest in finding the middle ground when it comes to educational theory. To do so would violate their unwavering worship of diversity, and the belief that students should not have any subject forced upon them, because it may offend their individual interests. Brown's WIDE-open curriculum always made sense to me, until I began to study the true purposes of higher education, and sought to find out why my university had become a breeding ground for anti-American thought.

Universities have always maintained a responsibility of preparing their youngsters for life, not just preparing them in a specific academic field. There is no doubt that a person's college years are just as much a transition into adulthood and citizenship, as they are an education in a specific field of scholarship. That's why people cherish their education so much, even people who never wind up using the knowledge they gain inside the classroom. College is the place where many sprout into the people they will be for the rest of their lives, and universities have a role in making sure the character of the student body is one of good citizenship. Dean Armstrong cited a time when Emerson challenged his audience to recognize their "civic responsibility to provide the cultural leadership needed by the still relatively new nation. He felt that defining the role of 'the American scholar' was work worth doing because fundamental principles of citizenship, nationhood, and culture were embedded in the way this vocation was conceived." Dean Armstrong went on to say that Brown has long agreed with the notion of academia holding a civic responsibility. "There is a long tradition at Brown of viewing scholarship and learning as having civic purposes" and "From the beginning Brown has conceived of 'liberal education' in terms of civic responsibility."

From reading Dean Armstrong's essay I came to realize that it was true; Brown did seriously recognize a civic responsibility. It's just that the responsibility it rendered itself to was sacrificing the patriotism of the students. For decades, Brown had ignored the functions of a core curriculum, one that helps achieve a common bond among American citizens by offering a familiar narrative of their culture's history.

Dean Armstrong fully admitted to the charge, however. He declared in another essay on Brown's curriculum, "Connected to this emphasis on the value and the challenge of epistemological diversity is a particular notion of citizenship. Instead of defining community by the things everyone needs to know or by assimilating a common culture, at Brown we think of ourselves as a 'community of communities.'" $_{(26)}$ Exactly. Above all things, Brown was diverse. *American* values were merely among the many. No better, no worse.

While reading his essay, Dean Armstrong went on to tell me that a core curriculum is based on the assumption that all students function from the same set of values, and he noted Brown's diversity (and the nation's as well) to defend an academic setting that places no restrictions or requirements on its pupils. The problem with a conservative education, Armstrong explained, "is not only that the traditional canon excludes valuable texts by women, African-Americans, Asian-Americans, Hispanic-Americans, and others and should be expanded to include them (a concession some conservatives are willing to make)." He went on to ask, "What, then, is the civic responsibility of the American scholar today, in a country defined by its irreducible diversity? How can higher education make pluralism a generative principle of hope, creativity, and possibility and help us get past the dangers of cross-cultural misunderstanding, indifference, and intolerance?"

I knew how Brown would answer this question. The answer was to expose students early and often to the diversity that awaits them outside the walls of academia, and in the process completely abandon (unless a student didn't want to) subjects that explore American civilization, or that would "assimilate a common culture." At some point Brown decided to have an appreciation for everything but our *own* home and history. Diversity became student obsession, leaving less room for honest investigation into America's past (an exercise that could have dispelled the leftist perspective of U.S. history). *Why take 'American History 101' when I can take a trendier course? Perhaps 'Lesbians in the Fashion Industry 101'.*

Dean Armstrong also asserted that an open curriculum provides "a model of how we can negotiate differences with one another in a spirit of civic dialogue and with an appreciation for how our differences can enrich our intellectual, cultural, and moral lives." Such politically correct poppycock was multiculturalism's window dressing, suggesting the University's good intentions, and providing the illusion of Brown's worldliness. But I escaped from Brown believing that these declarations of the necessity of diversity served as snobbish whispers of the elite class. Through this wordage I saw only an insulting assumption of *my* bigotry, as if when I arrived as a freshman I was a helplessly bigoted teenager needing a twist of Ivy instruction. That way, when I finally made my journey into the outside world I wouldn't be so judgmental, intolerant, and overly-patriotic. If I had my own business, perhaps I would hire some Hispanics. I certainly wouldn't be so quick to join the military. And maybe I would even befriend some black people! Brown would have saved the world from my Catholic upbringing.

Still, many of my classmates allowed the over-accentuation of diversity to channel their energy into extreme multicultural positions. The corruption and abuse of multiculturalism was the result. Certain campus groups would take Brown's diversity, and use it *not* as a tool for everyone to use in order to gain various perspectives, but they would use it to their own political advantage, portraying themselves as victims of a racist nation. They were the ones being burned by America's conservative base, those people who couldn't "get past the dangers of cross-cultural misunderstanding, indifference, and intolerance." The multicultural rhetoric and propaganda was powerful, and everyone was unremittingly subjected to it, teaching us that our nation was founded on racism and injustice, and remains immoral even today.

And even though anti-Americanism mostly spewed from the mouth of the student body, we should recognize where such hatred was born—straight from the faculty and administration. The perfect campus equation comprised of an absent ROTC program, multicultural learning, an open curriculum, and the most left-leaning liberalism had resulted in the creation of an anti-American think-tank called Brown University, and it was finally spreading its wings in the wake of September 11th.

"Give Me Liberty Or Give Me Death!"——Patrick Henry, 1775

"Give Me Diversity Or Give Me Death!"——Brown University

During the aftermath of September 11th there was much discussion on the safety of leaving our borders open to immigration. One of my classmates once expressed his understanding of the importance of diversity to American prosperity. He and his friend were talking in the cafeteria line about the possibility for our borders to become closed in order to keep terrorists from entering our country. As I eavesdropped, this male student remarked, "We have to allow for immigrants to come into our country. The reason America is great is because we're a Melting Pot." Well, at least he thought that America was a great place. Many of my classmates did not.

Knowledge had become a transitioned notion during my young adulthood and my college years. Higher education was just that. Higher. More in depth. It had been rightly emphasized my entire life, the high worth of the freedom won for us, and that is still provided by our country. "With liberty and justice for all" I was made to repeat. "The Land of the Free, and the Home of the Brave" I had sung, never with the full understanding of its significance. The notion of liberty is rightly instilled into our children to preserve the concept of our country's foundation. Yet, Brown wanted to impede this valuable teaching right before it could be fully understood. This indoctrination never became true knowledge because few took the time to understand the previous sufferings that resulted from the restraint of freedom, and why so many had given their lives to attain it.

Higher education was supposed to offer my classmates and I the opportunity to sift through our indoctrinations and ask ourselves "why."

If Brown was to uphold a civic responsibility, then we should have been meant to gain a fuller understanding of the value of our liberty, and its origin. Instead, the open curriculum teamed up with the most traitorous liberalism on College Hill to channel the rebellious minds of the youth away from our most vital lesson. So we remained youthfully ignorant, taking for granted our most precious prize, fighting petty prejudice, and under the impression that *all we have in common are our differences.*

Patrick Henry, in his famous speech to his fellow countrymen in 1775, told them that he had "but one lamp by which my feet are guided, and that is the lamp of experience. I know of no way of judging of the future, but by the past." Similarly, glaring down at the campus from atop the University's John Carter Brown Library is this quotation: *Speak to the past, and it shall teach thee.* But the University had decided to ignore its own advice, doing a disservice to its students and the nation as the WIDE-open curriculum allowed tomorrow's most likely leaders to escape from College Hill without learning anything about U.S. history.

Liberty has allowed America to grow into the most affluent and most powerful country in the world. Unparalleled economic and political freedom. Not our diversity, and not our open borders. Only the grandchildren of freedom could be kept under such a spell of ignorance, so far removed from the pain of oppression and the blood of independence. I suppose that's why liberalism has been able to embed itself within the academy. Brown's *New Curriculum* helped ensure that the gap between young Americans and 1776 would only continue to widen. We were only to hear the anti-American bias from our leaders on the left, lessons that taught Brown students to become enraged whenever America claimed a moral high ground, as they could now only see that as the highest form of hypocrisy.

Several decades had to go by to see the true ramifications of the *New Curriculum* when hundreds of Brown students marched in unpatriotic defiance of the will of their own nation to rid the world of terror. The Land of Liberty. The world's Champion of Freedom. The Land of the Free, and the Home of the Brave. Many of my classmates now perceived America as an immoral nation, a ruthless murderer, a barbaric imperialist devoted to selfish acts of greed and racism. Brown's Office of Student Life declares on its website that the Office fosters "effective life skills for living and working in a diverse community." That may have been true, but after September 11, 2001 I could now see that Brown's priorities were screwed up.

CHAPTER 14
An Ivy Inmate

Every Fall Brown's incoming class, always a spirited and wide-eyed platoon, makes their symbolic entry into the Brown experience by marching through the Van Wickle Gates, one of the University's most recognizable landmarks. The Gates are only opened one other time each year. This time, in the Spring, they open outwardly to allow the graduating seniors to accept their passage into the world that awaits them. The Van Wickle Gates stare downtown Providence in the eyes from atop College Hill, as if they are the watch-guards of the "Renaissance City." From their lofty and elitist perch they are not all that different from many members of the Brown community, offering a downward gaze toward those they feel are beneath them.

Most find this ceremonial entrance and departure from the Ivy passage a powerful and romantic gesture of a college experience. Brown undoubtedly views and attempts to portray this imagery as an entrance to a welcoming tradition of community spirit, a diverse and open-minded arena of thought and debate. No opportunity for an unpleasant encounter, just wonderful learning.

After much time spent inside Brown's now-closed entryway, I thought of the clang of the closing Van Wickle Gates. I had, at first, appreciated the symbolism of this ceremony, but now it seemed more like the sound of prison bars closing shut on the first night of a four-year sentence, not a romantic entry into a prestigious place of personal growth. I had stepped through this ritualistic passageway to witness a world of pity, a habitat for deception, and the cultivator of hateful energy. And I was the outcast.

Every word uttered, and every opinion expressed was insulting, telling me that my values and priorities were misplaced. The morals of a privileged white kid. My accomplishments were a result of societal advantage, not my work and sacrifice. Others had paid their way. Me, not so much. White and middle-class. Plus, I was an athlete. A football player. The worst kind. Unenlightened and dumber than the rest of the student body. *Of course he's a bigoted conservative. He's a jock. It just makes sense. Ignore him. He's simply incapable of understanding.*

I resisted these inferences because they didn't make any sense. I had come from a family that taught me to be kind and charitable. I had come from a beautiful religion that taught me to never judge, and to always forgive. Yet, upon my arrival on College Hill everyone and everything was telling me that I was not from a place of charity and understanding. If I was going to accept such a demeaning premise of my character, I was first going to investigate why I should consider myself so ignorant and cruel.

All of the University's messages—victimization, ultra-sensitivity, the whining, and the political wickedness—seemed to contradict everything that I had learned during the first 18 years of my life. Most of all, I recognized an absence of conflict, a mysterious deficiency of fight. Where was the resistance?

Happy? I'm not so sure I was overly joyous the day of graduation. Proud, for sure. I did take one of those long pauses. A slow glance around the Main Green. I was surrounded by those beautiful buildings, the historical monuments that encased my college experience. For the past four years I had never realized what was actually happening to me until the moment Brown was forcing me to leave. I was tossed into an unfamiliar world without a warning of exactly what it was I would encounter, and the only defense I had from Brown's political onslaught were the values of brotherhood, athletics, family, and Catholicism.

It frightens me to think of what I could have become. Another collegiate tragedy of wasted intellect. Another member of the Ivy offspring, infected with teachings of entitlement and a diminished sense of individualism. Politically indoctrinated, taught to view others as helpless, and assisting communal outlooks of discouragement. Was I to discount the American Dream as a myth? Was I to become discouraged, only to infect others with my pessimism for the rest of my life, crippling them with sentiments of victim-hood and hopelessness? It frightens me to think that, if not for certain circumstances, I too may have graduated from Brown with a burning disdain for America, shame-filled for my whiteness, and helping to handicap my countrymen by always catering to the needs of special interests. As for my duty as an American citizen, was my political instinct going to compel me to whine and coerce, rather than think and reason? I have often heard this called the "dumbing-down of America." Is there any better way to put it?

I headed for the second time toward the Van Wickle Gates. I would never be allowed to step through them again. My time was over. Others would follow, just as I had. It was a sobering moment, a reflection of my mortality. I took a final look at Brown University before departing. I was wearing a black cap and gown, standing next to my closest friends, and surrounded by others who did not appreciate me so much. For the last time, I looked at Brown from a student's perspective, and knew that I had done it right. The Ivy League liberals had come at me with everything they had, and there I stood. My values maintained. I had arrived four years earlier to witness their political indecency, their elitism, their unquenchable appetite for victim-hood. I saw little desire for individualism, just the urge to join the nearest rabble of ignorance attempting to define everyone by their respective group. My classmates seemed to have the remarkable ability to determine the amount of injustice any individual had suffered by knowing their sexuality, gender, or skin tone. But they understood nothing of sacrifice. The sacrifices of those before us, and the sacrifices we are called on to make. They simply lacked respect for the lives laid down for their liberty. An absent conception of freedom's worth. Then came the ruthless and unexplained attacks on the character of others. I could only be repulsed by my classmates' intellectual dishonesty, and their unjust charges of bigotry. Hatred for the greatest nation in the world. Pimps, protests, and pessimism. Startled and stunned, I asked who these people were. They told me, "We call them liberals." Why would I have wanted anything to do with any of them?

Standing before the Van Wickle Gates for the second time, I knew that the reason I had received the most out of my Ivy experience was not due to the welcoming and open-minded environment Brown claims to have. It was all due to the values I had arrived with. I resisted my indoctrination because it was the only way I knew how to be—proud and stubborn when it came to what I thought was right, and what was wrong. Thank God. For reasons I still have trouble explaining, I stood fast in the face of Brown's aggression. Others felt it was enough to just keep quiet, but I had something to say. For me, that was the only avenue toward gratification. I could only be content with myself if I left no room for regret. Regret for ever attending Brown University. And after spending a significant amount of time in my front-row seat to view the demise of a great nation, I knew I would surely regret sitting idly by as I watched the erosion of America occur right before my eyes. Speaking out was the only way for me to survive my time atop College Hill. It was the only way I could ever be proud to be *Out of Ivy*.

EPILOGUE
The Foundation for Intellectual Diversity

I'm not naïve enough to believe that shedding light on a problem is equal to its solution. A diagnosis is not a cure. There are some who will say that Brown University, several years after my graduation, does not have the problems it had while I attended. *All is well.* I am willing to submit that improvements have been made, but to even consider the possibility that *all is well* is to argue that, within only a few years, Brown has corrected a decades-long solidification of liberal culture. This is simply not the case.

Often times, movements of student conservatives flare up on college campuses. College communities suddenly become exposed to ideas that hail from the right of the political spectrum, challenging the monopoly exercised by radical students, professors, and administrators. These always seem like promising occasions, but all too often the discussion becomes a debate about debate itself—about the acceptable bounds of campus discourse. Little is ever accomplished in terms of long-term reform for one simple reason: the students responsible for these uprisings graduate before they have devised a plan to achieve permanent change. They are immersed in an educational river with a rapid current. By the time they realize the bias of the waters in which they are submerged, they're already wearing a cap and gown. The scheme of indoctrination seems almost too perfect, doesn't it?

Students are merely the passers-by, so the team of educators occupying College Hill, an overwhelming majority of leftists, must be the ones held responsible for ensuring the intellectual variance needed to achieve this modification. But with such a domineering body of leftists at the helm, how can we trust the faculty and administration to remain in charge of the University's academic freedom? Surely, they have already betrayed the trust of concerned alumni, passionate students, unsuspecting parents, and a hopeful nation. This makes the cure to Brown's most dangerous problem difficult to prescribe. And certainly, such drastic restructuring cannot be achieved overnight.

Sometimes conservative students are backed by a national network of organizations like the Young Americans Foundation and the Intercollegiate Studies Institute. But the nationwide reach of such organizations means that the actual funding they provide to individual colleges and universities is meager—insufficient to have anything of a long-term impact.

The Foundation for Intellectual Diversity, an organization in which I sit on the Board of Directors, offers a solution to the situation at Brown. The *Foundation* will raise money from alums, conservative benefactors, and other sympathetic parties. The proceeds from fundraising will be used to support conservative publications, speakers, and clubs at Brown in order to promote intellectual diversity on a campus that is dominated by leftist ideologies. Surely, this is the demise of liberalism—forced intellectual exposure resulting from scholarly confrontations (you know, actual debate).

It is expected that the *Foundation* will become a mechanism for ensuring that Brown's budding conservative movement endures and flourishes. The directors of the *Foundation* are recent graduates, so they are in an ideal position to link current student leaders to older alums who have the means to support their efforts. In addition to fundraising, the directors will mentor student conservatives.

Restricting the focus to Brown will guarantee that the dispersal of funding will be effective, but the influence of the *Foundation* will spread beyond College Hill. Indeed, it is our hope that the *Foundation* can become a model for other colleges and universities throughout the nation. For the thinking will be this: if it can be done at Brown, it can be done anywhere.

Please visit www.idiversity.org to learn more about the *Foundation for Intellectual Diversity*, and to find out how to make a donation.

TJR

Prologue

1. "Students surprised, disappointed by passage of gay marriage bans," *Brown Daily Herald*, 5 November 2004.
2. "Brown Should Create a new, improved ROTC chapter," *Brown Daily Herald.*
3. Lenczowski, John, "Emboldening domestic resistance to Communism—Address to the George Bush School of Government and Public Service, Texas A&M University," *The Institute of World Politics.*

Chapter 1

1. Allhoff, Hans, "When toleration loses its loveliness," *Brown Daily Herald*, 1 Novermber 1999.
2. Beale, Stephen, "Homosexuality inherently destructive to all societies," *Brown Daily Herald*, 13 March 2001.
3. *http://www.brainyquote.com/quotes/authors/t/thomas_jefferson.html*
4. *http://libertyonline.hypermall.com/henry-liberty.html*

Chapter 2

1. Brown U. website: *www.brown.edu*, Life on campus, Student Organizations.
2. Goldstein, Dana, "Still a hotbed of activism," *Brown Daily Herald*, May 2003.
3. Martin, Laura, "In memoriam of diversity," *Brown Daily Herald*, 27 October 2003.
4. "Defending Civilization—How Our Universities Are Failing America and What Can Be Done About It," *The American Council of Trustees and Alumni*, February 2002.
5. Ibid.
6. Phillips, Janet M., "Brown University, A Short History," p. 83.
7. Phillips, Janet M., "Brown University, A Short History," p. 89.
8. Ibid.
9. Letter-to-the-editor, "Racism exists in many subtle forms," *Brown Daily Herald*, March 2001.
10. Ibid.

11. Action for Safety Campaign, *Lesbian, Gay, Bisexual, Transsexual Alliance Newsletter*, 26 April 2004.
12. Goldstein, Dana, "Still a hotbed of activism," *Brown Daily Herald*, May 2003.
13. Brown U. website: *www.brown.edu, http://www.brown.edu/Student_Services/Office_of_Student_Life/randr/conduct/index.html.*
14. Brown U. website: *www.brown.edu, http://www.brown.edu/Student_Services/Office_of_Student_Life/randr/.*
15. Owens, Mackubin Thomas, "Brown's budding brown shirts," *Providence Journal Bulletin*, 30 March 2001.

Chapter 3

1. Levine, Jenny, "Dream Team a Real Sleeper," *Brown Daily Herald*, 1999.

Chapter 4

1. Sanders, Jon, "Diversity debate continues at Duke," *Carolina Journal Exclusives*, 9 March 2004.
2. Ibid.
3. Will, George, "Academia, stuck to the left," *townhall.com*, 28 November 2004.
4. Student Flyer, (see Ch. 10, David Horowitz's 2003 visit to Brown).
5. "International Socialist Organization leads vigil for peace," *Brown Daily Herald*, 19 September 2001.
6. "Students, profs walk out of class to protest air strikes," *Brown Daily Herald*, 10 October 2001.
7. Carlos, Marjon, "Same as it ever was," *Brown Daily Herald*, 17 November 2004.
8. "Students surprised, disappointed by passage of gay marriage bans," *Brown Daily Herald*, 5 November 2004.
9. Rowley, Travis, "LGBTA sex posters intended to generate controversy," *Brown University Heraldsphere*, 2001.

Chapter 5

1. Brown's Ethnic Make-up

2. Brown U. website: www.brown.edu, Office of Student Life.
3. Bernstein, Joshua, "Most students realized that not all was well on Wriston," *Brown Daily Herald.*
4. "Not on our campus," *Brown Daily Herald.*
5. Allen, Brenda; Greene, David, "A few words from Brown's administration," *Brown Daily Herald*, 28 April 2004.
6. "International Socialist Organization leads vigil for peace," *Brown Daily Herald*, 19 September 2001.
7. Goralnik, Nate and Youngsmith, Barron, "Bleed the red states dry," *Brown Daily Herald*, 12 November 2004.
8. Blumenkranz, Carla, "In talk, RIC professor calls slavery 'part of the American pedigree,'" *Brown Daily Herald*, 18 October 2001.
9. Goldberg, Jonah, "Diversity Prop," *www.nationalreview.com*, June 2003.
10. Brown U. Course Announcement, 2005-2006.
11. Brown U. website: *www.brown.edu*, Administration, Student Groups, ISO.
12. "May Day panel addresses Marxism, political climate," *Brown Daily Herald*, 2 May 2001.
13. *www.newsreel.org/guides/skindeep*, California Newsreel.
14. Kors, Alan Charles, "Thought Reform 101—the Orwellian implications of today's college orientation," *www.reason.com*, March 2000.
15. Ibid.
16. Brown U. website, *www.brown.edu*, Administration, Student Groups.

Chapter 6

1. Carnevale, Alex, "Squashing intellectual diversity," *Brown Daily Herald.*
2. Martin, Laura, "In memoriam of diversity," *Brown Daily Herald*, 27 October 2003.
3. Healey, Patrick, "Conservatives Denounce Dissent," *Carver County DFL*, 13 November 2001.
4. "Kerry supporters on campus react to concession: though mostly

subdued, students and faculty express sadness, concern," *Brown Daily Herald,* 4 November 2004.
5. Martin, Laura, "In memoriam of diversity," *Brown Daily Herald*, 27 October 2003.
6. Brown U. website, *http://www.brown.edu/Administration/EEO-AA/*
7. Horowitz, David, "My visit to Brown," *frontpagemag.com*, *http://www.frontpagemag.com/Articles/ReadArticle.asp?ID=10857*
8. Brown U. website: *www.brown.edu*, Administration, Student Groups, ISO
9. Goldstein, Dana, "Still a hotbed of activism," *Brown Daily Herald*, May 2003.
10. *Brown Daily Herald*, April 2003.
11. Keach, William, "Perle should have been disrupted," Brown Daily Herald, 9 April 2003.
12. Keach, William, letter-to-the-editor, *Brown Daily Herald*, 17 April 2003.
13. Ibid.
14. Ibid.
15. "Students, profs walk out of class to protest air strikes," *Brown Daily Herald*, 10 October 2001.
16. Keach, William, letter-to-the-editor, *Brown Daily Herald*, 17 April 2003.
17. Poses, Roy M., "Keach tries to silence his opponents," *Brown Daily Herald*, 16 April 2003.
18. Ibid.
19. Brown U. website: *www.brown.edu*, Student Rights and Responsibilities, Message from the Deans.
20. Keach, William, letter-to-the-editor, *Brown Daily Herald*, 17 April 2003.

Chapter 7

1. "In Washington, Brown students join protesters at Bush Inauguration," *Brown Daily* Herald, 24 January 2001.
2. Rowley, Travis, "Brown protesters embarrassment to community," *Brown Daily Herald*, 26 February 2001.

3. Shechmeister, Matthew, "College Dems not official protesters," *Brown Daily Herald*, 27 February 2001.
4. Wildau, Gabriel, "'Normal' point of view creates a problematic other," *Brown Daily Herald*, 19 April 2001.
5. Codrington, Wilfred, "Rowley's stance on race issues ignorant," *Brown Daily Herald*, 20 March 2002.

Chapter 8

1. *Brown Daily Herald*, 2002
2. "Activist says Greek and queer communities don't communicate on college campuses," *Brown Daily* Herald, 14 April 2004.
3. Brown U. website, *www.brown.edu*, Administration, Student Groups, Hi-T.
4. Brown U. website, *www.brown.edu*, Administration, Student Groups.
5. Mamedova, Tamilla, "International Fear of Bush," *Brown Daily Herald*, 12 November 2004.
6. Hinkle, Tom, "Spring is the time for PDA for all sexual orientations," *Brown Daily Herald*, Spring 2001.
7. Brown U. website, *www.brown.edu*, Student Services, Third World Center.
8. Beale, Stephen, "Reforming Brown," *frontpagemag.com, http://www.frontpagemag.com/Articles/ReadArticle.asp?ID=11097*
9. Beale, Stephen, "Reforming Brown," *frontpagemag.com, http://www.frontpagemag.com/Articles/ReadArticle.asp?ID=11097*
10. "Segregation at Brown," *www.erinoconnor.org/archives/000724.html.*
11. "Students respond to possible changes to TWTP," *Brown Daily Herald*, 19 April 2004.
12. Ibid.
13. **Frantz Fanon**
14. Brown U. website, *www.brown.edu*, Student Services, Third World Center.
15. Brown U. website, *www.brown.edu*, Student Services, Third World Center.

16. "Administrators did not disclose opening of TWTP to white students," *Brown Daily Herald*, 19 March 2004.
17. Ibid.
18. "Students respond to possible changes to TWTP," *Brown Daily Herald*, 19 April 2004.
19. Ibid.
20. "Administrators did not disclose opening of TWTP to white students," *Brown Daily Herald*, 19 March 2004.

Chapter 9

1. "Campus members gather to discuss U. response to assault," *Brown Daily Herald*, 28 February 2000.
2. "UDC report shows details of alleged assault," *Brown Daily Herald*, 11 April 2000.
3. Ibid.
4. "Student complaint from Ebony Thompson," *Brown Daily Herald*, 18 April 2000.
5. "Campus members gather to discuss U. response to assault," *Brown Daily Herald*, 28 February 2000.
6. "Students protest alleged assault, demand that action be taken," *Brown Daily Herald*, 28 February 2000.
7. "Campus members gather to discuss U. response to assault," *Brown Daily Herald*, 28 February 2000.
8. "Students protest alleged assault, demand that action be taken," *Brown Daily Herald*, 28 February 2000.
9. "Campus members gather to discuss U. response to assault," *Brown Daily Herald*," 28 February 2000.
10. Ibid.
11. Ibid.
12. "UDC report shows details of alleged assault," *Brown Daily Herald*, 11 April 2000.
13. Ibid.
14. "Statement—Witness 10," *Brown Daily Herald*, 18 April 2000.
15. "UDC report shows details of alleged assault," *Brown Daily Herald*, 11 April 2000.
16. Ibid.
17. Ibid.

18. Ibid.
19. "Statement—Witness 11," *Brown Daily Herald*, 18 April 2000.
20. "UDC report shows details of alleged assault," *Brown Daily Herald*, 11 April 2000.
21. "Campus members gather to discuss U. response to assault," *Brown Daily Herald*, 28 February 2000.
22. Brown U. website, *www.brown.edu, http://www.brown.edu/Student_Services/Office_of_Student_Life/randr/conduct/index.html*
23. Hope High School, Office of Student Affairs, 2002.
24. "Two Brown students arrested on Main Green Friday afternoon," *Brown Daily Herald*, 11 March 2002.
25. Ibid.
26. Ibid.
27. Ibid.
28. Ibid.
29. Ibid.
30. *Brown Daily Herald,* editorial, March 2002.
31. *Brown Daily Herald,* editorial, March 2002.
32. Suggs, J. William, "BUPS does engage in racial profiling," *Brown Daily Herald*, March 2002.
33. "Simmons, students discuss Friday arrests at open meeting," *Brown Daily Herald,* March 2002.
34. Iloabachie, Onyeka, "Arrest incident should mean no guns for BUPS," *Brown Daily Herald*, March 2002.
35. "Taking a stand against racial profiling at Brown," *Brown Daily Herald*, March 2002.
36. "Simmons, students discuss Friday arrests at open meeting," *Brown Daily Herald*, March 2002.
37. Ibid.
38. Payne, Joel, "Friday's arrests must impact Brown police armament debate," *Brown Daily Herald*, March 2002.
39. van Buskirk, Tom, "Arrested students' reaction understandable, *Brown Daily Herald*, March 2002.
40. "Student Complaint from Ebony Thompson," *Brown Daily Herald*, 22 February 2000.
41. Rowley, Travis, "Racial profiling a necessary tool of law

enforcement, students deserve expulsion," *Brown Daily Herald*, 18 March 2002.

Chapter 10

1. Blumenkranz, Carla, "In talk, RIC professor calls slavery 'part of the American pedigree,'" *Brown Daily Herald*, 18 October 2001.
2. Horowitz, David: *Uncivil Wars—The Controversy Over Reparations for Slavery,* p. 9.
3. Boucher, Norman, "The War Over Words," *Brown Alumni Magazine*, May/June 2001.
4. Ibid.
5. Paid Advertisement by Horowitz, David, "Ten Reasons Why Reparations for Slavery is a Bad Idea—and Racist Too," Brown Daily Herald, 13 March 2001.
6. Boucher, Norman, "The War Over Words," *Brown Alumni Magazine*, May/June 2001.
7. Ibid.
8. Ibid.
9. Ghebremichael, Asmara, "Free Speech Is Only For Those Who Can Afford to Pay," Brown Daily Herald, 15 March 2001.
10. Coalition flyer 1
11. Boucher, Norman, "The War Over Words," *Brown Alumni Magazine*, May/June 2001.
12. Coalition flyer 2
13. Boucher, Norman, "The War Over Words," *Brown Alumni Magazine*, May/June 2001.
14. Ibid.
15. Ibid.
16. Horowitz, David: *Uncivil Wars—The Controversy Over Reparations for Slavery,* p. 62.
17. Boucher, Norman, "The War Over Words," *Brown Alumni Magazine*, May/June 2001.
18. Ibid.
19. Keach, William, letter-to-the-editor, *Brown Daily Herald*, 17 April 2003.

20. Horowitz, David: *Uncivil Wars—The Controversy Over Reparations for Slavery,* p. 61.
21. 57 faculty members, "Full text of faculty letter sent to President Blumstein," *Brown Daily Herald*, 12 April 2001.
22. Boucher, Norman, "The War Over Words," *Brown Alumni Magazine*, May/June 2001.
23. Horowitz, David: *Uncivil Wars—The Controversy Over Reparations for Slavery,* p. 58.
24. Ibid.
25. Owens, Mackubin Thomas, "Brown's budding brown shirts," *Providence Journal Bulletin*, 30 March 2001
26. Boucher, Norman, "The War Over Words," *Brown Alumni Magazine*, May/June 2001.
27. Ibid.
28. Davis, Marion, "Anger at Brown still simmers over divisive ad," *Providence Journal Bulletin*, 8 April 2001.
29. Ibid.
30. Ibid.
31. "Cornel West stresses critical thinking in Tikkun conference speech," *Brown Daily Herald,* 8 March 2004.
32. "Fearing violence, Republicans withdraw invitation to Horowitz," *Brown Daily Herald*, 2 April 2001.
33. "Black Panther Branch founder speaks on need for reparations," *Brown Daily Herald*, 17 April 2001.
34. Horowitz, David, "My visit to Brown," *frontpagemag.com,* 18 November 2003.
35. Coalition flyer 3

Chapter 11

1. "Brown from A to Z—Your unofficial guide to Brownspeak," *Brown Daily Herald: 2004 Orientation edition*, 3 September 2003.
2. *www.geocities.com/topofthecircle/gameoflife.html*, Shulman, James; Bowen, William, "Damning View of College Sports is a Hard Read, *The Game of Life.*
3. Pollick, Josh, "Ivy presidents ponder future," *dailypennsylvanian.com*, 15 January 2003.

4. Gopisetty, Smita, "Balancing act: athletics and academics in the Ivies," *yaledailynews.com*, 7 April 2003.
5. Licht, Jeremy, "Players, coaches unhappy with Ivy changes," *yaledailynews.com*, 5 September 2002.
6. Pollick, Josh, "Ivy presidents ponder future," *dailypennsylvania.com*, 15 January 2003.
7. Rasmussen, William; Rohatgi, Rahul, "Ivy League debates recruiting reduction," *Harvard Crimson Online*, 15 May 2002.
8. Ibid.

Chapter 12

1. Various campus materials.
2. "Activist says Greek and queer communities don't communicate on college campuses," *Brown Daily Herald*, 14 April 2004.
3. Rowley, Travis, "Brown protesters an embarrassment to community," *Brown Daily Herald*, February 2001.
4. Rowley, Travis, "Brown protesters an embarrassment to community," *Brown Heraldsphere*, 2001.
5. Ibid.
6. Rowley, Travis, "LGBTA sex posters intended to generate controversy," *Brown Heraldsphere,* 2001.
7. *LGBTA Newsletter*, 10 February 2005.
8. Berger, Daniel, "Rowley makes assumptions about goals of LGBTA," *Brown Daily Herald*, April 2001.
9. Beck, Eric, "Students surprised, disappointed by passage of gay marriage bans," *Brown Daily Herald,* 5 November 2004.
10. Baruffi, Russell, "Posters depicting homosexual sex misrepresent gays," *Brown Daily Herald*, 28 February 2001.
11. Rowley, Travis, "LGBTA sex posters intended to generate controversy," *Brown Heraldsphere, 2001.*
12. Ibid.
13. Ibid.
14. Ibid.
15. Brown U. website: www.brown.edu, Administration, Office of Equal Employment and Affirmative Action.
16. Rowley, Travis, "Despite what feminists say, women still need men," *Brown Heraldsphere*, 2001.

17. Ibid.
18. Ibid.
19. Schendel, Rebecca, "Rowley misrepresents feminism in his pro-life stance," *Brown Daily Herald*, 22 April 2002.
20. Rowley, Travis, "If abortion is not murder, then nothing Is—Empathy and female empowerment are no excuse for the murder of the Innocent," *Brown Daily Herald*, 17 April 2002.

Chapter 13

1. "ISO leads vigil for peace," *Brown Daily Herald*, 19 September 2001.
2. Ibid.
3. "Students, profs walk out of class to protest air strikes," *Brown Daily Herald*, 10 October 2001.
4. "Defending Civilization—How Our Universities Are Failing America and What Can Be Done About It," *The American Council of Trustees and Alumni*, February 2002
5. "Media bias, U.S. imperialism subjects of anti-war panel," *Brown Daily Herald*, 4 October 2001.
6. Ibid.
7. Shapiro, Ben, *Brainwashed*, p. 103.
8. "Media bias, U.S. imperialism subjects of anti-war panel," *Brown Daily Herald*, 4 October 2001.
9. "Defending Civilization—How Our Universities Are Failing America and What Can Be Done About It," *The American Council of Trustees and Alumni*, February 2002.
10. "Impromptu peace rally draws 20 students to city's federal building," *Brown Daily Herald*, 9 October 2001.
11. "Students, profs walk out of class to protest air strikes," *Brown Daily Herald*, 10 October 2001.
12. Lourie, Kevin, "Terror war against the superpower," *Brown U. News Service*, 25 September 2001.
13. "Students, profs walk out of class to protest air strikes," *Brown Daily Herald*, 10 October 2001.
14. Ibid.
15. "More than 200 students join peace rally on Green," *Brown Daily Herald*, 21 September 2001.

16. "Brown profs see need for restraint in U.S. response," *Brown Daily Herald*, 17 September 2001.
17. "Students, profs walk out of class to protest air strikes," *Brown Daily Herald*, 10 October 2001.
18. "ISO leads vigil for peace," *Brown Daily Herald*, 19 September 2001.
19. Carbone, Michael, "Take your student protest to Afghanistan," *Providence Journal Bulletin*, October 2001.
20. "Brown profs see need for restraint in U.S. response," *Brown Daily Herald*, 17 September 2001.
21. "Defending Civilization—How Our Universities Are Failing America and What Can Be Done About It," *The American Council of Trustees and Alumni*, February 2002.
22. "ISO leads vigil for peace," *Brown Daily Herald*, 19 September 2001.
23. "Students, profs walk out of class to protest air strikes," *Brown Daily Herald*, 10 October 2001.
24. Ibid.
25. Armstrong, Paul B., "The American Scholar at Brown: Diversity, the "Open Curriculum," and Liberal Education."
26. Armstrong, Paul B., "Brown's Open Curriculum and General Education."